ORDINARY MAGIC

PROMISES I KEPT TO MY MOTHER THROUGH LIFE, ILLNESS, AND A VERY LONG WALK

www.mascotbooks.com

Ordinary Magic: Promises I Kept To My Mother
Through Life, Illness, and a Very Long Walk

Second Printing. This Mascot Books edition printed in 2019.

For more information, please contact:
Mascot Books
620 Herndon Parkway, Suite 320
Herndon, VA 20170
info@mascotbooks.com

CPSIA Code: PFRE0319B
Library of Congress Control Number: 2018901149
ISBN-13: 978-1-68401-757-7

Printed in Canada

ORDINARY
MAGIC

PROMISES I KEPT TO MY MOTHER THROUGH LIFE,
ILLNESS, AND A VERY LONG WALK

CAMERON POWELL

Hat man sein "warum?" des Lebens, so verträgt
man sich fast mit jedem "wie?"

Friedrich Wilhelm Nietzsche

He who has a why to live can bear almost any how.

Für Ingelein

AUTHOR'S NOTE

Most of the story told in these pages was written first in diaries and then posted on the blog CaminoNotChemo.com, by my mother and me, as the events were taking place. I've elected to preserve most of our original, less-filtered impressions as we wrote them at the time, and in the present tense, without the later, writerly additions of Memory, Poetry, fearlessness, expertise, and other tomfoolery.

Blog entries have been edited for brevity and clarity, and only occasionally revised for context or to make me look nicer or more clever.

Some names have been changed, including my own.

PROLOGUE

I was married once, and with a brevity I was surprised to find agreeable. The nature channels tell me penguins can boast of longer relationships, and all too often do. By the time a judge closed the file, in the fall of 2011, I stood with my mother—who'd had no happy unions herself—on a yellow-arrowed path, six thousand miles away, like characters in some twenty-first century update to the Wizard of Oz.

My sixty-seven-year-old mother was on this 500-mile trail because she wanted a cure for her ovarian cancer—or at least a break from worrying about "all the cutting and poison", as she put it. She had beaten back cancer in 2001, aged fifty-seven, ditched the emperor of all maladies in a fiery lake of chemotherapy. Then she ran and ran and would not look back.

Oh, the places I went! she would write later, in our blog at CaminoNotChemo.com. *Erlangen, Germany, where I was born, Switzerland, Venice, Amsterdam, and more. How my endorphins just went nuts with joy. I felt such a sense of well being, of wonderful peace, that I was in tears half the time. I said prayers of gratefulness and thanks for my eyes that could see the beauty. For my senses that could take it all in and amazement at the miracle that is our planet.*

But the emperor had returned with reinforcements just over a year ago, in April, 2010, as measured by the test for ovarian cancer known as CA (cancer antigen) 125. She was astonished.

"You mean it can come *back*?"

Surgery, said the surgeons.

Chemo, quoth the chemotherapists.

Radiation, recommended the radiators.

She felt besieged with choices and their risks: another horrible chemo, or death sometime soon—which was worse? Her first rodeo with chemo almost a decade earlier had been so excruciating that she cried whenever the merest idea of enduring it again came up. Chemo's ancestor, mustard gas, after all, had been used to blister the skin, lungs, eyes, and throats of soldiers in World War I. Besides, she still felt fine. She was still not symptomatic, and her cancer was unusually slow-growing.

"Not yet," Mom had told the doctors. "I want to do it my way first."

Though Doc, her primary care physician, would have preferred she do something "soon", he and several other doctors agreed there was no immediate need, even now, a year later. So now here we were, with backpacks and hiking poles, crippling blisters (her) and a torn calf (me), high on the wild-dog-infested and wind-swept spine of a mountain range in northern Spain.

Exhausted from the long road to divorce, I hadn't believed there were any answers for me here, so I had sort of convinced myself I wanted nothing. I stood at the foot of a high rubbled mound, holding my new Nikon SLR, which I'd rationalized buying, from Costco, for this very trip. The video was on. Mom had talked about this moment for months, and I am nothing if not a catcher, or perhaps I mean a chaser, of moments. She was picking her way up the mound, through the powdery rocks, gray and white like her short-cropped hair. Cousin Carrie, fifteen, had abandoned her own massive backpack and was watching the scene from my left. In a field to my right, an older man, very tall, with sturdy boots and a backpack, was weeping.

The mound was pierced at its summit by a 30-foot-tall oak post, about as big around as a telephone pole. The very top of the post was fitted with a cross bearing a tiny iron cap, like the sort of hat an English bulldog might wear, if an English bulldog had scored an audience with the Queen. The three free arms of the tiny iron cross ended in Boy-Scoutish fleurs-de-lis.

For thousands of years a mound of rocks had marked the summit of this mountain range. And for thousands of years, some version of the Cruz de Ferro had spied on the most intimate rites of countless pilgrims—first Celts and other Pagans, later just Catholics, now we pagans were back—as they formed meaning out of this very way station. A million pilgrims before us, along with shamans, druids, sundry witches, and Catholic royalty, had built up the mound with hand-placed relics from their own private rituals of letting go: of anger, of grief, of resentment, of illness—letting go, perhaps, even of the fear of death. Because that is what people do on pilgrimages, of any kind, whether they mean to or not. They let go. That's what the verb *to forgive* means. To forgive others, and, harder yet, to forgive oneself. In his brief life, Jesus told us what he knew about forgiving our neighbors and our enemies alike, but the bastards killed him before he could show us how to forgive ourselves.

An ancient tradition holds that pilgrims should bring to the Cruz, from their own homes, one small stone and one personal item, and to leave them both behind at the cross. I watched my mother: her newly short hair, her glasses on a red string. She was placing among the rocks a small stone she'd carried from a deep and ancient canyon near her adopted home in western Colorado. Then she began to search her trekking vest for the personal item she'd stored away for this day.

Previous pilgrims had left behind other, telling things. A tube of lipstick among the rocks. A postcard of Bruges, scrawled in a woman's hand. Folded pieces of paper and fragments of words in Spanish and English, German and Dutch, Korean and Basque. Underwear that raised certain questions. A Matchbox car that looked to my inner nine-year-old's eye like a '68 Corvette. A toy soldier with only one leg, and the half-eaten cookie on which he had been subsisting among the rubble. A German pilgrim had erected a small German flag among the rocks. Not to be outdone, so had a Belgian. Or vice versa, let's not start another war. The lower third of the cross itself was also littered with splashes of color and texture: a tacked-up orange baseball cap and a clip-less biking pedal, a black-and-white photo of a European peasant family, circa 1930s, a 1970s photo of a boy, in a white shirt with blue stripes, holding a Bible.

I hadn't brought anything, and I would not leave anything.

My mother, still with her back to Carrie and me, stood now at the top of the mound. The Iron Cross loomed over her, stout in the gathering wind. She knelt amidst the murmuring shades of the druids, she bowed her head. She cupped her offering with both hands and held it over her head, a modest proposal to the cosmos about what she should be allowed to let go of. When I saw her shoulders start to shake I began to cry, too, but quietly and with minimal shaking, because I was the expedition videographer, not to mention its chief biographer, photographer, legal counsel, and acting podiatrist.

I handed the camera to Carrie and went to join my mother.

BOOK I

"To be an artist means never to avert your eyes."

—Akira Kurosawa

CHAPTER 1:
CALLS TO ADVENTURE

"I see a bad moon rising."

—Creedence Clearwater Revival

About 14 billion years ago, in the soundless moments before the Big Bang, the entire contents of the universe were, according to a leading theory, stuffed inside a single point of zero volume and infinite density. All the galaxies today, all the stars and planets, the white dwarfs and red giants, even the supermassive black holes and all the makeup of your body and mine, once lay inside that point. This impossibly heavy point was pregnant with potential, about to burst, and with impossible speed. Once it did, nothing would ever be the same. What's more, change would become a constant. And then even change would begin to accelerate.

For me, the Big Bang happened in the afternoon of April 12, 2010. A year and a half before my mother would kneel at the Iron Cross, my wife, Melissa, walked out of our last marital counseling session. It was the beginning of the end. That evening, as I lay in my zero-gravity chair, facing the white-capped Three Sisters volcanoes from the home office of the 4,100-square-foot Bend, Oregon home I owned jointly and occupied individually, my mother called to tell me she'd finally heard from Doc about her CA-125 test results.

"Son," she began, and I knew something was wrong. "The cancer."

Her voice shook. "It's back."

I don't remember what I said. I knew I wouldn't be telling her about my divorce.

"I felt that something was wrong through all those appointments," she said. "But I would not be quiet. Doc didn't pay attention until a few weeks ago I asked him if he'd ever heard someone say their blood was singing. *That* got his attention."

She'd been having mysterious pains for months, and had them repeatedly misdiagnosed, just as her ovarian cancer had been belatedly discovered ten years earlier, in late 2000. Back then, Mom had reported excruciating abdominal pain to several doctors. She also told them, "It feels like there's a cyst on my ovary."

"Gas," one concluded.

"Women problems," said the next.

"Probably just menopause," the third one offered.

The symptoms of ovarian cancer—abdominal pain or bloating, nausea, fatigue, among others—are all shared with other diseases. Doctors call such shared symptoms "non-specific", and they're one reason ovarian cancer is often not timely diagnosed. But early diagnosis of ovarian cancer is critical: only if caught early can ovarian cancer cells be removed with surgery alone, without any need of chemotherapy or other treatments.

Mom and I were in Germany later that year, as my Uncle Gunter died of cancer, and my mother sought out a fourth doctor, a woman. This doctor asked more follow-up questions—"Have you ever had abdominal surgery or trauma?"—and concluded my mother was suffering from adhesions, or scar tissue, likely from the appendectomy she'd had in 1952. Crucially, this doctor also ordered the blood tests that identified Mom's low white blood cell count, and she recommended the exploratory surgery, in Colorado, that led to the discovery of the cancer in the precise location of the "cyst on my ovary," and beyond. The next surgery removed Mom's ovaries, many lymph nodes, and more, or as Mom had put it in a call to my sister beforehand, channeling both my Grandma Powell and Janis Joplin, "They're going to take out your old homestead and put in a parking lot."

Now, my mother's CA-125 score showed even more ovarian cancer cells in her blood, though not by much. The greater concern was the CT scan, which revealed three new growths. One tumor perched in her abdomen. One glowered out from the surface of her lung. And the last had curled up near her intestines and lower spine, behind the peritoneum, or abdominal cavity lining, and locked its gnarled and bony fingers around the veins of her aorta.

"Doc said I should consider *chemo*," she said. "But I can't do it again. I just can't. Not right now, if ever."

She went almost silent. I say *almost* because I could just make out that most terrible of sounds, the sound of a mother's weeping as it enters the ear of her son.

A decade earlier, during her own chemotherapy, my mother had once shaken so hard, trying to vomit, that she couldn't walk to the toilet. She simply stood rooted in place, shuddering and trembling, trying to vomit, but nothing came, nothing but the pain of having nothing to vomit, and the urine that ran down both legs. She fell to her knees, still dry-heaving. At length she began pulling herself along the floor, down the hall toward the bathroom, until, exhausted, she laid her hairless head on the back of the cold tub. She began to sing German hymns to herself. "*Großer Gott, wir loben Dich / Herr wir preisen Deine Stärke.*" "Great God, we praise You / Lord, we need your strength." She imagined cancer cells devouring her healthy cells. She imagined herself dying. She felt such longing for her children and grandchildren, and with such ferocity and sadness, that she had begun hiccupping with sobs. I had just gotten a job in Portland, Oregon, so she'd concealed almost all of her misery from me.

"The doctors said they probably can't get the worst tumor out without risking my life," she said now. "Why didn't anyone make sure I understood I could even *have* this cancer again?" We both remembered what the doctors had said ten years earlier, about the growth near her aorta. "If that ever gets cancerous," they had told her, "it may be impossible to get it out safely."

Probably no one made sure she understood things for the same reason she was so often avoidably misdiagnosed: doctors are far more human than most people (including doctors) think, or prefer to believe. About one of every five diagnoses is wrong or tardy. I didn't know it at the time, but a fuse had been lit in me.

But what could I do now? "If you ever have to do chemo again," I said, "or need me in any way, I'll be there this time. You won't do it alone."

CHAPTER 2:
YOU WANT TO DO *WHAT?*

"I'm restless. Things are calling me away.
My hair is being pulled by the stars again."

—Anaïs Nin

M om's brief, happy career as a professional chef, at a five-star Colorado resort, ended when the cancer first hit, in 1999, and she began the long months of chemotherapy. What she didn't tell me is that she insisted on working through the chemo, cleaning offices and houses, in spite of being nauseated by the cleaning chemicals. Afflicted with the money-anxious DNA of her Pfannenmüller clan, she would throw up, clean, throw up, clean. "Because that's what you do, you know?" she told me later. "I needed some money." Even with that money, she couldn't afford to pay for CT scans at $8,000 a pop, or for treatments priced for sultans, as I angrily told the boss of a hospital financial counselor who'd browbeaten my mother over the phone until she cried.

After the chemo, Mom began cooking for friends and held private dinners, taught teenagers to cook, and taught etiquette to children. Mom agreed with Julia Child that the best kind of people were people who loved to eat. She made ends meet with careful budgeting—she prided herself on a near-perfect credit score— her small social security check, and a little help from me.

It made me happy to see letters like the one from fourteen-year-old Sydney: "Several years ago I took part in Chef Inge's manner's classes. Ever since that time, no matter where I go, I am always complimented on my 'exquisite' manners." And the one from twenty-three-year-old Jamie, "Little did I know how this [cooking] experience would ignite a long, lasting passion. I have since tried other jobs but nothing was as exhilarating, or satisfying. I have now enrolled in a culinary arts institute to become a master chef. Thank you, Chef Inge."

She named her cooking business Gourmet du Jour, and I built her a website for it. She printed up business cards and menus that featured a colorful illustration, by my lone German cousin, Fiona, of a lobster lounging amongst assorted vegetables. One of her most popular meals was a recreation of the last dinner on the Titanic, which consisted of creamed barley and whiskey soup, chicken *Lyonnaise*, duchess potatoes, minted green pea soufflé, and strawberry Romanoff. Her sauerbraten was peerless. You could smell the sweet, vinegary aroma of the pot roast's marination from a block away. Mom had a gift and a lifelong passion for food—for getting it in the first place, for she'd grown up always hungry, among the ruins of late '40s and early '50s Germany, and, once gotten, for transforming it into wonderful things for friends. To offer food was to love.

In early June 2011, I flew from Bend, Oregon, to even more rural Montrose, Colorado, for the annual birthday party Mom threw for herself and her friends. In her backyard among the guests she looked great, flushed from the high of the party and healthier than she'd been in a long time. After the diagnosis of her cancer's recurrence over a year earlier, she'd designed a menu of sugar-free, red-meat-less, macrobiotic vegan, and vegetarian meals for herself. To every dish she'd brought her own culinary genius. I watched her now as she ran through her story again, boasting that the kids who came into her orbit *specifically asked* for her cooking, though it now contained little or no sugar and no fried animal protein. She'd dropped 45 pounds from her 5'9" frame, and felt her energy blossom. One of her tumors had disappeared and another had gotten smaller. (The third, the dangerous one lodged near her aorta and spinal cord, had stayed the same size.) Her easy gait also told me that her painful plantar fasciitis was now gone.

As always, she was a consummate host. She wore a ready smile, full of kindness. You could hear her from anywhere, welcoming, making and laughing at her own goofy jokes, hugging, serving food, talking about doctors. If a relationship didn't get close, a person might not even notice that my mother was doing all the talking. She was so lively and charismatic, her stories so fun, her laughter at her own jokes at once infectious and disarming. She'd also convey a performative note that drew attention to the fact of the joke, or herself as the maker of the joke, and since the time I was a teenager that had made it less funny for me. "Other people think I'm funny," she'd say to me, and I'd marvel at the sheer improbability of it.

I had just returned from two weeks in Israel, where I'd gone to reward myself for outlasting my divorce, and to get a feel for the land where I'd situated the first in a planned trilogy of novels I'd spent eight years researching. But no one would hear much about that because my mother was on a roll, and the wall of sound was underway. I once wrote her, in the late 90s: "When you hold court, you speak as if, were someone to interrupt you, you would never be able to speak again."

I felt I'd come to an understanding about why she was like that, and who the primordial interrupters of her past likely were, but at someone else's home, it could be a bit much. I looked over at Monika, one of Mom's many German friends in Montrose, remembering how she'd once described meeting my mother. About eight years earlier, Monika had just arrived from Germany. When she walked into the home of Silke for her first Montrose *kaffee klatsch*, my mother was already there. "She was talking, talking, talking. Which I was not used to," Monika told me. "A big woman coming in. She was in the room and the room was hers. She was taking over the talking. But she was also very friendly. Everybody liked her." Well, today, it was Mom's party and she was catering it with food you couldn't get for hundreds of miles in any direction, so no one minded that she was also the entertainment.

After everyone had gone home, I helped her with a final clean up.

"Since I lost all this weight," she said, as we unloaded the dishwasher, "I can finally walk and move. I'm getting itchy-footed. I need a bigger challenge now. Not just around the neighborhood." She drew an air circle around her head. "I don't want to think about all this surgery and chemo and radiation anymore...Remember when we went to Lucca?"

I did. When she was undergoing chemo in 2001, she had taped up on her television cabinet a picture of a town square in Lucca, Italy. "In between vomiting and general misery," as she would put it later on CaminoNotChemo.com, she would imagine walking through the colorful market in the piazza. She'd hear the cries of the vendors offering their wares. She'd walk to the church tower and climb the stairs: one... two... three—all the way, for no particular reason, to fifty-two.

And then one day in late 2001, still shattered from chemo, she learned she'd won. "No Evidence of Disease," Doc said, waving her file. Still bald as a billiard ball, she flew to visit me in Portland and I drove her to Cannon Beach, where she ran zigzag and pell-mell through the sand, yodeling *wooohoohoohooooooo!* and tearing off her blonde wig to toss it high in the air.

Three years later, she would write, *I had the good fortune to go to Germany with my BFF, Irene aka Muschi, a friend from Montrose, and my son. My German cousin, Renate, generously lent us her Lincoln Town Car. With Cameron at the wheel, chafing because not one of us could read a map, we drove to Switzerland to visit my brother, Horst, and my sister-in-law, Rösli. On we went through Italy. Staying at wondrous places, seeing beautiful old towns, villages, and countrysides. Then we came to Lucca. And there it was...the tower. I nearly fell to my knees with the joy of actually being there. Of being alive to see it. The gratefulness I felt was overwhelming. I ran over to climb the steps and yes, there were fifty-two of them.*

Mom now kneeled to open a cabinet. "I want a sunny spot for my future," she said. "I want some more moments of joyful recognition like that." She stood. "A few days ago, on my German TV, I saw a movie, and then a documentary, on the Camino de Santiago. It's a pilgrim path established over a *thousand* years ago. Just about 500 miles long. Have you heard of it?" In 2011, I was still among a large majority of

15 *ORDINARY MAGIC*

Americans who hadn't. I shook my head.

"The scenery was so gorgeous," she went on, her voice rising. "It's in Spain. Old cobblestone paths leading to small, ancient chapels. Winding roads through beautiful forests, up hills past blooming lavender fields. Peasants sitting in front of their villas, waving or offering food or water. Mountains in the rising morning mist. People from all over the globe, walking, calling out 'Buen Camino'. People who have walked this path say it hums with energy," she said. "There's a cross at the top of a mountain, an iron cross, where it's said that people sometimes experience miracles."

She turned to put the kettle on as my heart sank. Miracles? What could bring more crushing disappointment than to invest hope in the impossible? I couldn't bear to see my mother suffer.

"I really want to do this," she said.

Was this really a good idea? On the other hand, was is it really surprising that my mother held out some hope that even more statistical improbabilities, if not outright miracles, could be in store for her?

For example, when my mother was eight years old and living in Erlangen, West Germany, in 1952, her appendix ruptured and had to be removed. My Oma spent some very scary hours with her at the hospital. A nurse comforted Oma with the plain fact that Oma would still have three other children. But in 2000, the abdominal pain from that appendectomy is what ultimately helped doctors unravel the thread that led to her cancer's discovery. And even after the scar tissue from the appendectomy was diagnosed as the likely cause of her pain, the cancer itself may have remained hidden if Dr. Gilham, her surgeon back in Colorado, had not decided to cut deeper than a mere laparoscopy, on a hunch: *I wonder why she's always talking about her ovaries.* That's how they finally found the cancer, swelling her ovaries to three times their normal size. Dr. Gilham also told me, in the waiting room, his eyes wide, that her fallopian tubes had *flipped upside down* and kinked like a garden hose, possibly helping to slow the spread of the cancer.

What if this new hope of hers could alleviate more suffering than it caused? Could I really know what would be good and bad for her?

On a wooden tray my mother now placed the porcelain teapot,

two teacups, a colorful array of tea bags, agave syrup, whipped cream, and slices of a peach tart she'd just pulled from the oven. I followed her into the dining area and sat down at the table with her. Then she sprang her trap.

"Will you go on the Camino with me?"

* * *

Two days later, back in Bend, I walked out on my deck, seeing the town below and the Cascade volcanoes to the west. In the east rose Pilot Butte, the cinder cone, or mini-volcano, that was also one of my mood elevators. I slipped on my minimalist footwear—almost no padding, with each toe in its own compartment, like fingers in a glove, or very small racehorses in their very small gates—and walked out to my car. I thought of my mother's request.

"Jesus, Mom, I'm trying to get divorced here."

That's what had gone through my mind. But if I had expressed the resistance I felt, she might not have asked again. So I'd just said, "But you're not even Catholic anymore."

"All sorts of people walk it now, for their own reasons," she'd said. "It's not the religious element I want."

"I'm just not sure I can leave right now," I'd said.

From Pilot Butte's parking lot I walked to my usual starting line, clicked my smartphone's stopwatch, and began a slow jog up and around the small conical butte, as a paring knife circles an apple. I slowed down as the sand got deeper and the circling path steeper. I missed hiking this hill with Jazzy, Melissa's soulful Great Dane, but the dry, velvety aroma of the junipers was like a balm, mixing like a potpourri with the dirt and the sage and grasses. I trotted along, scouring my lungs to raise my estimation of the future, along with my spirits.

Short of my being comatose and in traction, or dating a Nobel-prize-winning supermodel with a fear of flying, my mother could not have picked a more inconvenient time for me to leave behind a thousand and one responsibilities and walk unproductively across a country without serious mountains. I was desperate to be divorced, after all of Melissa's crazy-making foot-dragging. I'd contracted to sell my big empty house for a huge loss. A year before, soon after the bankers turned our economy upside down, I'd been laid off from my latest startup company, and there still weren't many jobs—certainly none for me in Bend. Resilience dripped out of my body with every month I was not making money, or feeling attached to a sense of purpose.

Anxiety was writ all over my face and body. I knew this because my body talked to me. It has always talked to me, and chattered at others. To my mother's dismay, since I was a child the knuckles of my hands have needed frequent cracking. I could get two, even three pops out of a single finger. I didn't know why one arm sometimes wanted to stretch out, vaguely, reaching for nothing, until it was completely straightened out, and when my mother walked with her arm in mine and it happened, I was forced to wonder things like, *Is this because I have some kind of issues with my mother?*

When I sit in a chair, at least one leg is hammering up and down like a pump jack. If I'm not wearing shoes—*Get on the good foot*—my toes want to be turned under, so that the knuckles are tops-down on the floor, and the downward pressure of my weight then deliciously pops one to four toes' worth of knuckles. In case I ever lose the use of both my hands, I can also pop all of these joints using the other foot. I can also do all of these things during yoga or meditation class. Or, as a boy, in such a way that my mother *can't hear herself think.*

When I'm really stressed out, as I was during a big trial on a constitutional case at the Department of Justice, I may start jerking my neck to the side quickly, preferably for a little pop. *At first I was afraid, I was petrified.* I'll crank on my head with both hands, something only chiropractors are lawfully permitted to do to other people. I can hear fibers stretching. It's somehow satisfying. Necessary. I suspect it's also the reason I ruptured a disk in my lower neck during that same trial, though at the time and for years after our victory I blamed gentle *Ron Spritzer*, the supervising attorney on the case who was culpably sitting in my office at the time my neck self-destructed. What is my body saying?

My body is saying (in addition to, *He did the mash, he did the monster mash*), *You have fucking Tourette's, man.*

Tourette's. A *little tour,* indeed.

It was Melissa who, a few years earlier, had gone searching the Internet. One evening she called me over to look at an article, on her computer, about Tourette's Syndrome, a little-understood neurological or motor disorder. As Melissa pointed out, I rocked many of the symptoms. *Let it roll, baby, roll.* I had also pioneered tics not even on the list.

Since then, I've learned about the condition mostly from the gentle pen of Dr. Oliver Sacks, who observed that Tourette's is "characterised by an excess of nervous energy, and a great production and extravagance of strange motions and notions: tics, jerks, mannerisms, grimaces, noises, curses, involuntary imitations and compulsions of all sorts, with an odd elfin humor and a tendency to antic and outlandish kinds of play." Tourette's can come with lightning thought and reflexes, even a musical and rhythmic genius. It's "a sort of 'missing link' between body and mind" caused by an excess of excitor transmitters in the brain. What that means is: I've often excelled at things that involve quickness, along with swats in school, citizenship grades of D-, and the knowledge I'll likely leave many social encounters with some residue of strangeness, difference, or even offense.

Tourette's requires a vocal tic. If yours is severe and uncommon, like *coprolalia* (Greek: feces talk), you'll curse and hurl obscene insults, loudly, uncontrollably, at strangers on the street. Some have *echolalia,* annoyingly repeating what other people have just said, or random words, or their own phrases. I don't have these severe versions, though I admire virtuosic cursing and I do tend to *riff—riffolalia?*—without filters on things people have just said. I seem to be fascinated with sounds, and in a typical afternoon I may speak or sing in the voices of outraged Scotsmen and Louis Armstrong, sly rednecks and Ray Charles, Steve Martin and posh Englishmen. I have a talent for seeing what's wrong with something and how it can be improved, and a less popular habit, or impulse, of pointing it out. Stir in my free-associations and I can probably seem off-puttingly glib, facetious, arrogant. "Coarse chutzpah," is how Dr. Sacks summed up his most famous patient, Witty Ticcy Ray.

In school, I spoke up too much for about half the teachers, usually by getting their hopes up, by raising my hand, and then dashing them with creatively incorrect answers. In third grade our teachers called a class summit to decide on a signal that would let me know I was running my mouth too much. My classmates gamely proposed various hand signals, face touchings, honking sounds, and other *discreet* ways of *letting me know*. Nine years later, the same bastards voted me Wittiest and Most Likely to Succeed.

Until the diagnosis, I feared other people assumed my behavior signified someone who was just overeager, over-sharing, self-absorbed, anxious, rude, insecure, impulsive, a poor manager of stress, attention-seeking, inappropriate, twitchy and weird, or, of perhaps most concern to my mother, impatient and irritable. Since the diagnosis, I've still worried about these things, and what's more that they were true, and no knowledge of the condition has done much to allay my guilt over my impatience and irritability with my mother in particular.

At my finish line, where Pilot Butte's incline evened out onto pavement, I stopped the watch—eleven minutes—and forced myself to keep walking. I took in the view of the Three Sisters, to the south, Black Butte to the west, and the rest of the Cascade volcanoes to the north. I paused for a right-legged Half Chaplin, walked a few more steps, and then popped a left-legged Half Chaplin, for a sweet double.

In over 40 years, I'd never had the outbursts or grand bodily tics of severe Tourette's, the dances, the little rituals, as choreographed as any Charlie Chaplin bit. But now, every x number of steps—the number changed with stress—I stepped forward and a bit to the outside with my right foot, at an angle of about 45 degrees, and planted my foot firmly, whereupon the upper body quickly twisted to the left so that the right knee joint turned inward and popped and the body could then be permitted to walk on. It was satisfying, if not useful in a Chinese circus performer kind of way. The Half Chaplin, as I called it, seemed ill-suited for a 500-mile walk. I was surely also operating on historic lows of patience.

I stopped and stretched.

The thoughts crowded round my head like a dozen crazed magis, come to squash in its infancy any new idea. I didn't even *like* walking. And I wouldn't have any weed in Spain. After some embarrassingly belated study of the matter, in my thirties, I'd concluded cannabis helps with Tourette's. (Still, not so much that whoever didn't approve couldn't fuck off). The last thing in the world I could imagine would be planning, and then taking, a very long walk across northern Spain—and be in the company of my mother, day and night for weeks, for the first time since I'd started first grade.

Just a few weeks ago, she'd called me to complain about a contractor, adding that he'd been rude to her. As proof, she read me a text from him in a condescending tone.

I was instantly exasperated. *That's so her.* "That tone isn't in the text you just read me, Mom," I said. "You supplied it."

"Oh, so I'm always the one who's wrong."

It was so sudden that I could see the path forward was hopeless. "I don't want to argue with you, Mom," I said, "I'm just saying I think you hear slights that aren't there."

"I'm sorry I'm such a piss-poor mother!" she'd said, before hanging up on me.

Her hypersensitivity had never been easy, perhaps not least because I saw myself in it, and I did not like what I saw. My mother couldn't bear the thought of having done something wrong, or worse, thinking she was the source of someone's pain, but her overreactions made it that much harder for me to offer constructive criticism or even advice, let alone have a grievance of my own. For me more than anyone in the world save perhaps my sister, it was hard to spend a lot of time with her.

Will you go with me?

I ran back down Pilot Butte in the fine, hot sand.

CHAPTER 3:
MEMOIRS OF A
FORGOTTEN BOYHOOD

My relatively limited knowledge of my past comes from two primary sources. One is other people, and none more so than my mother and sister. The other source is the journals I've kept since I was nineteen, in part because I knew even then that my memory was not like other people's, and in larger part because I was trying to explain myself to me. But before I started my journal, in my sophomore year of college, there was precious little documentary evidence to tell me what happened in my life. With one notable exception.

Written on a Big Chief brand tablet with a fat pencil graspable by small fingers, the surviving two (of three) sheets now bound by tape and yellowed with age, these four pages of text titled *Christopher* tell the story, in a single, majestic paragraph, of my first nine years of life. At the risk of critics pointing out that I was a better writer at age nine, I'll quote from it here.

On a certain day in a bar,

the autobiography begins, introducing a prose style that will remain at once elliptical and specific,

a black haired man in the army called Jim met a woman called Inge...

Jimmy, as he was actually called, was stationed with the U.S. Army, in 1968, at Ferris Barracks, in Erlangen, West Germany, my mother's hometown. He first spotted my mother at the Fasching carnival in February. Inge, twenty-three, was hard not to see, with her long auburn hair, red cowboy hat, red boots, a leather gun belt, long legs, and a skirt, short, with a leopard print. Jimmy was a handsome, polite southern boy, his short, slicked black hair parted on the side, Buddy Holly's black-rimmed glasses on his Elvisy head, and sideburns big enough to swab the deck of a small sea vessel. He loved to spend time with me when he had a day off and Mom was working, taking me into old Erlangen to sightsee and people-watch. I was not quite three when my mother and Jimmy decided to move to Jimmy's sweet home Alabama. Daddy was going to leave the Army at the end of his enlistment and follow in the footsteps of his father, a sheriff whom Daddy called Daddy and whom I would call Big Daddy. Daddy was going to become a police officer, and I was going to become a police officer's son.

> Chris stayed with his Grandparents while they went to get married in Alabama. They came back, got Chris and went to "live" in Alabama. They had good times.

Since the first time I read this little autobiography as an adult, gazing upon its infestation of quotation marks, I've wondered what my nine-year-old self was up to. Were the fussy quotation marks applied by a boy wholly lacking trust in the permanence of things, in the veracity of (adult?) claims of reality, in the reliability of identity, or of relationships? Was this my first verbal tic, and one that revealed as plainly as if through glass my anxiety or doubt about each word?

Mom got a job at a restaurant at the airport in Huntsville, a town stocked with both Germans and rocket scientists we'd never meet. But I was still made to wear *lederhosen*, and once again the local government refused to intervene. We soon bought a new house in a subdivision on Danman Drive. Meanwhile, my mother was only dimly beginning to realize she'd chosen just the sort of relationship she'd had with her father. *Why can't I tell you how I feel without being ridiculed or humiliated?* she wrote Jimmy once, nine months after we got to Alabama, after Jimmy had asked her for a divorce, and suggested she go back to Germany for a trial separation. *I wonder if there is a place,* she wrote, *where people care about each other.* He'd slept around soon after their wedding, and maybe before it, for all she knew, but now he wouldn't even talk to her, she complained, nor show compassion. What hurts more than being hurt is the indifference to our pain; we wilt beneath a lack of compassion.

My mother and Daddy decided to stay together, and in second grade Daddy signed me up for a tackle football team with the improbable name of the American Eagles and jerseys of even more unlikely hunting-vest orange. CHEATHAM, my jersey said, on the back, in dark blue letters, just above the "41" I had chosen as a tailback.

"You know," my mother told me, many years later, "for all of Jimmy's faults, he was very good with you. He used to play with you a lot. He'd say, 'Throw the ball. Good! Very good!' He'd put you on his shoulders and ride around with you. He was always talking to you." My introduction to football came from Daddy, with big assists from the 17-0 season of the nearby Miami Dolphins and the even closer Alabama Crimson Tide's ninth national championship. (Between the two bowl games, my sister Candy was born.) Neighborhood kids descended upon our giant front lawn to play football with us. Turned out I was fast. I could feel where other bodies were, how fast and in what direction they were moving, and change directions instantly. I was very hard to catch.

But the coach put me at defensive end, which annoyed Daddy, who wanted me in the backfield, where I belonged, where there was glory. But decades later he recalled overhearing two fathers from the opposing team discuss my work at defensive end. "Ah think my boy'll be alright long as 'at Cheatham kid don't kill 'im." He was so proud. He was even happier when, in the second half of the final game of the season, I was finally put in at tailback, and I ran wild, ran for three touchdowns, two of them on very long breakaway runs. In my brain's wiring I can find even now traces of how wonderfully empty the wide path to the end zone looked, and how the longer you ran, the louder the crowd roared.

I was O.J. Simpson.

"You'll be even better next season, son," Daddy told me.

Chris loves him, my mother once wrote in her journal, calling me the name I went by until the moment I first introduced myself at law school, *with such a devotion and so powerful for his few years that it seems incredible.* In one of the many letters she addressed to Jimmy but may never have sent, she wrote that while Jimmy's family may often remind him that "Chris is not yours, YOU are Chris's, I have not seen any other child being so devoted to a Father."

But then Jim went out with other women. Trouble began, they were still married 5 years. And then wanted a divorce.

"I have one memory of that time," I told my mother once. "I was trailing Jimmy back and forth between the house and his red and black Chevy SS in the driveway. He was stuffing his police uniforms and dry-cleaned shirts into the trunk. I remember I said to him, 'Where are you going, Daddy? Where are you going?'"

"I don't think that could have happened," my mother said. "You weren't there when he left."

Memory, as the Czech-French writer Milan Kundera has said, is not the opposite of forgetting, but a special form of it. Not recollection but reconstruction.

Then after a while they got divorced. Chris was 6 now. And Inge bore another child before they had got divorced. Her name was Candis Renee Diane 'Cheatham'. Across the street there lived people called the 'Wittens'. Candy and Chris usually went to watch Mr. Witten with his gardening.

Mr. Witten, fifty-five, retired from NASA, was my best friend. He let you follow him around his yard of wonders and he'd stop and explain anything you wanted to know about.

> They were big help to Chris, Candy, and Inge. Once they even bought them $60 dollar groceries! Candy, Chris, and Inge were thankfull. Even though Candy didn't understand very well.

It was around this time that I promised my mother that when I grew up, I was going to give her sixty-five dollars *a month*.

> Now Jim wanted to see Candy and Chris every Saturday and Sunday. And he did. Now he started liking another woman called Janine. Then 'it' became marriage. Janine was a stepmother to Candy, but was mean to Chris and Candy. She couldn't whip very hard so either she would send them to their room or let Jim whip them. Whenever one of those happened Chris cussed at them silently. But Jim started more trouble he made Inge go to court and Inge always won.

I have no memory at all of any spanking, and I doubt I was doing any cussing. Probably the trouble I was referring to had to do with the time sheriff's deputies arrived at our house, somehow equipped, by an actual judge, with a court order to take my sister and me to the house Jimmy shared with Janine, whom he'd *started liking* far earlier than I knew here. When I confirmed to one of the officers that my name was, in fact, Chris Cheatham, he pried me off my mother's leg to carry me out of my home and into a police cruiser.

> He got Chris and Candy for 10 days.

The judge restricted my mother to thirty minutes of visitation per week, which thirty minutes Janine measured, as my mother cried afterward, "with an egg timer!"

Then back to court. And Inge won.

After ten days we were allowed to go back home. In my sister's case, my mother had no choice but to fight the custody suits that Jimmy would file every few years. For me, the solution was closer at hand.

"You're going to go by your real name now," she told me.
My what?
She took me in her room and pulled my birth certificate from a dresser drawer. There it was. My name was *Cameron Christopher Powell.* Also, I'd been born in Colorado.

Chris's name was Cheatham even though Jim never adopted Chris, they changed his name legally on papers...

I saw the familiar name after *Mother*—Ingeborg Amanda Pfannenmüller—but what was this series of words with letters after *Father*, Clark Powell? And who the hell was Cameron? "From now on you're going to be Chris *Powell*," my mother said.

"I remember that you sort of backed into the subject," I once told her. "The way I recall it, you told me you'd read a story in which a little boy is told that his real father had left before he was born, and he, the little boy, becomes hysterical, angry at his mother. And you asked would I have done something like that, if I had been that little boy? Well I knew the answer to that. 'No,' I said, 'I wouldn't do that.' And then you told me, basically, that I had a real father, and he'd left before I was born."

"I didn't tell you about reading some story," Mom said. "I think you must have added that. But," she said, "I'll never forget how you wailed, 'Now I've had two daddies and now I don't have any!'" During the dark and heavy days of my split with my wife and the return of my mother's cancer, I sometimes wondered if the grammarless part of me was feeling something along the lines of *Now I've had two women in my life and now I might not have any.*

At school, the day after I learned of my provenance, I sat on Mrs. Burdette's lap, crying, "They're going to take away my name, Mrs. Burdette. They're going to take away my name." The rupture with my life in Alabama was as abrupt as a lightning strike—Mom and Dad are getting divorced they don't like each other your daddy is not your daddy your real daddy left before you were born and your names aren't your names and the new daddy wants to take my sister away and makes my mom cry about bankruptcy. At the very time I might have either clung to Jimmy or properly grieved the loss of him, he was using the legal system in ways I could see were devastating my mother and our family—ways, I decided at the time, that were not in good faith. As a seven-year-old, I first began to have to choose, and quick on the heels of the amputation I chose came a cauterizing move to Colorado.

> But he started more trouble and Inge couldn't take it. So she moved to Colorado.

I was in the middle of my third-grade year when my mother told me we would be moving to Colorado to live among a large group of people to whom, she claimed, I was related. *The Powell Family.* Why not go back to Germany? It's impossible even to imagine how much different our lives would have been there, as relatively urban members of the democratic socialist German middle class. But she may have answered that question in an unsent letter to Jimmy, dated 1970: *Remember when you said to go back to Germany? Darling, where to? To what? I don't belong there either. I will NOT go back home.* She thought it would be good for me, in Colorado, to be surrounded by so many relatives. And after the judge's outrageous order to let people have custody of me without requiring proof of either parentage or guardianship, a decision so harebrained as to be corrupt (I remember hearing that the judge and Big Daddy were buddies), she agreed with Mr. Witten that she would never get a fair hearing from the judges in Huntsville.

She packed my sister, me, and Squeaky, our Doberman-chasing Chihuahua mutt, into her Chevy El Camino. Jimmy came by the next day and saw the house vacant, then ran across the street to the Wittens', where Mr. Witten then told the second lie of his life—after lying about his age to join the Army and then help liberate over two thousand civilians from a brutal Japanese prison camp—and said he didn't know where we were. In fact, ol' Mr. Witten knew we were driving over 1,500 miles from Huntsville, Alabama to Rangely, Colorado, where I would begin to learn about a history and family I had never known.

My sister was three, Squeaky was five, and I was a month shy of nine. I had never heard of Rangely, or of Colorado, or of any of the nine pairs of aunts and uncles and the dozens of cousins who were alleged to live there independently of my awareness of them. And I'd only just learned my *real father* lived nearby.

But where will we live? I asked, as we drove.

At first we'll stay with your Grandma Powell.

Who?

Your father's mother. Grandma Powell is Clark's mom. She's always liked me better anyway. Ha ha!

Before I was born, when my mother was working as a stewardess for Scandinavian (SAS) Airlines, in New York, an unlikely chain of events brought her back to her hometown of Erlangen. The Second World War (to choose an arbitrary beginning) had led to her family's poverty, which meant hunger, which led to an accident at age seven involving a squirming stolen chicken, a hatchet, and her brother Gunter, and the accident, though Gunter picked her up and ran with her several miles to a hospital, led, at age twenty-two, to a problem with her leg that she could only afford to treat by using the universal insurance to which she was entitled as a German citizen. Remove any piece of that chain and I'm not born.

For a few months, she went to work at the U.S. Army's Ferris Barracks, as a clerk at the EUCOM Exchange System. It was spring 1966 and the Righteous Brothers were in the air. With her friends she sometimes found herself in a bar called Hubertus and sometimes in a bar called Der

Walfisch, or The Whale. Hubertus was less colorful than Der Walfisch, which a group of American Green Berets regularly trashed on Saturday nights and regularly reimbursed with a check on Mondays. But it was in Hubertus that she met one of the leaders of that group of rowdies, a handsome, high-speed soldier, the handsomest man she'd ever seen.

For several months he courted her assiduously, the Ranger from the 101st Airborne. He was a highly trained killing machine, and he was buying my mother flowers and taking her to movies. At around the time he shipped out to Vietnam, she returned to Long Island, and her job with the airline. She sang "Unchained Melody" to herself. She wrote my father letters almost daily. They were both twenty-two and one of them was in love.

My mother had been in Long Island for a few months when she found out she was pregnant. "But I have friends here," she said to my father, when he came through New York on leave. "I have a good job. I don't want to leave all this for a safety-pin marriage."

And my father then said to my mother words that would achieve a kind of immortality between us.

"What kind of a sonofabitch," he said, "do you think I am?"

So she decided to find out. She agreed to leave her life and career in New York to go to Colorado.

They came to Colorado and wanted to get married,

as *Christopher* explains, with its characteristic economy of style. But they didn't get married. Clark was flirting with the girls on the train to Denver, my mother told me later, stood her up for three blood tests in rural Rangely, and later brought his new girlfriend to the Powell Ranch, where my mother was staying with my grandparents before and for ten months after I was born.

But Clark had to go out with the "Green Bay" [Green Beret]. When he came back Inge had bore a child, he was named after hid Grandfather,

Christophe, Cameron Christopher powell. But Clark said he had to go back to war, to fight for Vietnam. He went there a stayed for quite a while ...

In mid-February 1967, my young mother lay in her bed at the Rangely Hospital, naming me. Cameron, a Scottish surname, was a name she'd recently seen used as a first name, and Christopher she took from her father's Christoph. Unmarried and well-riddled with Catholic guilt, she assumed my last name would be her own: Pfannenmüller. Which, as I used to tease my Uncle Horst, means *pan miller*.

But when morning came my mother looked up to see my grandfather, Les, standing in the doorway in his trademark khaki pants and shirt, twisting his battered cowboy hat in his hands. "Howdy, Sis. I, uh. Well, look here. At the end of the day a man's word is all he has. And no grandson of mine is gonna be a bastard." He peered at the infant in my mother's arms. "He can have my name." And so it was.

When I learned of this story as a boy, I was delighted. I decided it meant I had gotten my name not from my father but from my grandfather, who, by all accounts, had really doted on me. "He'd put you on his knee and just talk to you," my mother said. "Your Grandma said he didn't do that with his own kids!"

But within ten months,

... she got tired of waiting [for Clark] and went back to Germany.

I never saw my grandfather again.

It was January 17, 1976 when, having fled Alabama, we returned to western Colorado as if for the first time, to the snow-covered desert, to the tumbling Russian thistle and the hard earth, harder, as my new Grandma would admit of her two-day-old biscuits, than th' back a God's head. I was innocent of cursing at this point, so it was Colorado at least as much as Tourette's that showed me the profane face of my true self. If my new cousins scandalized me with their enthusiasm and proficiency, my grandmother—a quarter Cherokee and three-quarters gristle—was unlike anyone I'd come across in any of the primary theaters of grade school, children's books, and network television. We passed her sayings around like nudie magazines, like *samizdat*, like Lemonheads candy.

Goddamn, that's an ugly kid. You'd have to tie a pork chop around his neck to get the dog to play with 'im.

I wouldn't piss up her ass if her guts was on fire.

That'll freeze the balls off a brass monkey. Colder'n a witch's tit!

Goddamn, it's rainin' like a cow pissin' on a flat rock.

She's uglier'n a bucket a worms.

"Gramma, where's Bert?"

He went to take a shit n th' hogs ate 'im.

Grandma Powell made one prophecy that I recall. "He's gonna be the one to write a book about this goddamned family," she told people, referring to me. "And I don't wanna be around when it happens." We are now near the end of *Christopher's* single (and still majestic) paragraph:

> And Chris saw 'his' Grandmother and other
> relatives. But his Grandfather had died of Cancer
> to the lungs when Chris was 6 1/2. He had seen
> the grave at the cemetary. Clark Powell was
> married and living in dinosaur.

Did I expect that once we moved to Colorado I would come to know, or even be accepted by, my father? I have no recollection, nor any record. A few months after we'd graduated from Grandma Powell's bunkhouse on the ranch to a trailer in town, I woke up to voices in the hallway outside the bedroom I shared with Candy. A man, with my mother. Somehow I knew.

"Why didn't you marry my mother?" were my first words to him, from the top bunk. And his last words, for several years, would be

"Whaddya say we go drivin around or shoot some cans on Thursday? Pick you up at five, sharp."

"That was just like Christmas!" I told my mother, the next day. On the appointed Thursday, I ran home from school and sat down on the porch to wait for my father. I was probably in my thirties when my mother corrected my misremembering the origin of *Christopher*. I had recalled writing the story for the emotionally neutral reason of a school assignment, rather than something I wrote, at my mother's suggestion, after she took me back inside to go to bed, after my father failed to show up. She'd always found writing helpful, even necessary, she said. *Christopher* may have been my first act of writing in an attempt to make sense of the world.

Somehow, with the resilience of a child, in the second reconnaissance I took the fight to him. I have no memory of it, but it took place several months after the first. I went behind my mother's back to find out his birthday from Grandma Powell, and on the big day I staked out his oil field company's office on Main Street from the post office next door. When he pulled up in his red truck, I leapt up and ran across the street, and, according to the office's longtime secretary, Marguerite, I reached out to give him the birthday card I'd written. "He took one look at it and got back in his truck," Marguerite told my mother.

Mornings before school, the boys huddled around outside and told stories in the four dialects—hunting and shooting, motorcycles and four-wheeling, sports, and fighting—of the love language of rural American men. That's how I began to hear about the legends surrounding my father. That Clark, as a young man, had jumped out of a tree onto an elk's back, armed only with a knife, which he used to slit the animal's throat as it ran. That as a teenager he'd tracked and killed mountain lions, across the backcountry, on snowshoes. That he'd gotten a Purple-Heart as an airborne Green Beret in Vietnam. He'd been a Pathfinder in LRRP, the long-range reconnaissance patrol, the lone wolf who dove into the jungle for a month at a time, kill or be killed, sometimes with no more companionship than his M14. After the war, while building oil fields in Saudi Arabia and Iran, he'd gotten run all the way through by a Saudi's saber. He was a badass, man.

I didn't know, then, that he'd gone into the Army to avoid jail time for beating up my grandfather. Since I first met my father, and began to hear stories of him, I accepted as axiomatic that he was the expert at whatever manly things he did, and, what's more, that he was the very template for being a man. So what did it say that he wanted nothing to do with me? I was weirdly alert to his big red oilfield services truck driving around town, but, aside from his own reconnaissance missions, he made sure he and his family and mine were never in the same place, at the same time, as me.

By the third recon, we had moved next door to a larger trailer—a 14 x 70—which was 6 feet longer and 2 feet wider than the first one, had three bedrooms instead of two, and sported a blue stripe across its length instead of the brown one we'd suffered through next door. It was late at night and my mother and I were watching George C. Scott in "Patton". Suddenly, on the porch on the other side of the screen door, like an apparition: my father. He held a purple-sacked bottle of Crown Royal in one hand. "Hello, Clark," my mother said calmly, politely. She remained seated on the larger couch. "That's a damn fine movie," Clark said through the screen door. I sent tumbling the pile of books that always ringed my smaller couch and walked outside on the porch to talk to him. Ten minutes later, he was gone.

Then, when I was in sixth grade, I met the oldest of my three half-brothers, three years younger than me, on a father-son fishing trip of the Elks Lodge. Corky had come to the pond near Massadona, Colorado with his mother's father and I was there with Mr. Hilkey, one half of an older couple who showed my mother and me great kindness when we lived in Rangely. I knew who Corky was and told him so. "We're *brothers*?" he said, and for the rest of the trip we were inseparable. We slept in the bed over the cab of his grandpa's RV, a super-cozy, fort-like space, with its low roof, little windows, and tiny curtains, and we laughed our asses off. In the daytime we maxed out the daily allotment of fish we could catch. Instead of just handing us shotguns, someone had stocked the lake with such a surplus of fish that they jumped on your hook as you were still trying to untangle it from Mr. Hilkey's tackle box.

The first time I called my new brother, after the trip, he told me, "My mom and dad said we're not brothers. Just cousins."

"Oh," I said. "I see." I thought I really did. I recall feeling a curious pride about how perceptive I was, how restrained. Didn't even argue.

The next time I talked to Corky, he said we weren't related at all. Maybe he'd gone and check-mated his parents with the obvious question about our supposed cousinhood: "Well, then whose kid is he? Which aunts and uncles?"

It was at the end of my senior year that Clark initiated our fourth and final recon. I was swearing under the torn-up dash of my car, formerly Mom's, a 1976 Cutlass Supreme, where I was wrestling with the installation of a monstrous new stereo system. My picture was all over the county, on the front page and above the fold of *The Rangely Times*. I was the town's first ever Boettcher Scholar since the full-ride statewide scholarship was first introduced in 1954. I'd won a National Merit Scholarship, and been an all-conference tailback, student body president, and record-breaking hurdler. My father's truck rolled up and he got out to tell me it looked like I'd done pretty good for myself and if I wanted to go to the Air Force Academy, why, he knew a certain full-bird colonel. I thanked him—it was a year late to start that process, and my eyes weren't good enough to fly jets—and told him I was going to the University of Colorado at Boulder to study aerospace engineering.

Four years later, in my senior year of college, Grandma Powell suggested I invite Clark to my graduation. She called me to make the probably apocryphal claim that he was "having a hard time" with "his guilt." Could I invite him? It would mean a lot to him, she said. I spent about two months trying to craft a short note without a false note. I made clear what the invitation was not about—"I'm not inviting you to suggest you had any role in any of this, or deserve any credit, for that honor goes to another"—and what it *was* about—forgiveness. And he came, and when the College of Business mistakenly named someone else its valedictorian, he went with me, sort of father-like, to the administrative offices as I worked it out. Afterward, we were standing on a low hill overlooking the campus when, as if answering the first question I'd ever asked him, thirteen years earlier, he said, "When I's your age, all I wanted to do was jump outta airplanes 'n tear down whorehouses."

After that, I did the recons, visiting him and his family, at his isolated mountaintop home in the high desert, when I came to Rangely during law school breaks, for Corky's wedding (in his own Army Ranger uniform), or, with Adam, to deliver the baccalaureate address to middle brother Les' graduating class. Clark and I had little but DNA in common, but I tried to make conversation. He asked me no questions about myself. He stared into his coffee. When a man of few words meets a man of too many they'll eventually both just start squinting into the distance. When I invited Clark to my law school graduation, I warned him, on the phone, that the campus was going to be jam-packed with *people*—of whom, I'd come to believe, he was not at all fond. "You sure you'll be okay with that?" I said. He said nothing to me about the offense he took, then or ever, but I found out years later that he'd complained to my Aunt Jayne that he'd been all over the world with all kinds of *educated people* and he could go goddamn anywhere and talk to anybody of *any* goddamn level of education, no problem.

One day a dozen years later, I was driving south of Portland on I-5, with Melissa, telling Clark over the phone how I was about to cash out of a startup company. This meant trying to explain stock options, which is not something most people have any occasion to know about. He wasn't grasping my explanation, and I gathered—"Well I work real hard for my money"—he was worried I was asking him for money. He began to mumble, and I told him, more than once, I couldn't hear him over the road noise. He got frustrated, and then I lost track of his voice again, and said so. "Aw, goddamnit," he said, "I'll call you back."

I never heard from him again.

"When will you stop letting him disappoint you?" Mom said to me, when he did not respond to the wedding invitation I sent a few months later.

"I know," I'd said. "I thought I had it down to nothing."

My mother never had much luck with material things, nor with men, but she had, beneath her palpable insecurities, a profound inner strength, and a survival instinct that was unrelenting. Now she was again wrestling a more implacable enemy than any Greek hero ever squared off against: cancer. And with the Camino my mother seemed to have found a purpose as powerful as any handful of blockbuster drugs. People who have a sense of meaning and purpose can even change their *genes* for the better, according to recent research, something that was considered impossible just a few years ago. I had read a lot of the research showing that simply cultivating positive thinking and emotions produces near-miraculous effects on mind and body. We know now, with scientific certainty, that the best things in life—health, resilience, longevity, happiness—come when we seek meaning rather than merely avoiding discomfort, when we cultivate gratitude and compassion in place of complaint or resentment. I knew that my accompanying my mother on this adventure would be the best thing for her healing—and also the best thing for her belief, should things later get difficult, that she had at least *lived*, by which we mean lived with meaning. How to go to one's death without having found a story with meaning in it? I remembered my mother's distress, when she'd worked at the elder care facility in Montrose: "No one comes to visit some of these people. No one!"

If Mom believed the trip could make a difference, then it could. Back in my big empty house in Bend, I called her up.

"Okay," I said. "Let's go."

"Oh, that's wonderful!" she said. "I have a feeling that it could be good for you too. They say you walk the Camino to meet yourself."

* * *

In western Colorado there is a 95-mile-long natural wonder called the Black Canyon. The Gunnison River, the carver of the canyon's stone, roars through the canyon like a waterfall in only mild recline. Some parts of the canyon are so deep and narrow that they see sunlight for only a few hours a day, and that's how the great granite gash came to be named the Black Canyon. "No other canyon in North America," according to the U.S. Park Service, "combines the narrow opening, sheer walls, and startling depths offered by the Black Canyon of the Gunnison." This was the stunning cathedral of my mother's religion.

In the deepest part of the canyon, 2,722 feet down, you could stack about two and a half Empire State Buildings end to end. Once at the bottom, you can touch rock that, at 1.7 billion years of age, is some of the oldest exposed rock on earth. It was born in the drifting of one volcanic island arc, now in Wyoming, into the volcanic island arc of south-central Colorado. Tectonic specialists, people who dedicate their lives to watching things barely happen, like to sex-up this imperceptibly gradual process by calling it a "collision".

If you were so fortunate as to be a peregrine falcon wheeling above the canyon's rim in July 2011, you would have seen coyotes, rabbits, elk, and the figure of a lone woman with a slight German accent and sensibly short white hair, cursing, because the used boots she'd bought were too small. On this morning, just a few weeks after surgery that had cut out the cancerous spot on her right lung, she had laced on her boots, left the little house I had helped her buy as a reward for surviving her first round of cancer, gotten into her Kia car, and driven to the south rim of the Black Canyon. Mom took sustenance from the natural majesty of the canyon, its silent brooding depths. In her darkest hours, my mother took refuge in nature. *Instead of chemo*, she thought as she walked, *I'm going to walk the Camino.* On the blog I soon built for her at CaminoNotChemo.com, she would write:

> Everyone has heard of the Grand Canyon. The Black Canyon
> is God's smaller, more compact miracle. I love going there. Espe-
> cially in the morning, when all is quiet, except for an occasional
> bird calling, before the tourists show up. The pictures do not give
> justice to the dizzying depths. Makes one feel insignificant before

such wonders. How lucky am I to live so close and get to go any time I want? VERY lucky, indeed.

Alone today at the canyon at 6:30 a.m. with backpack, water, and a sandwich. Beautiful, cool, and peaceful. I became aware of the click-clack sound my poles were making. Everything moving in tandem. Step-clack step-click, inhaling well, heart pumping, lungs expelling without much pain from the surgery.

I met a doe. It did not move, just stood at attention, watching me. The Gunnison River was below. I could hear it rushing and thundering.

I thought of Quasimodo, the handicapped bell ringer of Notre Dame, and the beautiful Esmeralda. They became my invisible companions. Quasimodo had a weight on his back, which he couldn't take off. *Mochila* is backpack in Spanish but I will name mine Quasimodo.

I was shaken out of my reverie by the piercing cry of a falcon. I started singing old folk songs. Then I thought of my parents. Hard working, honest laborers. Giving me the gift of tenacity, perseverance and courage, and a good dose of optimism from my mother, who sang even when she was despairing. Gifts worth more than money. I hope I passed them on to my son and daughter.

When I got home and took Quasimodo off, the sudden liberation unbalanced me for a few steps and I zig-zagged like a drunken bee.

She walked the trails around the canyon's rim several times a week. Once she'd bought a larger Quasimodo and other gear, she began walking with some weight on her back. She was training for her Camino, her *camino*, or path.

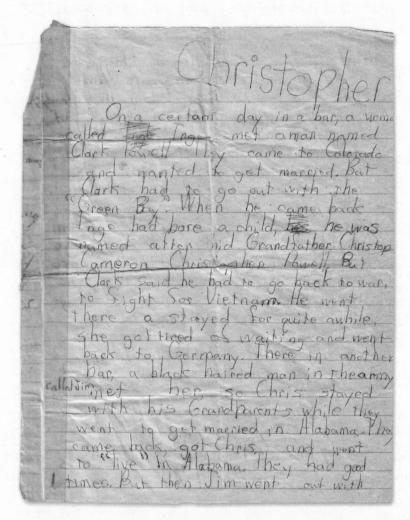

Christopher

On a certain day in a bar, a woman called Inge met a man named Clark Powell. They came to Colorado and wanted to get married. But Clark had to go out with the "Green Bay." When he came back Inge had bore a child, he was named after his Grandfather Christopher Cameron Christopher Powell. But Clark said he had to go back to war, to fight for Vietnam He went there a stayed for quite awhile, she got tired of waiting and went back to Germany. There in another bar, a black haired man in the army called Jim met her, so Chris stayed with his Grandparents while they went to get married in Alabama. They came back, got Chris, and went to "live" in Alabama. They had good times. But then Jim went out with

The first page of my autobiography, Christopher, *from 1976.*

CHAPTER 4:

A DARK WOOD

Midway in my life's journey I came to myself on a dark blue sofa with light blue stripes in Jersey City, New Jersey. Jersey City Heights in 2011 was a *transitional* neighborhood, which is another way of saying there were no Starbucks there. What was I doing on my friend Adam's couch? I certainly didn't go to live in gritty New Jersey, so far away from the legions of lovely and talented women in Manhattan, let alone far-east Brooklyn, who *would not* traverse a bridge or tunnel to New Jersey if it were the only place fine shoes could be found. No, but I'd rented out all three levels of my house in Bend, so I decided to spend the month before the Camino at Adam's, but as often as possible in Manhattan, on a picaresque of first dates.

"Nothing to be said," I'd said to him, as I'd walked in the door with my bags. Mom had just gotten the results of her most recent test: the cancer had likely grown some more, albeit slowly.

"Nothing to be said," he'd said.

Adam always understood my allusions, no matter how obscure. That, combined with the fact that he almost never took me personally, had been the recipe for a long and uncomplicated friendship. I'd met Adam in our first week at Harvard Law School. He was from New Jersey, had graduated *summa cum laude* from Princeton with a degree in Latin American studies. He'd written his thesis in Argentina and taught English in Madrid. He wore his dark brown hair in a ponytail, and sported a trimmed beard, so that he looked like Robert De Niro, if De Niro were selectively kosher. We each lived with a roommate on the fourth floor of Hastings Hall, the law school's oldest and largest dormitory. Our suites consisted of two bedrooms, a large living room, and a working fireplace. We even had balconies, if you never-minded all the signs forbidding our being on the fire escapes. Mine looked out to Austin Hall, which had once housed the entire law school, as well as toward the two-story white house of the Harvard Law Review, where a skinny 2L named Barack Obama sometimes came outside, all angles, to smoke cigarettes. We weren't acquainted, but we were in law school for the same reason: to get into politics, to make life better for people like our mothers.

One day Adam had the idea that his fireplace was designed to boil Jägermeister, in a pot I'd lent him. It was the end of the pot, but the beginning of a long friendship in which I approached his ideas as with oven mitts. He was a gentleman wrapped inside a gentleman. His credo, from which I'd never seen him stray, was always to be unfailingly polite. He strode the campus dressed as formally as our emeritus professors, some of whom would die that very year. His style, if you will, made people think Adam was serious about the law, or at least spiritually the oldest person in our class, but the critical fact here is that he would wear the same clothes—I don't mean just the same style, but the original pieces of clothing—for the next twenty years. Consensus was general that Adam had no time for any modern culture after the Council of Trent (1545–1563), or perhaps it was the Treaty of Ghent (1814), I can never remember which. Years later, when we got an opportunity to attend a singing lesson, Adam would bring sheet music for "O Isis und Osiris", from Mozart's "The Magic Flute", and I would bring, on my iPhone, karaoke tracks of Otis Redding.

After law school, Adam joined a New York-based law firm in Houston, because he hated the cold, and I went to Denver for a one-year clerkship for an unethical federal judge, who, *inter alia*, never read a party's brief or the opinions I wrote when he signed them, and then I moved to Washington, D.C., to work for the Department of Justice and to turn in the judge. Adam married his college sweetheart, for about nine unhappy months he didn't get around to mentioning until they were over, got divorced, and then found himself working as a consultant for McKinsey & Co., which hardly seemed fair. I jumped to a firm in D.C. to practice intellectual property law and learned after three years that I did not like law firms, litigation, interpersonal conflict, measuring my life out in tenths of an hour, or the average law partner. I joined a D.C.-based best practices consultancy until a few months after Adam got hired at an internet startup and then I left D.C., the city where I still have the greatest number of friends, to join the startup, just before Adam and I saw it was doomed. I returned Adam's cronyism by hiring him into two startup companies, in Portland and Seattle.

And then I got married, at last, largely on the strength of a storyline of my own making. My motivated reasoning went as follows: I was feeling resistance to the relationship because something was wrong with me, something related to the separations and abandonments of my childhood, so the reason I couldn't feel what I wanted to feel was just *fear* speaking and I simply needed to *push through the fear.* Or, as my lyrics-drenched mind sometimes put it, to *Break on through / to the other side.* Once I began to see through *that* story—the idea that a good argument can ever trump how something feels—I was euphoric. I never felt so fearless in my life as when I knew that I should not be married any longer and why. Those were the kind of days old sports call halcyon. They emitted their own light, those days did, whenever afterward the mind touched upon them.

What else was there to fear? Getting divorced, one of the worst things I'd ever feared happening, had happened, and I was still alive. As a young Winston Churchill learned during his first cavalry campaign, there is nothing more exhilarating than to be shot at without result.

For most of my life, I thought I had to actually prove others wrong, or at least to have a reason, well-argued, for my feelings and decisions. But now, at last, it was enough to simply say, *This doesn't work for me.* In the spring of 2010, I was ready to stride across oceans. I could have swallowed the moon.

So why was I, over a year later, doing little but treading water? Aside from being simultaneously without salary and unmotivated to find one, apart from Mom's cancer being on the move, there was Melissa's failure, inability, how much does it matter, to show up, in any way. She had not received penance or apology, she had not offered any. She would not meet, even with a therapist, to express her grievances. She would not discuss our joint business, nor the marketing of the book I'd spent eighteen months of spare time ghostwriting. She reciprocated no gestures toward friendship. Then she wouldn't show up for the divorce itself. How had I not seen any of this coming? I was, like the God of the Old Testament, almost continually, and never pleasantly, surprised.

The Camino still seemed like a detour from the particular search for meaning I was sure I was on. I spent the month before the Camino on Adam's living room sofa, sleeping there, still dreamlessly, reading there, but still reading fiction, oddly, no more. When I awoke each day and perched the super-light laptop I'd bought for the Camino on my stomach, the sofa became my office. I'd try, and often fail, to work, to create, to reach out, to do any of the things I thought I should have accomplished or been able to do by now, sixteen months after the world first went all bollocksy. Where had the time gone, and how had nothing gotten done in so long? *Where had the time gone?*

All that energy, all that willpower, gone.

I might have sensed that Adam's pitilessness would be a cool balm both to my simmering resentment toward my future ex-wife and her three terrible lawyers, each incompetent in his own way, and to my self-pity about how unreasonably long it had all taken to produce a simple settlement agreement and get back to a life that made sense. Like a proper Zen master, Adam listened without either judging or indulging my storylines, and without at least seeming to judge me for indulging in them myself. (Happily, he did not expect the same courtesy from me.) He was rarely encouraging, but he also didn't pity. Adam was, in fact, the least sentimental person I had ever met, and I had in mind J.D. Salinger's useful definition of sentimentality, from one of his *Franny and Zooey* stories: to give to a thing greater tenderness than God would give it. I had never, not once, caught Adam (in contrast to God) feeling sorry for himself, even when, as the gentle reader will see, he had every reason to.

I went to REI in Manhattan to buy the last items I'd need for the trek. I also tried jogging—I try this every three or four years—and I tore a muscle in my calf. And though I waited ten days, until it was no longer sore, on my very next jog I pulled it so hard I thought I heard it snap. I tried to stay off it after that.

Meanwhile, Mom was gaining another ally in her quest.

Laurel and daughter Carrie came from Grand Junction yesterday and we all went to the Black Canyon to see the Beauty. Carrie's grandmother is Cameron's oldest cousin, though Cameron has never met her, or Laurel and Carrie. So they're my shirttail relatives.

I managed 5 miles in 90°F and that was a bit rough so short a time after surgery. The altitude, 8100 feet, made my lungs burn. Carrie, a great young lady of 15, and I talked about the possibility of her coming along on the Camino. It would be a once-in-a-lifetime experience. I told her we had to have some ground rules, though. I'd taken teenagers to Europe before, and I'd said never again. So: no primping, cell phone, iPad, whining, makeup, or sleeping in.

Carrie asked me, "If I promise I won't do those things will you take me?"

She was beside herself with excitement. When I showed her some clips of the Camino on YouTube back at my house, I got re-inspired, excited, and totally committed no matter what. I am not going to listen to my own objections nor will I give in to my fears and doubts. I went by myself on a train when I was five, to the next town, because I wanted to travel. I went to Nürnberg to visit my aunt by myself, on the bus, with nothing but my doll in a shopping net. I went to live in Munich by myself when I was fifteen and to England when I was seventeen. I can do this!! This I know for sure. I am going on the Camino de Santiago and nothing will deter me.

In early September, two weeks before we would all leave for Europe, she wrote one more post.

I am amazed that this trip is reality now. I am actually going. When I awoke, very early again, due to those nerve-wracking crickets, I lay there in wonder. Breathing in the cleansed, moist mountain air from the great rains, once more I was buoyed up. I was in awe. I am steady and straight. I have great energy. My mental faculties are present. (Well, most of them anyway.) I have a sense of well-being that is not supposed to be in conjunction with this "cell problem". This divine force which propels me to the Camino, clear and bright. Hope. Can't beat it down. There it is. A new, little sprig, green and fresh. All the while I pray the same prayer: please let this pass. I want to see the beauty of this gorgeous world just a little bit longer. I want to see my son and daughter happy and my grandchildren graduated. I want to have my friends over to share food and laughter. If I wanted to have an adventure, my choice would've been one with lots more comfort (and gourmet food). Not to walk so many miles in whatever condition. But, it's a strong voice and I'm heeding it.

There will be a P.E.T. scan/bloodwork exam upon my return. Shall we dare to hope? Yes! Buen Camino, indeed!

We shall see.

CHAPTER 5:

BASECAMP BILBAO

Blog, Day 1: The Return of Don Julio Angel Redondo

September 17, 2011. The adventure begins. Mom and Carrie, whom Mom is now calling her niece, "if not by blood then by mutual consent and love", are flying from Denver to Bilbao. Against all odds, Carrie got permission to take five weeks off school to join us on the Camino—not only from each of her divorced parents but from her school district. She just went to the school principal and pulled out a map on her phone to show him the route, explained why she was going, said Mom was her aunt, wanted natural alternatives to chemo, and was inspiring to her. The principal said simply, "You might learn more on this trip than you will here."

I fly from Newark to Bilbao, and, true to his word, my new friend Julio meets me at the airport. We embrace and sit down at a café to wait for Mom and Carrie. I'd emailed him a few weeks earlier. *Don Julio*, I began, *my mother wants to walk the Camino de la Santiago*...I'd met Julio just a few months before that, in mid-May. Adam and I had landed in Brussels for what we thought would be a twelve-hour layover en route to Tel Aviv, but a fuel problem would leave us stranded in Brussels for another day, and thirty-six hours, as everyone knows, is hardly sufficient to learn Belgian. "Neat," Adam said. "And second prize is *three* days in Brussels."

We ended up having dinner with the most Chinese-looking bald Spaniard I had ever seen. The physiognomy of his face and head hinted at centuries of ancestral battering, by both Roman centurions and the mountain sheep of the Basque region. "He looked like a wiry version of Mussolini," Adam would later say.

This was Julio.

"So why are you going to Israel?" I asked him. Of course he must be going there to see Jerusalem, then to take a bus to the Sea of Galilee and the Dead Sea and the nearby fortress at Masada, like any other tourist.

"I am going to *walk* from the *north* to the *south!*" he said.

I could see he was of advanced years, so I spoke more clearly and this time from the diaphragm. "What," I bellowed, nearer to his ear, "will you be doing in Israel?"

"*Seven* years ago," he said, in a staccato, "when I was *feefty*, I retire *early* from Banco San*tan*der and grab my *ruck*sack." The vibrating bald man grinned mirthlessly. "I could not put up with the *bull*sheet!" Julio said everything emphatically, even explosively, and with an accent as sturdy as the stone of a Spanish villa. Now he puffed on his cheroot, drank from his beer stein. "I remember when I was in the bank," he went on, "they offered me to go to work in Madrid. I said to them, 'What am I going to do in Madrid, four hours from the sea?' No fucking way."

He began to hum the theme to Sesame Street.

Adam and I made eye contact. "What I love about Latins," he said, "is that they have the lack of inhibition that I lack."

Our waiter returned. Julio asked him in fluent Italian for another beer. So did Adam, who in the 1990s had taught himself Italian from the *libretti* of operas. Julio turned back to us. "I think nature is often the answer," he said. "But when I mentioned to my *friends* that I was going to *Ees*rael for a month to do *walk*ing, they said, 'Julio,'" and here he smacked his forehead, "'*please* go see a psy*chi*atrist!'"

The next night, just after midnight, in the Tel Aviv Airport at last, we said goodbye. Julio went north to meet his longtime trekking buddy, Andy, an engineer from Germany. Adam and I took a taxi to Jerusalem and settled in with a friend of his. Over the next few days we toured the great old city, then took a train north to splendorous Haifa and the Baha'i Gardens. For a day we walked and drove around Tel Aviv, which was modern and therefore of no interest to me, and the next day we rode a slow, creaking bus to the mystical hilltop village of Tzfat, the highest in Israel and one of the four holy cities of Judaism. Then, down a cobbled alleyway, I spotted him. The tireless walker from the Basque country, the retired banker and guru of the good life, the grizzled and explosive Don Julio Angel Redondo of Bilbao.

"Cheesus Chrise!" he shouted. We ran toward one another, like in the movies, then found the only place in town that served drinks. Afterward, having wrought some havoc on the local beer supplies, we traded email addresses as we said goodbye.

Now, in the Bilbao airport bar, Julio orders beer for himself, a San Miguel, and black coffee for me. He lifts my pack—a 55-liter, 28-pounder—with a grunt. "Too heavy," he says. "Even if you are strong as Meester Mike Tyson, you will be very unhappy after you carry thees for six or nine hours." Then he begins to tell me about the Camino.

"No matter what religion, beliefs, anything, still good idea." Julio agrees with the Internet that the most popular pilgrimage route, "the one done by thousands," is the Camino Francés—the French Camino. Francés crosses the Pyrenees mountains from St.-Jean-Pied-de-Port, France, and goes through several cities: "Pamplona is the bullfighters' place, the one from Hemingway, and then you reach Logroño, Rioja's heart, then Burgos, León, and Santiago in the end. The last three have all the great cathedrals. All along this Camino you will find hundreds of places to get food, water, and relax."

Julio had already walked all or part of the Camino Francés five times. In addition to fluent Spanish and French, and reasonably fluent Italian and English, he spoke passable Basque and Catalan. He was also hilarious. What were the odds of meeting in Brussels, and re-meeting in tiny Tzfat, such a person? And what were the odds he lived next to the Camino and became your Camino guide? Well—not as good. In response to my email, Julio had also written that he could not join us because he would be joining friends on an annual trek they all took elsewhere in Europe.

Julio and I now gamble that we can take a bus to Bilbao's old quarter, the Casco Viejo, and find a hotel before we need to be back at the airport to meet Mom and Carrie. We walk outside, where it is raining and overcast. "Eet has been raining every day for a month," Julio says. "Terrible." We ride a bus to old Bilbao, where I reserve a suite in a small hotel. We hurry back to the airport and find Mom and Carrie wandering about, looking for their packs.

"Hello, son!" Mom says, and I can hear that Julio and I have arrived back at the airport later than she'd have liked. She's knackered. We hug. Carrie smiles radiantly. I only know Carrie from a few pictures I've seen on Facebook—studs, rings, blue hair, and a smile like a thousand mid-sized suns.

"You're only a second-cousin," I say, having taken her measure. "Or once removed or something."

"I know," she says. She shrugs sweetly. We hug.

"Hello, Cinderella!" Julio says to Carrie. "How was your treep?" He turns to Mom. "Miss Ingeborg," he says, with exaggerated gravity. "*Ju* are my *he*ro!" He steps forward and gives her a hug.

Mom beams. "It's *so* very nice to make your acquaintance," she says to Julio, displaying with mock formality the English accent she'd first learned as a teenaged nanny in England. "It's a beautiful place. Hilly, cobblestones, geraniums, and greenery. Very European. I am so excited!" she said, with accompaniment from her waving hands.

"Julio," I add, "is neither a Basque nor, tragically, a Sherpa. But he can *speak* some Basque."

"Basque and Catalan were both forbidden during Franco times," Julio explains. "Because I start my working days in a rural area almost forty years ago, I was forced to manage in Basque."

"People back home were telling me to be careful of the terrorists here," Carrie says.

"Not to worry," Julio says. "They have just laid down their arms. The only time I had any sympathy for the ETA," he adds, using the initials of the infamous Basque terrorist organization, "was when the government put a nuclear reactor outside of Bilbao. If you want nuclear power in Spain," he cries, "put it in fucking Madrid! Next to the *king*!"

Day 3: Bilbao to St. Jean

We are up at 6 a.m., and we are downstairs, as agreed, by 6:40. It's dark out. The streets of old-town Bilbao are empty and shiny-black, wet from yet another night's rain. Last night Julio took us to a wok restaurant, in a largely successful attempt to get Mom her first cancer-smart meal in several days. It's harder to find a restaurant in Bilbao that will cook a meal before 8:30 p.m. than it is to get into Yale Law School, so if you want to eat prior to the time a morning person like my mom goes to bed, you are limited to the bread-heavy *pintxos* (peenchos), known outside of the Basque Country as *tapas*, and which, whether containing brie or salmon or crab, sport dollops of what appears to be the regional spice of choice, mayonnaise.

Happily, and by avoiding the mayo she loathed, Mom enjoyed herself. "Oh!" she said, as she raced around the salad bar, waving tongs and serving spoons. "My cells are loving all this fresh food!" She piled green and red and yellow bits onto her plate. "Don't eat only beige food," she said to me, seeing my plate full of noodles and orange chicken and other beigery. I caught Julio's eye and motioned to the bottle of red wine. "In my country," he said gravely, "we only ask the *dead* eef they want more to *drink*. If the person ees *alive*, you jus' start pouring." I poured.

Julio walked us back to the hotel afterward and told us he'd escort us to the bus station in the morning. I insisted he didn't need to, but he waved me off. He began to walk away, then turned. "I must tell you," he said, looking around like a co-conspirator, "after your first email, I tol' a friend of mine, 'This American sent me an email about his mother walking the Camino de Santiago and I waited to see if he would perhaps stop smoking marijuana and send a correction.'"

In the morning, Julio is waiting downstairs. There are hugs all around. "I'm so excited to get started," Carrie says. Julio stands there with his backpack and looks at his feet for a moment before raising his head. He clears his throat. He looks at my mother.

"The first time Cameron tol' me about the Camino de Santiago," Julio says, "with you, not to mention Cinderella here"—he nods at Carrie, who laughs—"I thought it was a dream, a joke, everyone in Europe know that a large majority of Americans take the car to go from the kitchen to the bathroom. I wanted to meet this person suffering from cancer, this woman of a certain age, as a Frenchman would say, who has decided to walk just about 500 miles on foot with a backpack." He's quiet for a moment. "Bwell. I said to myself, 'Fine, I will pick you up at the airport and take you to the Camino trail and point you in the right direction and that will be the end of it.' But later I found out your cancer and it hit me here"—he smacks his fist into his chest—"and I could not think straight for three days."

"Oh!" Mom cries.

Julio takes a breath. "My mother and father both died of cancer at seventy-five, within a few months of each other, in the same 'ospital. They"—here he looks to the sky—"went to heaven. So it hit me *here*." He slaps his chest again. "I was talking to my sister on the phone last night and I said my friend Cameron is doing the Camino and she say to me, 'Julio, your voice sound very different.'"

And now he has run out of words. He looks from one of us to the other. "Bwell," he says, to Mom, "*ju* are my *hero*. I would like to join you on your journey. For the *first* two weeks."

"Oh, how *wonder*ful!" Mom cries. She launches a hug in his direction. He withstands the assault with the gravity of a matador.

"Yay!" Carrie says.

Julio and I do a fist bump. Things are looking up. Mom will have more people to talk to, and I'll save some energy and have more time to myself.

We walk through the empty cobblestone streets of Casco Viejo with a spring in our step, and, in my case, the occasional Half Chaplin. Julio bounds off to use a payphone. A young man with a backpack approaches the rest of us.

"Excuse me," he says, in Dutch-accented English. "Do you have a map of Spain?"

"No," Mom says, "we don't have a map. But our friend will be back in a minute."

The guy's brows knit in confusion.

"We decided to bring a Spaniard instead," I explain.

CHAPTER 6:
THE CAMINO DE SANTIAGO IN HISTORY

"Santiago" refers to Saint (Santo) James the Greater, one of the twelve disciples of Jesus. *Iago* or *Tiago* is how the ancient Hebrew version of James, *Ya'akov*, was first rendered into Spanish. (Tiago later became Diego.) *El Camino de Santiago* then means, literally, *the Way of St. James*, which is exactly what the British alone insist on calling it. You can find descriptions of the Camino that are as varied and contradictory as the accounts of Jesus' activities in the Gospels, but most begin with this impressive fact: the tradition of Catholic pilgrims walking the Camino began over 1,200 years ago. The ground ought to be measurably sacred by now, as Mark Twain once said of the cathedral at Notre Dame—and many generations of pilgrims have believed it was in fact sacred.

Here's what we know from history. In 711, the Moors, as medieval-era Muslims and Arabs in Spain and northern Africa were then called, poured into the Iberian Peninsula and, over an eight-year period, conquered most of present-day Spain and Portugal. They called the land they conquered Al-Andalus ("Land of Vandals"), which today gives its name to the southernmost region of Spain known as Andalusia, the land of bullfighting and flamenco, *Don Juan* and *Carmen*. But the Moorish emirate in Spain never quite wiped out the resistance in the Basque country, in Spain's northeast corner; or in Asturias, in the northwest; or in the Cantabrian mountains that run from east to west in the north of Spain.

It was an Asturian nobleman named Pelayo, who, in around 722, led the first band of Christians to victory over the Moors. The resistance soon spread west of Asturias, to Galicia. There, after Pelayo's dim-witted son unsuccessfully challenged an actual, live bear to a fight to the death,

Alfonso I became king of Asturias. Alfonso, with a ragtag band of warriors that Moorish chronicles would refer to as "thirty wild donkeys," managed to expel the occupying Moorish army and incorporate the territory into his own kingdom.

But Muslim-controlled forces remained alert to finish the job. Because Spain is a land bridge from North Africa to Europe, Moorish generals continually threatened to cross first Spain and then the Pyrenees—the mountains we'd be crossing tomorrow— into the rest of Europe. And the Moors did briefly cross the Pyrenees a few times, including in 730, when 50,000 Moorish soldiers swept into what is now France like "a desolating storm," as one source put it. They were famously pushed back by Charles "the Hammer" Martel in 732. But Christian Europe remained afraid, so the re-conquest of Spain, or *Reconquista*, became the defining aim of Spanish monarchs and the Christians of Europe for nearly eight hundred years. But the *Reconquista* sorely needed soldiers, and for soldiers it needed money.

Europe at the time was awash in fake relics, each authenticated by a tall tale. Churches throughout the land boasted splinters of the One True Cross, or the Ark, and others boasted bits of Jesus' seamless robe, or his foreskin ("the Holy Prepuce", it's called), or milk from Mary's breast. Unverifiable legends were, in fact, the bread and butter of the tourist and pilgrim business. My greatest admiration must be reserved for the competing monasteries that each claimed to possess the head of John the Baptist. To resolve the conflict, it was decided that one had John's head from his youth and one from his old age.

The Biblically insignificant James was almost certainly not the Camino legend makers' first choice, as I illustrated in an irreverent footnoted novella I wrote for my mother's amusement, *True History of the Camino de Santiago: The Stranger-than-Fiction Tale of the Typo that Invented Spain and the Biblical Loser Who Became a Legend.* Consider that, in the Gospels, when James learns a village up ahead does not welcome Jesus and his disciples, he asks Jesus to rain fire down on the village's inhabitants. When Jesus calls James and his brother John *Sons of Thunder*, I am guessing he was mocking them. But all the good saints had been taken, and a scribal error in copying an ancient document—a kind of typo in which the Latin word *Hierosolyman* (Jerusalem) was copied as *Hispaniam* (Spain)—had already led to a legend that St. James went to evangelize in Spain. So legend makers devised a fanciful story of how the bones of St. James, after his beheading by Herod in Jerusalem, had made their way back to Spain, where the bones were needed as a source of strength against the Moors.

Even more of the Camino legend makers' work had already been done for them: it just so happened that in the late 700s there was already a pilgrimage in Galicia, in northwestern Spain. And the Celts and other Pagans had walked a similar path across Spain for centuries, maybe millennia. They had walked west to east because that's how their particular mythology—that the world is criss-crossed by ley lines of energy—said it should be done. But Catholic monarchs knew all the soldiers, farmers, and money were far to the east, in Europe, so the Camino, like the bounty of the sun, would need to run east to west.

The Camino legend begins with another Pelayo, this one the sort of full-time pilgrim we know as a hermit. Hermetic Pelayo was said to have been led by a star to a field in northwestern Spain, where the star pointed out to Pelayo the bones of James the Greater, cousin and disciple of Jesus, along with two of his own disciples, Athanasius and Theodore. The Asturian King Alfonso II, "the chaste one," as he was known—but surely known to responsible historians as the Fonz—was said to have been the first pilgrim to come to see the apostle's bones. At night, it was said, the Fonz II was guided by the Milky Way, which mirrors the route of the Camino Francés. In 814, at the site of the bones Pelayo had supposedly found, Fonzie began construction of a wooden chapel that, over the next eighty-five years, would grow into a mausoleum, a cathedral, and eventually the crown jewel of the capital of Galicia, Santiago de Compostela. According to one theory, the word *compostela* has its source in the Latin *campus stellae*, "field of stars." Under other theories, it does not. For example, *compostum tellus* is the Latin term for a cemetery.

As the pilgrimage's legend grew, so did its reach. Kings along the Camino set up a series of hospitals and hospices, and put them under royal protection. By the middle of the tenth century, pilgrims from beyond the Pyrenees were making the trip to Compostela. The popularity of the Camino soared along with Catholics' passion to retake Spain from the Moors. The Camino reopened channels of communication between isolated Asturias and the rest of Europe that hadn't been active since the Celts and Romans. Badges and souvenirs were hawked and sold—indeed, Camino vendors probably invented history's first tourist tchotchkes. Other pilgrims came from the farthest reaches of Christendom, walking double or even triple the length of the Camino Francés just to reach St. Jean.

Not by chance, these pilgrimage routes also served to unite Europe by sea and land. As writer and Camino pilgrim James Hitt put it, "The Camino de Santiago was one of the most effective means of transmitting culture in European history. Many Central European cultural influences travelled to Iberia through the Way of St. James, from the Gothic and Romanesque styles to the Occitan lyric poetry." The Camino de Santiago, by creating an attraction for all of Christian Europe, was a masterstroke of human ingenuity, military recruiting, PR, and economic engineering.

The pilgrimage itself began to fade in popularity in the 1100s, but by then the legend was being put to maximum use. St. James became the very symbol of the Spanish military. As far away as South America, Spanish armies cried "St. James and strike for Spain!" on their way into battle. Legend makers had James ride at the head of a Spanish army in the made-up Battle of Clavijo, where he helped them to slaughter 60,000 Muslims in a single day (53,000 Americans died in the entire Vietnam War). Here we see a wish fulfillment of genocide on a scale that would not be technically feasible until the 20th century, though by then Jews would replace Muslims as the supposed scourge of Christian Europe. Cathedrals commissioned giant paintings depicting the saint on horseback and in full military regalia, sword in hand, slicing away at the Muslims writhing at the horse's feet. James became, in effect, the very god of war that we see in incipient form in the Gospels. The pilgrimage wasn't revived until the late twentieth century, but it now sees a quarter of a million pilgrims a year, almost none of whom are there for the legend.

CHAPTER 7:
THE FRENCH SIDE OF THE PYRENEES

Day 3 continued: In the Land of Bayonets

On the bus to Bayonne, France, 7:30 a.m. The rain continues, but the fog and mist add a cozy spice to the lush forests of the Pyrenees. Now we wend our way up through the dark green hills, lulled by the hum of the bus and the sound of water against the tires. In the forested cleft of a misty mountain to my left, I notice a sinuous thread of fog in the shape of a question mark.

Across the aisle, my mother and Carrie are looking out their window, pointing things out to one another. I am writing this blog post, on my laptop, largely in order to take my mind off the 6 feet and 1 inch of my body that's contorted fiendishly in seats that appear to have been designed and manufactured for, and perhaps even by, very small children. When the three-hour ride is over, I will require the services of both a chiropractor and a shrink.

Somehow, we arrive in Bayonne, in the southwestern extremity of France. I am happy to learn the word "bayonne" is the source of the word *bayonet*. We grab our packs from the bus' side compartment and walk through town toward the train station. Mom is in high spirits, clacking her trekking poles together the way she usually does a knife and fork. Julio introduces us to a woman named Marie Anne ("Mariana!" when in trouble, we would find), whom Julio introduces as a friend. He'd told us about her on the bus, all the walks they did together. "Bring her along!" Mom had said. Marie Anne, who has bright auburn hair, was born in Morocco to Spanish parents and moved to France when Morocco won its independence. She teaches Spanish and French for a living, and she's passionately involved in local theater. Her English is rudimentary, but her face can say just about anything. Carrie will write, "I really enjoy her company even though I can't understand much of what she says." Mom is thrilled. St.-Jean-Pied-de-Port, the traditional start of the Camino Frances, is only an hour away by train.

St.-Jean-Pied-de-Port: Traditional Start of the Camino Francés

We have arrived in St.-Jean-Pied-de-Port, henceforth "St. Jean" so as to ration our hyphens for the rest of the trip. It's a charming village, a World Heritage site. The River Nive runs through the village, and a citadel presides over it all. St. Jean sits in a valley *pied de port*, or at the foot of, the Roncevaux Pass—the one we'll try to cross over, back into Spain, in the morning. We're still in Basque Country, but the Spanish has been replaced by French and the *jamón* (a ham delicacy) by *jambon*. The narrow streets are winding and cobbled, lined by old white stucco buildings with orange slate roofs and bright red shutters as far as the eye can see. English remains a luxury. The village has been overrun by pilgrims. It's so busy!" Carrie says, of the bustling foot traffic. She's thrilled, overwhelmed. She'd never been on a plane before a few days ago, never met a foreigner. "I just want to buy it *all*," she says in the shops. "But I can't carry it all."

Mom flutters here and there, hoisting wheels of cheese and sniffing kaleidoscopes of spices set out in weathered wooden buckets. She is fairly skipping and clapping with anticipation. *I absolutely love Saint Jean*, she will write. *I am in high spirits with looking, tasting, and walking up and down the town. Lovely flowers everywhere, cute shops and tiny cafés. God's gift to us: color. Walking the cobblestone streets on a beautiful autumn day, well, my cells are happy. Then, a lovely meal with our friends in a lovely restaurant.* In the restaurant,

Mom regales Julio, Marie Anne, and assorted other pilgrims with her tales of misdiagnosis, doctors, cancer, and healthier eating.

After dinner we check into our *albergue*. Albergues on the Camino Francés, in 2011, cost between four and twelve euros per night per dorm bed, while the *donativos*, which also contain dorm beds, operate on donations. Like the operating room in "M.A.S.H," an albergue is an open dormitory with many beds, the odd puddle of blood, an occasional crucifix, some screaming, and generally clean sheets. Pilgrims are expected to stay only one night and must check out by 8 a.m. Albergues may be run by the local parish, the local council, private owners, or pilgrims' associations. You can occasionally find very similar *refugios* in Spain's monasteries.

Our dormitory is a single rectangular room with white walls and eight sets of bunk beds made of red metal tubing. A small window reveals a glorious view of the village and valley. Sixteen people will sleep here tonight. An older Frenchman is here with his grandson. A couple, the woman from Peru, who live in San Francisco. In these close quarters I am forced to notice that she has great legs. Four Koreans, all in black-rimmed glasses, and three already asleep. On a bed near Marie Anne is an older woman from Philadelphia. Near the door, two men lay in their bunks, one sleeping on his back and sawing away. Carrie and Marie Anne giggle. I pass around a container of earplugs, but no one accepts them.

My pack weighs about 28 pounds without water—about 9 pounds heavier than the recommended weight for long-distance Camino trekkers, which is ten percent of your body weight. Mine is heavier mostly because of the trail shoes I will rarely wear, my 3-pound laptop, several cameras and lenses, voice recorders, lots of cords, and a tiny tripod.

As we brush our teeth in the bathroom, Julio says, "There are no words to tell you what I thought when I first imagined your mother and Carrie in the first stage in the Pyrenees." Tomorrow we'll need to walk over 16 miles, climbing 4,200 vertical feet to the top of the pass, crossing back into Spain, and descending another

1,600 feet to one of the albergues nestled among the buildings of the eleventh-century Roncesvalles monastery. What Julio doesn't know is that, only two months before, Mom had surgery to remove one of the three tumors, the one on her lower lung, and for a seven-month period before that she suffered from acute plantar fasciitis, a painful inflammation at the bottom of her foot, that left her unable to walk at all. Meanwhile, Carrie is packing a disarming smile, but also a pack almost as heavy as mine. She told me she'd walked "a little" to train, but never with a full pack, or for more than a few miles.

CHAPTER 8:
GRIT

Day 4: St. Jean to Roncesvalles: In the Footsteps of Charlemagne

No one has slept past 6, and many of us didn't sleep much before that either. It turns out the grunting fellow from last night is in fact a *champion* snorer, the Paul Bunyan of nasalsawyers. Surely a local university's Richter scale picked up the violence done last night to the continental plate.

"A most *interesting concert*," Julio says to me, stretching his arms in the bottom bunk. Julio has stayed in many albergues. He knows that with the low cost and camaraderie come trade-offs, such as privacy, quiet, and modesty.

Julio begins talking, in French, to the older Frenchman, who has done the Camino eight times. The man says he is here on the Camino again because he wants his grandson "to be more human, instead of playing video games and watching TV all day." Then he looks over our shoulders at the women in our group.

"It's the first stage," he says solemnly, "that breaks people. St. Jean to Roncesvalles. Today."

Carrie stumbles by, one eye still shut. "Oh gosh," she says, "it's pitch-black outside. This is going to kill me."

When we've finished breakfast, we step out into the dark morning. Across the cobbled street squats an ancient water fountain, which we allow to fill our water bladders and bottles. We set out, still before first light, in high spirits, following the yellow-arrowed road, the Rue de la Citadelle.

"Out the door and up the hill, right, Inge?" Carrie says, repeating one of my mother's mantras. Mom smiles and nods, unusually focused.

It is beginning, at last. We head down the narrow road, with red-shuttered houses on both sides, their lights a warm yellow in the gloaming. A fog covers the hills beyond the town. Julio sings French and Spanish show tunes. We will be taking the Route de Napoleon over the Pyrenees, which the man himself preferred for getting his troops in and out of Spain. Early pilgrims also preferred this route because it stayed above the trees, where the bandits lurked.

The air felt cool when we started, but within about 2 kilometers I am sweltering beneath two layers of high-tech wool (wool breathes, wicks away sweat, and, unlike synthetics, doesn't stink). I take off my pack and stuff a layer back into it. Then I find myself annoyed by Mom's jangling tin water cup, swinging from the back of her pack. We stop and I stuff it inside her pack. We begin walking again. Now, the scallop shell she bought yesterday bangs into a carabiner.

"I'll walk behind you," she says, seeing my teenage-boy face. She is breathing heavily, but walking steadily, soaking her cells in adrenaline and happy endorphins. We walk in fog for a good while, but as we get higher and the sun burns off the fog, we can see the beauty of the hills.

"My, how very gorgeous," Mom says. Later, she'll write, *Then I notice how steep it climbs and my heart sinks. I have to go up there? With this pack? O.K. then. Let's start. It's one thing to read about it and see pictures but quite another to actually have to do it. I set one foot and the next onto the path.*

Most of the pilgrims seem to be carrying smaller packs, and certainly without the density of the electronics store I have packed. A few even wear tiny backpacks of a size popular among preschoolers. These people, we learn later, are using a taxi service to transport their larger *mochilas*. Meanwhile, Carrie is carrying about 22 pounds, which, at her size, is like schlepping around a small furniture store. Her art teacher had given her assignments that required oils and paintbrushes, all of which she has with her now.

"Are you also carrying canvases and frames?" I ask. She laughs. By the first break she will leave her weighty Spanish-English dictionary with an albergue's book collection. Mom soldiers on.

On and on and on. Mist is rising and the surroundings are green and dotted with cows and houses. I stop to catch my breath. After a couple of hours climbing, my spine is on fire, pushing Quasimodo into my intestines. My thighs are shaking, my throat parched and dry and my feet hurt.

I feel my torn calf muscle tugging at me, nagging for my attention. I decide to ignore it. I catch up to Julio and we are soon way ahead of the others in our group. My calf, now warmed up, has stopped hurting.

We continue to gain altitude. We walk through the mud and shit-grimed stones and over the half-foot-tall turd cathedrals of a rather athletic breed of cow. I am already running on spaghetti bolognaise fumes, and I'm grateful for the granola bars I packed. Julio and I decide to stop for lunch at a few boulders with a panoramic view for miles. We throw down our packs and I pull out my laptop and sit on a rock to write. We watch the sun burn off the fog over a valley dotted with trees and the white houses and ochre-orange roofs of St. Jean below. A bird of prey wheels through the sky over off-white cows who stand aslant on the steep hillsides.

I take pictures while Julio begins cutting bread and *jamón* on a nearby rock. He shares it with me, and I share my chocolate and granola with him. Dozens of pilgrims pass us. We exchange *Buen Caminos*.

About an hour later, Mom heaves into view, puffing hard. "Hey, there!" she says. I walk down toward her and turn on the video camera, addressing her in an overwrought French accent. "I can feel the incisions," she says, holding her side. "Pish, pish, pish." She makes a motion with her fingers from her belly outward. "*And* I've got a bloody hemorrhoid too!"

"Ve are on ze cameraaaa," I sing.

"Oh!" she says.

After lunch, we all climb into our backpacks. As we pass some resting pilgrims, they point at my minimalist footwear, with its separate, glove-like containers for each toe, and they titter as school children will, at one of their fellows who has been born a hunchback in a society without universal healthcare. I walk with Mom, Carrie, and Marie Anne for a while, and Julio goes ahead. Once again, though, I feel restless, the pent-up energy of the past months fairly popping and sizzling through my body. Mom says she's doing okay, so I tell her I'll see her later.

I pull out my iPod and dial up the fast-paced mix I've labeled "Songs in the Key of Speeding Tickets". I insert my headphones. The Rolling Stones. The Doors. And then I grow wings. Chuck Berry. James Brown. Up above tree line I hike, through grasses and gorse, stepping lightly over the matte-black grenades of sheep dung, reeling in one Frenchman after another, but *sacre bleu!* there's a bottomless supply of them. I haven't sustained such a high heart rate in a very long time. It feels great. I pass the Koreans from the albergue, kerchiefs wrapped around their faces, wearing hats and gloves, glacier glasses, and long sleeves. I am well above tree line now, surrounded by rolling grassy hillocks, when I come upon a group of horses lolling in the sun. To protect myself in the event of an international incident, I make a video of the proposition I make them, but not a single one of the useless quadrupeds is interested in taking me over the Pyrenees.

I pass a fork in the road and initially take the wrong path, a metaphor I choose not to dwell on. I am concerned that Mom and Carrie might do the same, so I set up shop on a nearby boulder and write most of the words of this post. For a while, I listen to my iPod. I do some stretching. I relieve myself nearby in the short grass. From the dark yellow I decide I am not drinking enough water. I drink water. Then I turn off the music and just sit, cross-legged, and stare at the grass, and some broken brown eggshells.

I hear the bells of cows, or perhaps some of the belled horses I had seen earlier, from far away. Birds cheep in the grasses nearby.

When I lived alone in Bend, on many days yoga class was my only contact with other humans. One day a yoga instructor asked, as they do, if anyone in the class had any injuries she should know about.

"I've got a crick in my neck," a woman behind me said, reminding me of how many westerners say *creek*.

"I've got an entire river delta in mine," I said, to the usual general puzzlement.

"How does that feel?" another instructor asked, at another time, when I was in the upside-down shoulder pose whose name might sound like pinch-a-meyer-asana if Jews were naming yoga poses several thousand years ago, which I think they were not.

"Temporary," I had said, cracking my knuckles.

I try now to imagine just sitting and watching the grass during the madness of the summer of the Half Chaplin, and I fail. I couldn't have done it. Had there even been birds, in Bend, this summer? Everything that could have gone wrong had. I felt bad about dashing Melissa's high hopes; she'd been so excited, so happy and in love. I felt bad about words and actions that had hurt her. Telling her—never mind the context, which inevitably seeks to let us off the hook—that she was a nasty piece of work. That there was—and again, never mind—something wrong with her brain. That she was, even if true, "immune to reason".

I felt bad that I had lost a lot of money on my latest startup, after the Great Recession, and that there wasn't more money in my bank account, a measure of importance and success I knew was absurd but could not shake off. When you start so far behind, even being good enough isn't good enough. Only better is good enough. Here was a recipe for unhappiness. And instead of building on the successes of my teens and twenties, my thirties and early forties had seen me take many creative and financial risks with little but an increase in my resilience to differentiate them from failures.

I define a mid-life crisis as the simultaneous affliction of two thoughts: one, *I haven't accomplished or become as much as I hoped I would*, and two, *It's too fucking late*. A proper midlife crisis also requires an unhelpful story about the past, and past self, coupled with a depressing story about the future, and future self. My stories about both selves were at near-all-time lows. There are few better times to begin a proper, full-blown, midlife crisis than after getting laid off and divorced in a recession, particularly if one's stories about oneself, like mine, already combined the Jesuitical complexity of theological debates with the self-fascination modeled for us by Narcissus.

Carrie will write in her journal, "It was hell. Straight up hill almost the whole day." Mom tells Carrie, *who is soldiering on and trying not to moan, that we have to remember how eager we were to do this. On and on, up and up. Past cows and sheep, past other Peregrinos. Suddenly, my right boot hurts and my sole is on fire. I change to my sandals, drink water, walk on.*

After about an hour, the three women come into view on the path below. They confer at the junction. Mom looks up. "Is that my son?" she asks Carrie. They walk some more. "Hello, handsome!" Mom calls out.

"*Bonjour!*" Marie Anne calls. She waves her sticks with bonhomie, and likely with other French attitudes as well.

Mom is dragging, but still in good spirits. "I could never have done this when I was fat," she says. "I wish I hadn't been so cheap," she adds, referring to the too-small used boots she'd tried to have stretched instead of replaced. She gives me a knowing look. Spending money, at least on herself, always made my mother very anxious, just as it had her parents. She was the daughter of my Opa, whom I once saw peeing in the dark, the bathroom door ajar just enough to let in light from the hallway. So she had decided to make do with the wrong boots. I remember her complaining about always having been given her sister's shoes, hand-me-downs, when she was a girl, though Christa's feet were a size smaller.

"Julio ees ahead?" Marie Anne asks. Yes, I tell her, probably far ahead.

The climb continues. *"High were the peaks, and the valleys deep / The mountains wondrous dark and steep,"* says the "Song of Roland", an epic poem set in the Pyrenees. Soon our group is bringing up the rear among all the pilgrims. We will only fall farther behind as the afternoon wears on.

I move ahead again and catch up to Julio, who's sitting on a rock.

"Ju are my hero," he says, and jumps up to walk on with me.

It is still a cloudless day. We walk now among belled sheep and horses—the cows have long since given up—and sometimes over short, carpet-like grass. We are a little more than halfway to Roncesvalles, at around 14 kilometers (8.6 miles), when Carrie, a few hundred meters down a hill from Julio and me, begins to cry. "I felt like I was dying," she'll tell her journal, "wondering what I got myself into. I felt like I was hopeless, like I wasn't going to be able to finish this trip, missing my mom and sisters, and like I was going to let Inge down." We watch and listen from our higher elevation as Mom and Marie Anne, now joined by a woman from Philadelphia, try to cheer her up. "Ask for what you need," Ms. Philly is saying. "The universe will give you whatever energy you need, but if you don't ask, nothing will happen."

"A very good *point*," Julio says to me.

The women huddle around Carrie and reassure her. Julio and I continue to watch from the spine of the hill above them. After a while, Carrie regains her composure and begins to walk up the even steeper hill between us. "I pulled myself together," she'll confide to her journal, "with all of the ladies' help. We prayed to the universe and laughed together about how we all were doubting ourselves but we couldn't stop now."

The terrain changes and we are on sharp white rocks on a trail lined by beech trees. This is the Roncevaux Pass. We stop at the Fountain of Roland, a happy coincidence of one medieval legend passing through another. The modern Camino pilgrim is still working to digest the thin gruel of the Camino legend when she is confronted by the watery sauce of the Legend of Roland, or, as a Monty Python fan might refer to him, Brave Sir Roland.

There may have been a real Hroudland, or Roland, as attested in an account of the Battle of Roncevaux Pass written by the Emperor Charlemagne's courtier and biographer Einhard, but the real Roland, a Frankish military leader under Charlemagne, met with a bad end. According to Monsieur Einhard, in real life, in 778:

> [Charlemagne] marched into Spain with as large a force as he could mount. His army passed through the Pyrenees and [he] received the surrender of all the towns and forti-fied places he encountered. He was returning [to France] with his army safe and intact, but high in the Pyrenees on that return trip he briefly experienced the Basques.

In the context of the ensuing Basque slaughter of Charlem-agne's army, the phrase "he briefly experienced the Basques" ranks, as understatement, with referring to the bombing of Pearl Harbor as "that time some Japanese dropped by." The real Roland was killed, and in around the year 1000, as further punishment, his story was turned into the world's first heroic poem, "The Song of Roland". If you have consumed any book or movie about the legendary deeds of a hero, your enjoyment owes a debt of grat-itude to the chanson de geste, an epic literary form that flour-ished between the eleventh and fifteenth centuries. To whip up the emotion needed to send French soldiers to battle the Moors, "The Song of Roland" simply substituted Moors for the slaugh-tering Basques.

Another hundred meters beyond Roland's Fountain we see a sign marking the border with Spain. Carrie is amazed by the fact of the border, and she takes many pictures of it. Another sign says it is 18 kilometers back to St.-Jean-Pied-de-Port, and 8 to Roncesvalles.

Marie Anne is feeling blisters form, so she, too, changes to different shoes. But she is still in good spirits. "This is the last top," she keeps saying to Mom, pointing her poles toward what would turn out to be yet another false summit, and each time Mom says, "'The last top, the last top'—you said that the last time! When is it *down*hill?" And Marie Anne giggles at this, and Carrie grins slyly.

I am limping now. My calf has gone on strike and will not work for the rest of the day and night. I can feel my hips groaning after hours of carrying the pack uphill. What must Mom, at sixty-seven, with her own pack, be feeling? I motion to her to remove it and she hands it to me with obvious gratitude. I sling it around my right shoulder. Eventually we reach the saddle between two modest hilltops and we see below us a valley, a thing that, when you see it, means there is no way to go but down. Mom and Carrie exult: "Finally!" But the only downhill path we see goes straight downhill, at a steep grade, with no switchbacks. When your thighs are already spent, going downhill is tortuous, and going downhill without switchbacks is a serviceable definition of Hell.

Mom says she can take her pack and I give it back to her. Then Julio and I get ahead, as usual—it is less painful to sort of fall downhill at our usual pace than to try to arrest our momentum—and we just keep going. My limping gets so pronounced that I have difficulty keeping up. At fifty-seven, Julio is still walking with a spring in his step. Since his retirement, he's gone on long walks over 250 days a year. I am no longer talking much, so we walk, and walk, in silence. Up ahead, Julio says something.

"I'm sorry, Julio," I say, "but it sounds like every word you're saying is *cerveza*. That's all I can hear. *Cerveza una cerveza de las cervezas, y por favor una cerveza.*" He laughs. And then, at last on the perimeter of the monastery grounds, we come upon a black stone sculpture of Roland himself, Messiah-like, sitting, spent, on the ground. The monastery in Roncesvalles, founded in the eleventh century, is a massive building, and is easily the most impressive site of any albergue on the Camino. The monastery was renowned for its hospitality to pilgrims. A twelfth-century poem sang its praises, but it could have been stating the credo of all the Camino hospitals of old:

> The door lies open to all, to sick and strong,
> Not only to Catholics but to pagans too
> Jews, heretics,
> idlers, vagabonds,
> In short, to good and bad, sacred and profane.

At half past 6, about eleven hours after our start, we reach an outdoor café and I crumble into a chair. A clutch of Dutch pilgrims sits nearby, drinking and joking wryly, as they do. They think my footwear amusing. When I get up for the bathroom, I try to hide my limp, so they won't think I am limping because I am a moron who walks in absurd footwear. Julio and I decide that he will go back to meet the rest of our group. Marie Anne arrives soon after he departs. Unknown to me, Mom is in engaged in a great challenge:

I know I cannot rest because I could never get back up. Carrie is getting exhausted as well but I tell her we have to get out of this forest as we have no more food nor water. We can not rest. Well, she gets her second wind at that and walks past me.

Finally, we see sunlight and there stands Julio. I nearly cry with relief but am too tired to produce tears.

This was a 12-hour trek over rough and difficult terrain. BUT...we've made it. I have seen grown men shake with exhaustion and frustration, but here we are. Carrie, my brave teen, and I.

Mom and Carrie collapse into chairs. Marie Anne, Julio, and I cheer the new arrivals. "Good job!" I say to them. "That was *not* an easy hike." I try to stand up. This does not work out. "In my heart, Mom," I say, "I am hugging you."

"*Magnifique!*" says Marie Anne, embracing Carrie.

"I thought it was never going to end," Carrie says.

"For what you *did* today," Julio says to my mother, "you are my *hero*ine."

"I almost cried all the way down," Mom says. "But I was too tired. I have never worked so hard for so long, except when I saved my life that time in the mountains." In the summer of 2000, on a day off from cooking at the Colorado resort where she was chef, she had gotten lost in the wilderness for a harrowing twelve hours. She'd had to conquer her fear of water to make her way back to her car, crawling along a rock face overlooking a wild river. "A few times I just wanted to sit down and sleep," she says now. "I had to make myself like a robot, not thinking, just to keep moving." She plops into a chair next to me. "I compare it to childbirth," she says. "Something you do once and then say, 'Never again!'"

We've completed 25.8 of 799 walking kilometers, or 3.2 percent of the Camino. As Carrie lifts her camera to frame a picture of Mom standing next to a road sign that says *Santiago de Compostela—790 km*, Mom throws her head back melodramatically and claps the back of her hand to her forehead. Marie Anne's feet are torn up and she is utterly spent. Carrie is exhausted. I am hobbling around. Julio is simply annoyed that he can't find a cigar and, for all I know, that he is being prevented from walking with it this very night to light his way to Pamplona.

I see Julio again just before bed. "The test was more than overcome," Julio says. "But it is clear we will have to pay in the following days. To be honest, I cannot imagine—apart from faith, if that exists—how your mother was able to manage."

"When I was a kid," I said, "she used to call herself a tough old broad."

* * *

Rangely, Colorado, turned out be an isolated oil town, closer to Utah than most parts of Utah are, with an economy the size of a stockbroker's heart. When our German relatives visited, it made the local paper. Mom took whatever jobs were available. We did not think of ourselves as being in poverty, though I can now look up the government definition and see that we fit easily within it. Year in and year out, I quietly qualified for free school lunches. Mom worked as a nurse's aide, as a bartender, as a jazzercise instructor, as a women's career counselor and cooking instructor at the community college. One summer she wielded, for five dollars an hour, a weed cutter that left her hands bloody at the end of every day. In her hardest jobs, she was the only woman, and several bosses told her she worked harder than the men. She came home to shower and change before going to the Ace-Hi to tend bar, or to the community college to teach German. Often she worked two jobs at a time, sometimes three. Once, for a few high-wire months when I was sixteen, there was no work at all, and I worked eighty hours a week to pay the bills. I saw my father driving around town in his great shiny red trucks. His sisters said he was thrifty, cheap, that he had cash accounts at many different banks up to the FDIC maximum. When my mother realized men were making more money in construction, she went into construction—as a laborer. Within five years of our arrival in Colorado, she owned a house with five bedrooms, a fenced yard, and the only blue spruce tree in town.

CHAPTER 9:
SPANISH BASQUE COUNTRY

Day 5: Breaking Bread in Zubiri

The automated klieg lights of the monastery's largest alber-gue flip on at 6 a.m. We're all in one large room, each of our beds surrounded on three sides by a low divider, like office cubicles, but with less privacy. Like a small child, I think that if I put my hands over my eyes, the lights will go away. Ten seconds after I sit down in the bathroom, the automatic light turns off. The toilet is a good 12 feet from the light switch. Short of adding probiotics, Mom's flax seed, and laxatives to my diet, there is nothing to be done.

As we stuff our things in our backpacks, Mom says, "I was in so much pain last night I don't think I got to sleep before 2 or 3 o'clock. How did you sleep, Carrie?"

"Like a rock," Carrie says. "Once I get down, there's no waking me up."

"There's no way I can move today," Mom says. "I'm just locked up. Everything hurts."

"My feet hurt so bad," Carrie says. "I feel like my back is tied into a pretzel."

We decide Mom will take a bus to Zubiri, and Carrie and I will accompany her.

We took the bus and Quasimodo went underneath, Mom will write. *I will say that I had absolutely no separation anxiety.*

In Zubiri (48.2 of 799 km), we find an unsmiling and unhelpful woman at the public albergue in town. She is cleaning, so I figure she is, in fact, the cleaning woman. She cannot possibly be the public face of an albergue so heavily trafficked by pilgrims from around the world. *I can feel my energy seeping out,* Mom will write. *Bread, carbs, eggs, fries and then...again.* Carrie is quiet. This means, she says in reply to my question, she's in a bad mood. Her whole body hurts, and she's still wondering what she got herself into. She's going through "Facebook withdrawal." She misses her mom.

We visit an ancient bridge that's disappointingly not of Roman vintage and then return to the albergue to find the cleaning woman, now changed out of her blue cleaning outfit, presiding over the registration desk, and not noticeably more excited about customer service than when she had been the cleaning woman. We pay only six euros each, though, which raises my mood. Mom inspects the cooking facilities and announces that only stew will be practical; she and Carrie go shopping for ingredients. I nap while Mom makes a peerless stew of carrots, potatoes, spinach, and several magical spices she'd bought in St. Jean.

An Australian couple who have been living in London asks if they can join us, and of course Mom says yes. Julio and Marie Anne emerge from their showers and grab their plates. Never mind her pain and exhaustion, Mom's in a state of flow, and soon the whole table is chattering and laughing. Sharing meals is surely one of the oldest Camino traditions. Jesus is portrayed in the New Testament as constantly eating and drinking wine with strangers. The religious scholar John Dominic Crossan has made a persuasive case that communing over meals was in fact an integral part of Jesus' ministry.

"I have no idea what anyone is talking about," Carrie tells Julio, "but I'm having the time of my life."

Day 6: Back on the Trail in Basque Country

We are up before light. There is really no choice in the albergues. The nighttime policy that turns out lights at 10 p.m. works well to allow people to get to sleep, but pilgrims have worked out no agreement for how (or how early) they get up in the morning. Small, clumsy children, and most breeds of cattle, could be quieter in a small room. Pilgrims crinkle plastic bottles while they *whisper*, stomp around in their boots (while *whispering*), or even call out to their fellows in the next bunk in the sort of *library voice* that would be most appropriate if one were in a library to which one had accidentally set fire.

We're all walking again today. Mom sends Quasimodo ahead with a local taxi service. "I'm not the person who works out a lot," Carrie says. "But I'm happy I'm here." Julio and I walk abreast as we leave Zubiri. "Oh, my *God!*" he cries. "That woman at the *albergue!*"

"You mean," I say, "the cleaning-cum-attendant lady?"

"I wanted to *ask* her, How much do you want for a *smile?* Two or three *euros?* Cheesus *Chrise!* Bloody *spinster!*"

The trail in the morning winds through bucolic country. Parts of it are so lush I am reminded of the Pacific Northwest. A stream burbles on our right for a long way and we walk in shade. There is only the sound of our walking sticks clicking, and Julio's occasional irruptions of singing and jokery.

This Basque country is beautiful, Mom jots down in her diary. *Some of the Camino is sun-dappled forest, with great paths along the hillside. Some other people join us and we have nice conversation, usually in four languages. At one point I hear a snappy, lively tune out of an open window and I break out in some happy dance steps.*

We take a break in a small, unmarked store. "Julio ees ze king," Marie Anne announces, for no reason I can ascertain. "Cameron, 'e is ze prince," she adds, which puts me in mind of regicide. But only a half hour later Julio falls into a stream so small it could not have snuffed out a lit match, and Marie Anne announces, with some sadness, "Julio ees no longer ze king."

The Lost Joys of Wasting Time

It has been a very long time since I spent my time so point-lessly. For the last year and a half, I would wake up in the morning feeling on my chest the entire weight of the mountains I needed to move. Like a caricature of an overachiever, I began each day unforgiven. Now, as we walk, I'm not sure what to think about. I'm not thinking of the vast majority of things that have occupied my thoughts, to near obsession, over the prior sixteen months. I don't even catch myself thinking about where to live next. In fact—and this is even crazier—I don't even worry about my failure to plan.

Instead, I look at rocks and trees and think about what to write in the blog, what picture I can take and share. It feels suspi-ciously like being alive.

Julio finds some blackberries and hands some to Mom. "Sour!" she says. "But that makes you feel happier."

Near a pasture, I bend down to regard a particularly fine-look-ing cow, a dishwater blonde. She draws closer. Into one another's eyes we gaze. "You have beautiful eyelashes," I say to her. She reaches out a large pink tongue and licks me right between my upper lip and nose. Carrie's camera clicks.

Marie Anne decides to offer Spanish lessons. "*El cielo es azuuuuul!*" she cries, pointing her walking stick at the sky, which is, in fact, blue. "*El cielo. Es. Azuuuuuuul!*" she repeats, and vainly does the sky attempt to parry her walking sticks' blows. "*Las flores son amarillas!*" Now the flowers are yellow.

"Mariana!" Julio snaps. "You have forgotten to take the second *pill* again! *Come* on! *Be* serious!"

Marie Anne sighs. Mom is laughing. She is reveling in this experience.

Later, Marie Anne labors to protect me from Julio's own Spanish lessons, both advertent and inadvertent. In what I think is imitation of Julio's habit of addressing passing male pilgrims as *patron*, or roughly bossman or governor, I am cheerfully calling every older man on the trail a *cabron*.

"Hello, cuckolds!" I say, in Spanish, waving my poles merrily.

Marie Anne is scandalized. "No, no, no!" she says, shaking both head and finger. "You cannot say zese sings." She chastises Julio most terribly in Spanish.

"Ju use the imperative so many times," Julio says to her. "Ju remind me of this fellow from Germany weeth the mustache."

Mom laughs at this.

"He is de*ci*ding to be his *own* man," Julio says, shrugging. He turns to me. "*Ju* say what you *like*."

Mom points out flowerpots in the windows. "Makes the heart smile," she says.

This causes Julio to launch into some operatic love arias.

"Sing some marching tunes," Mom says to him. "Something we can walk to."

"I do *not* want to sing *marching* songs!" Julio says. "I learned them all in the *army*, and I do *not* want to *think* of *Fran*co!"

Marie Anne begins to sing the Marseillaise.

"*Allons enfants de la Patrie—*"

To this Julio barks, "Mari*ana*! You should have taken *singing* lessons when you are a leettle *girl*!"

Mom now sings songs she sang when I was a boy. "My Fair Lady" ("All I want is a room somewhere, far away from the cold night air"). "The Sound of Music" ("Doe, a deer, a female deer" and "I am sixteen, going on seventeen"). I smile as I walk ahead of her, thinking I will remember this for many years. How is it that everyone listens to, talks about, reads about, and buys music and yet no one is singing to anyone else?

Carrie hums along. What a sport she has been! Most *adults* in Europe, Americans at least, kvetch more than she does. What's with this teenager? What do we have to do to break her? We've thrown everything we've got at her: easily more than three types of food, the teenage maximum; miles and miles of hiking with heavy packs; group living amongst some of the finest snorers in the Old, New, and Asian Worlds; foreign languages and conversations exclusively among adults, often with references to history and politics; and a total inability to check a smartphone or Facebook page for days at a time.

And not a peep.

Still well above the valley, we come upon a few houses, quaint and crumbling farm buildings. We are starving. On the cobbled road outside of one of the houses there are two sleek vending machines, standing out like sore thumbs, but now, with a strange tingling of my intuition, I know there is an entrepreneur in the area. Then I hear something making a noise against a plate.

"I just heard a plate," I say.

"Oh, yay!" Mom cries. "I was about to eat my shoes."

Around the corner, we find a line of pilgrims that leads to a man and his wife serving up hot dogs, beer, and something that looks like a combination of pizza and quiche—something that runs out right before my hungry eyes. A shy young Korean woman, who has been traveling solo, offers me her own. I thank her, but I can't bring myself to accept. About twenty pilgrims, arrayed with food around a long picnic table, are looking very pleased. The prices include an obvious convenience surcharge, and probably a desperation tax, too, and we all pay it gladly. Mom is tired, so it's Julio who holds court before the assembled pilgrims.

I've seen Julio help one stranger after another with every aspect of Camino travel, from language to luggage to extending a hand through boulders to be climbed.

"Thank you!" they say.

"Come on!" he cries. "Be serious!"

Whatever language he speaks, people laugh. He is a character fit for his own TV show.

After about half an hour, we are back on the trail.

"I am drunk!" Marie Anne announces. She begins to sing.

"The second pill!" Julio cries.

CHAPTER 10:
MOUNTING CHALLENGES

Days 6-8: The Fine Little Town of Pamplona

Pamplona is a fine little town, strong and true. In the Casco Viejo the streets are narrow and cobbled and in the cathedral you will see fine examples of medieval art. The Jesus y Maria hostel in Pamplona (69.6 of 799 km) sits squarely in the middle of the old town. *Our refugio is in an old monastery,* Mom writes. *It's clean and bright with a very nice kitchen.* As Ernest Hemingway might have put it when he found his voice in this very city eighty-five years earlier, during a Running of the Bulls, the albergue shower is hot until the twenty-five seconds have passed and then the water is not hot because it has turned off.

"This city has the best energy to it," Carrie announces. The most famous of pilgrimages that run through the streets of Pamplona is not the Camino de Santiago but *Sanfermines*, a week-long festival held in honor of Saint Fermín, patron saint of the province of Navarre. And the most famous event of the festival is *el encierro*, which you know as the Running of the Bulls.

If Ernest Hemingway could see what had come of the festival, he would surely shoot himself again. He loved Pamplona but when he wrote of *el encierro* he brought it to the attention of the entire world. Still, for over three hundred years, foreigners were already coming to the festival to eat and to drink and to puke and to be gored, and sometimes to puke again and be gored again. And from heaven above Darwin did grin. Julio tells us he himself ran with the bulls "in Franco times", which Marie Anne and I agree explains a great deal.

The bulls run through Pamplona in July, so we need to go online to see the goring. In one video, we see bulls charge idiots across the cobblestones. We see the idiots run for one of the wooden barriers that line the streets. The first idiot gets one leg over the fence when the first bull rams him. The idiot is wearing high-top sneakers and a Barcelona *futbol* jersey and he looks awfully surprised and falls back into the street. Then three more idiots run into the walls with bulls' horns in their backs, and they all get gored just like that. When a million and a half people crowd into the Casco Viejo, the bulls are able to find them more easily. In one video, raven-haired women show their breasts and the young men surf on the crowd because until the goring they are brave and good and strong.

In Boston, where I lived for three years of law school, there was once an even more dangerous pilgrimage to Filene's Basement, a well-known discount department store, for a one-day-a-year sale of deeply-discounted wedding dresses. The event was famous for the spectacle of brides-to-be and their helpers, all wearing matching t-shirts and communicating with whistles, bursting into the store as it opened. Police officers were on hand to break up fights and make arrests, and in those days we called it the Running of the Brides.

Julio begins his albergue-arrival routine; he trades his boots for sturdy clogs of blue rubber and he clogs with his blue clogs into the shower, where, with an enthusiasm equal to the talent of José Carreras, he runs through a medley of Spanish shower songs. He always emerges a new man. He disappears for a while into Pamplona, and when he returns to find us resting in our dormitory beds, he's got bags of lentils.

"We are going to have *two* pots of lenteels," he announces later, a five-gallon steel pot hanging from each arm, looking very much like a toreador. "One *weeth* cholesterol, and one weeth*out* cholesterol." One of the two pots has chorizo sausage and one does not. There is so much food we are obliged to press it upon an Irishman, an Israeli, a young English couple, and all seven Koreans. "Oh, my gosh!" Carrie says. She points to her bowl with her spoon. "Lentils are amazing!"

I complain we never have enough wine on hand to get drunk. "Always these damnable half measures!" The Irishman disappears for a while and when he returns he is brandishing three bottles of Rioja, which is a good start. I turn on my laptop and out spills Dean Martin—*When marimba rhythms start to play*—and the Gipsy Kings—*Baila, baila, baila, baila!* We sing. Julio performs his escaping-rabbit-made-from-a-handkerchief trick on one of the younger Korean boys. *We laugh so hard that we cry over Julio's rabbit antics,* Mom will write. Mom and Marie Anne sing and join arms and rock to and fro. Mom serenades a bottle of wine, and later gives Carrie a talk about boys and the advantages of not getting pregnant in high school. "Pamplona is a fine town and aren't we all having fun now and I love you," I say.

"We had the best night," Carrie will write, in the morning. "It was so lovely." We decide to stay here for another day. We go to an open-air café-bar in another part of the old town. Bulls clatter by on the cobblestones at intervals. The woman tending bar calls out to me. "You look like Robert Redford," she says, "when he was young." I leave an appreciative tip, finish my coffee, and walk the sunny streets to find a place to get a haircut. There are several *peluqueros* in the winding streets of Pamplona and some will cut a man's hair for thirty euros but it is possible to have your hair cut for only eighteen euros if you are willing to have your cheek sliced with a razor. "This is my last and best and truest and only haircut," I say to the clumsy *estilista*. I walk back to the bar and my mother looks at me and says the hair is good. The bartender says, "You are very handsome *today*." My mother thinks this is just grand. *Today*.

Day 8: A Rest in Cizur Menor

There were good restaurants in Pamplona when Hemingway stayed in it. He loved the short walk to the Iruña Café for coffee and a smoke, and he talked there with men who had fought in the Great War. On our second morning in Pamplona, we walk there for coffee before our short walk to Cizur Menor. It's 8:22 a.m. Inside, I see elaborate carving, a giant wooden bar, glazed mirrors, and no people. Outside, we are locked out. "Teepical," Julio snorts. "Suppose to open at 8 a.m."

I see two young officers of the *policia* and turn to Julio. "Go now and ask the *policia* to yank the owners out of bed."

Julio goes to the sturdy *carabinieri* and the men laugh and answer Julio in the way young men do when they know nothing of death. I see Julio waving his arms around, but the one *carabinieri* only smiles and the other bites his toothpick and neither of them will do anything useful today.

We go to another bar and eat croissants and drink black coffee and pour bowls of almonds into our pockets. Mom needs more time to recover so she's taking a taxi to the albergue at Cizur Menor, just 5 miles way.

Julio and I walk alone. We're falling even farther off our pace to Santiago.

"I am reading your blog," Julio says. "I am not this gentleman you write about."

"Nonsense," I say. "You don't have a let-someone-else-handle-it bone in your body. You see a need, you act. No hesitation or ado. By comparison I am diffident, even lazy. I don't even feel like putting a period at the end of this sentence"

He shakes his head, still somewhat puzzled. At last he grunts but does not respond.

I ask him about women. At this point, I am still unclear on whether he and Marie Anne are friends or lovers.

"Bwell," he says, as if approaching a subject of some enormity.

"I am using—" he rummages for a word. "I have been using—"

"In English we say *prostitutes*."

"No, *not* prostitutes. That was in *Cuba*." He squints at the sky baldly, as much Patrick Stewart as Clint Eastwood. "Recently I put an adver*tise*ment for *some*one to travel around the *world*. For *one* year. Man or woman. Most of the responses I received were from women. And they were not so interested in *trav*eling as in finding a *hus*band. So that's that." He shrugs. "Maybe I weel try *again*."

"But what about dating?"

"I tried it *twice* and it did not work," he says.

"Do you think you could be what we call a commit-ment-phobe, Julio?"

"Maybe," he says. He thinks for a moment. "It could be."

"I used to think I was," I say. "I thought something was wrong with me and the solution would be to get married."

"Jes of course," he says.

Day 9: To Puente La Reina and the Bridge of the Unknown Queen

Morning, Cizur Menor. "Bwell," says Julio, from his bed, "there was no concert last night."

"Oh yes there was," Mom says. "David"—another pilgrim—"and my son. My son snored all night. I was hoping someone would adopt him."

I think this is one of the funniest things I've ever heard my mother say. I laugh out loud and give her a big hug.

"How you doin', Mom?"

"Not great," she murmurs. "But I'll show up."

"I feel like I'm in heaven," Carrie writes in her journal, "the bed isn't comfortable but everything else is amazing."

We start out at 7:30 a.m., Mom will write, *and walk approx-imately 8 km, have a decent lunch, and walk through beautiful countryside. Large fields, now empty and harvested, cypresses and blackberry bushes. My foot starts to hurt again and it is getting hot, but I will not complain.*

My left calf is stiff and tender, but now there's a new flash of pain on the top of my foot. Happily, it's on the left foot, so one limp takes care of both injuries. Stick, stick, stick. I do a walking meditation as I learned it from the Shambhala Center in Portland, Oregon, attending to the sensations of my feet hitting the ground, the way they roll from heel to ball, noticing the feel in my ankles and knees and hips. "Walk as if you are kissing the Earth with your feet," says the writer and teacher Thich Nhat Hanh.

The night before, I received an email from Melissa, declaring me responsible for all the bad that had happened in the world in the last half-century, with the possible exceptions of the Kennedy assassinations, the extreme and modern concept of *jihad*, and the open and notorious use of unnecessary quotation marks. So sometimes I am not in the present, the only place where joy is found. Sometimes I am in the past, resentful, and at others, I am in the future, worrying, planning. *Ungrateful...take responsibility... ow...foot...hungry...who's that?...interesting landscape...Jesus she's pretty...wind turbines...like north of San Francisco...wonder where she's having lunch?...online dating...New York...where will I live?... thirsty...then we'll have chocolate...*

Mom sings German lullabies and folk songs. I film her as she sings "Hänschen klein", or Little Hans, a song so familiar in Germany that in the German-dubbed version of Stanley Kubrick's "2001: A Space Odyssey", it's the song the malign computer Hal creepily sings as it's deactivated. "Hänschen klein" is like the parable of the prodigal son, except Hans isn't leaving because he's wronged anyone but because his mother complains a lot, and when he returns home at last it's not forgiveness he gets from his mother but recognition: she is the only one who recognizes Big Hans.

"I used to sing that when you were young," she says. "Before I started yelling."

I hear the old theme. I don't want her to lash herself anymore.

"You didn't yell that much," I say, which is both not true and probably not a thing a person with my memory could say with confidence anyway.

"I was always so stressed out," she says. "I always wanted it to be later on so I couldn't *be* in the moment. 'Oh, if it was only ten years from now!' I'd say. Now I'd do anything to get those years back."

* * *

She did yell, though it was her anger that had scared me, far more than any fear of physical harm. Anger is the quintessential rejection: her face got red like Opa's, with veins in her forehead, and that powerful, throaty, enraged voice. Some words were in German, magnifying their terror. When I was well into adulthood we had an argument, probably involving my accusing her of self-pity or self-absorption, that found us both shouting like that. "Are you going to *hit* me now?" she'd cried, and I had been confounded. "Opa's not here, Mom. He's gone."

* * *

Even as a child, I told myself I understood her stressed behavior. The custody battles with Jimmy had drained her financially and emotionally. She struggled to raise two kids on minimum wage. None of us had health coverage. My own father, living in Dinosaur, 19 miles away, had gone AWOL from any child support responsibilities. Mom sacrificed several of her own teeth after diverting the money for dental work to pay for things my sister and I needed.

One didn't really have *conversations* with my mother, in the sense of her asking questions and listening, then replying with something relevant to what one had said. One of the saddest things my mother ever said to me was that she hadn't learned, in her Dickensian childhood or after, "how to do that." I got easily frustrated with her. I would say something and she would nod, as if either distracted or impatient, and respond with something irrelevant either to the emotional or literal content of what I'd just said. If what I said sounded to her like criticism, she had other ways of not hearing me, such as by throwing the same criticism back at me, or detonating the entire conversation by pressing the victim button. ("Sorry I'm such a terrible mother!") Her reflexive response to my cosmic web of strategies, solutions, and ideas was No. She often didn't want to try it or consider it, whatever it was, and seemed not to grasp how to discuss it.

"I think everything I do irritates you," she once said.

This was roughly true, give or take a thing or two. That had been one of my biggest concerns when Mom asked me to join her on the Camino.

All my life I suffered from the hurt my irritability caused my mother. Why was I so irritable, if that was the right word? When I was young I went through the Freudian checklist. Was I angry at my father for abandoning us? Was I angry at my mother because as a kid I saw her angry? Did I resent the helpless-seeming part of her personality? Was I angry because my childhood had been foreshortened, even burdened, by her craving for attention, affirmation, emotional support? Even as a kid, I was embarrassed and troubled, in ways I couldn't yet explain, by the way she boasted about me. In my mid-thirties I read an arresting excerpt from the child psychologist D.W. Winnicott:

> The mother gazes at the baby in her arms, and the baby gazes at his mother's face and finds himself therein...provided that the mother is really looking at the unique, small, helpless being and not projecting her own expectations, fears, and plans for the child. In that case, the child would find not himself in his mother's face, but rather the mother's own projections. This child would remain without a mirror, and for the rest of his life would be seeking this mirror in vain.

I wondered, when I had looked into my young, storm-tossed mother's eyes, had I seen myself reflected there, or my mother? I began to see my irritability with my mother—and my own small-n narcissism—in a new light. Then the diagnosis of Tourette's just muddied the water again. Children with more severe Tourette's, I read, were often subject to terrible rages. Was my irritability the lame-Tourette's version of rages? What if whatever I felt was even partly from neurons misfiring, as happens with Tourette's? What if hearing interruptions or having to repeat myself felt, to me, the way nails on a chalkboard did to some people, or how the sound of other people chewing drove some people mad? What if I wasn't, at last, or at least not primarily, an asshole, an egotist, a bad person, an insufficiently loving son?

The day a Portland neurologist confirmed the diagnosis of Tourette's, I was years away from linking the condition with more subtle behaviors like irritability or glibness. But I was still surprised, when he told me, to feel tears well up. Maybe I was not an itchy twitchy bag of neuroses, a person with the character defect of being unable to handle anxiety, or other people, normally. Maybe I was a bit weird, but at least I wasn't a *weirdo*.

* * *

Stick, stick, stick.

"I could never have imagined in a million years I'd be here," Mom says. She gives thanks to her brother Gunter, now deceased eleven years, and his wife, Elfriede, dead now four. "I'm grateful that they earned the money, and Elfriede saved it and left some of it for me when she left. That money gave me breathing room. It let me travel." Yes, when Elfriede left my mother a third of her small estate, it caused a stir among the blood relatives she had passed over. But it was my mother who flew to Germany to take care of Elfriede for several months when her encroaching dementia had left her unable to care for herself, and her relatives were nowhere to be found.

We catch up to Marie Anne, sitting on a boulder with her head hung low, ironically, and an impish smile on her face.

"We were expressing gratitude," I say.

Marie Anne says, "Ze dinner in Pamplona is my *favorite* moment of ze Camino. It's not ze town," she goes on, "but ze people. You know?"

"Son?"

I turn to Mom.

"I am dizzy," she says. "I'm not sure how much farther I can go."

"Do you want to sit?"

"No, not yet. Let me try a little more. You go ahead."

We are quiet for a while as we walk on. Carrie, by herself between our two groups, is determinedly plying her single walking stick against the earth. Her earphones are in and she is singing quietly under her breath. Julio darts off the path and over a low fence to steal a rose, and when he jumps back he presents it to her. It's obvious she adores him.

The Bridge of the Queen and the Running of the Very Small Bulls

Finally, we come to Puente La Reina [94 of 799 km], Mom writes in her journal. *I made it! Lots of movement in town, with people sitting all over outside, picturesque houses, lots of flowers. Carrie has made a friend. An older gentleman and artist. We go to see the old bridge and I take pictures.* Online back at the albergue, Carrie is excited to talk to her big sister, who is her best friend, and it makes her a little sad afterward. "I want to go home to see them," she says, "but it reminds me how very lucky I am to be here."

In the courtyard of the albergue, I meet a social worker from Tel Aviv, Schlomit, who first heard of the Camino only two months ago; a young Brit, Jethro, who's been walking for three months, starting in Britain; and a dashing Italian, Marco, who runs a hostel in southern Brazil and walks in a beret. Mom and I explain to Jethro that English accents make everything sound more intelligent, even funnier. Except, I add, when he himself speaks. But he is in fact quite witty.

In the plaza nearby, there is a brass band comprised of men

in their fifties and sixties, and one long-haired young tuba player. Across the small plaza there is also a DJ spinning modern pop songs so loud that we can't hear the band. *We get our little family together*, Mom will write, *and go to see the bulls being run.* Two economy-size bulls are run back and forth to exhaustion by a band of gelled-up teenage boys in sneakers and soccer shorts and basketball jerseys. There are also a few older veterans, one of whom does actually grab one of the bulls briefly by the horns.

The people in the plaza dance, each holding a beer in one hand and the much-abused beat in the other. *A DJ plays good loud music and Marie Anne and I dance. It is so much fun.* Mom raises her head above the crowd and pumps her arms. In the same plaza, in 1315 and again in 1345, Jewish men were burned alive as sodomites, so running bulls as public sport could reasonably be seen by some people as an improvement. Tonight, a young man doesn't get out of a bull's way soon enough and finds its horns dug into his back, throwing him face-down onto the street. He lies there motionless and is surrounded by locals, until, after a while, he finally sits up.

Jethro says he is out of money.

"Join us for dinner," Mom says. "We'd love to have you as our guest."

Marie Anne somehow turns rice and mushrooms and other ingredients into a great risotto.

* * *

That night, I have a flying dream that I do not put in the blog: I start to take off, but Mom grabs at my legs and holds on, grounding me. I scream at her. *If you ever do that again you will never see me again!*

Day 11: The Long Road to Estella

In the morning, Julio is beside himself. It is going to be nearly 100 degrees, he says. "We should have *start*ed at quarter past *six*," he says. "It's going to *melt* all the Camino."

"I'm *melting!*" Carrie and I cry, like the Wicked Witch, but with our hands pulling at our faces like in Munch's *The Scream*.

From Puente La Reina to Estella will be 23 kilometers, with some climbing and descending. The country has grown drier since the lush riverside we found on the way to Pamplona. We walk through vineyards for much of the day. The others find the heat overbearing, but, perhaps because I am wearing a thin, wicking, breathing wool shirt, it doesn't bother me much.

In the village of Cirauqui, a Basque term meaning "nest of vipers," we come upon the cobbled stones and flagstone borders of a Roman road, and, after a while, a Roman bridge. While many parts of the Camino follow the course of the Roman Via Traiana, the best-preserved remains of the entire route are here. The cobbled Roman road continues for a few time-travelling kilometers, until we wind through more of the same dry, beautiful country, through hills where hermits came to live a thousand years ago, including in the still-extant Ermita de San Miguel. In a tunnel, amongst the graffiti, someone has written, "The Camino has nothing to do with Compostela. The Camino is right here, right now."

I call her the elusive, Mom will write of Estella. *I was under the impression that Estella was only 19 km from Puente La Reina, but the walk seems to go on for a long time. We see lovely vineyards, hills, olive trees, and figs. Julio picks some of each and offers them to me to make up for the lack of veggies. We walk up the hill and I am really breathing hard. When I reach the top, there is my little family, giving me a standing ovation.*

"My hero!" Julio says.

"I love you so much," Carrie says, hugging her. Marie Anne

offers Mom some water, and soon we are off again. "My legs are sunburned and red like lobsters," Mom says. And then, some kilometers later, we are at last in Estella (116.6 of 799 km).

CHAPTER 11:
MI HIJO

Day 12: La Bruja en Los Arcos

I am in some kind of narrow enclosure. Melissa is advancing toward me, naked, looking beautiful, being friendly, wanting something from me. I am not tempted. Once awake, I decide this must be evidence of my moving on. I wake up many times in the night, and I know I am sick. I can feel it in my chest. I feel weak and have chills.

When I get out of bed, my Achilles' tendons are once again painfully tight and inflamed. I hobble on them to the bathroom as on stilts made of glass. Julio sees me stagger in as he finishes shaving.

"Is this what it's like to be an old man, Julio?"

"I *would* not *know*," he says crisply.

I decide to take the bus to Los Arcos rather than suffer through a 20 km walk. Mom will write, *I could not face another day spending most of the time in 100 degrees Fahrenheit, so we make a good start in the cool morning mist. The stars are shining and we hear the click-clack of the walking poles. I have two BFFs, Preparation H and ibuprofen.* The countryside we pass through—I on the bus, the others walking—is gorgeous, all greens and browns and yellows, everywhere rolling hills and citadels and *iglesias*, with high granite cliffs in the distance.

As the wheels hum beneath me, I reflect on the nature of my days here in Spain. We walk rural trails through small towns that are largely emptied of the young (and even the middle-aged) and have few cafés or nightlife. I don't have books. I am reminded of meditation retreats, where people want to run away. When you watch your mind you see things that you aren't keen to see. Resentment, cravings, attachments, irritability, annoyance, jealousy, rage, desire, rejection, self-absorption, discomfort. Meditation doesn't make the unpleasantness go away—it just allows us to better manage negative thoughts and the emotions they lead to. Keep walking. Stay on the path. Just follow the yellow arrows.

It had been a long time since my mind was not continually gnawing over the future or, just as unhappily, the past. But in Spain, my mind is rarely occupied by anything more complicated than the next meal. I don't check my phone for emails or texts—because there are none. Some of the Tourette's tics are largely in remission, a fact I take as the clearest, most objective evidence of change. I haven't seen the Half Chaplin in about a week.

Every mid-morning, we begin to entertain fantasies about Second Breakfast. It's usually similar to First Breakfast—bread, cheese, yogurt, and *bocadillos*, sandwiches made from bread cut lengthwise— but we eat a lot more of it. We're thirstier, and water and juices replace the coffee of First Breakfast. We talk, break bread, say *buen Camino* to passing pilgrims and *hola* to locals. Soon we're back on the trail. About two hours after Second Breakfast, I am pining for First Lunch.

I wear a camera case in front of me. Hank, a Dutch pilgrim, tells me it looks like a codpiece and wonders if it interferes with my manhood. During walking breaks, sometimes even while walking, I whip out of it my notebook and pen, or my camera and either of two lenses. I write in cafés and on boulders. Walking long distances on purpose is one of the fundamental differences between humans and animals—as is creativity. Perhaps it's no coincidence that walking heightens creativity. After checking into a hostel in the afternoon, I take a shower, then I lie on my back on my dorm bed, put my MacBook Air on my thighs, and sum up the day's journey as pilgrims nap around me.

It's a very uneventful day, but it's more than enough.

Today, once I reach Los Arcos by bus, I walk around for a bit, finding the stores, the *albergue municipal*, and a café-bar called "abascal" whose owners have apparently lost their capitalization permit. I eat a green-and-red-pepper omelette *bocadillo* and drink hot rooibos tea. I leaf through a Spanish magazine to catch up on which American celebrities are sleeping with which other American celebrities. Back outside in a small plaza I sit staring at my hands with old men who seem not to have stirred since Franco.

* * *

The Albergue Municipal in Los Arcos (138.4 of 799 km) is staffed by two volunteers, a Belgian couple from Flanders. The man, rotund and pink-cheeked, is pleasant enough. I check in and have barely gone upstairs to Bed #6 when I hear Julio arriving downstairs for #7. I hear the woman from Flanders telling Julio that, no, he cannot reserve any beds for Mom and the others, though they are only minutes behind and he is holding in his hand their passports and Camino credentials. I turn and walk back downstairs.

Julio is looking at the woman like she has a *backpfeifenge-sicht*, which is the word Germans use for a face that's sorely in need of a fist.

"You are saying," Julio says, "that if a *person comes, first* time on the Ca*mino*, has *can*cer, you cannot put her near her *son*?"

"It is not allowed to make reservations in advance," the woman says, as if she is referring to well-settled principles of international law. "All Spanish outside," she says, motioning to him.

Julio's eyes grow to saucers. He makes a face at me and motions at himself to calm down. Then he walks back outside, to Table #1, to fill out his papers. I follow him. "Bloody hell," he mutters. "They don't know what they are doing. Can you believe what she says to me?"

"Volunteers," I say, trying to avoid a conflagration.

"Yes, we are volunteers." The husband has sidled up to us like curdled milk.

Julio digests this for only a moment. "Eef you are volunteers," he says, "then you have no right to complain."

Meanwhile, Mom is soldiering on. *The many hills that I have to climb don't elicit any more comments from me,* she will write. *It is what it is. It is all I can do to place one foot in front of the other.* She arrives exhausted. She's done a lot of mileage the last few days. "It was so hot!" she says. "I had to borrow Carrie's pant legs because my sunburn was so bad." She lifts her hem to show a painfully burned calf, red as the roof of a magic mushroom. I jump up to fill out the forms they need to sign at Table #1 so that they can then be permitted to approach the forbidding Flemish woman at Table #2. Julio takes the papers from me and presents them to the woman. He offers a new solution: he and I will simply move out of our dorm and into the one Mom is assigned to.

The woman shakes her head! She crosses her arms and cites to Julio one made-up rule after another, rules that don't exist in other *albergues.* This goes on for some time. My mother, exhausted, stands there next to Julio clutching her papers. The woman turns to her.

"Do you speak English?" she barks.

My mother nods.

"So what's the problem?" the woman demands. On her visage is the implacable calm of the righteous.

Mom seems confused. "I don't have a problem," she says quietly. "I'm just waiting here."

"He arranges everything for you?" the woman demands, pointing to Julio. "Even though you speak English? Why do you not handle this *yourself?*"

"I'm sorry," Mom says, "but I feel really sick, and right now I can't even manage writing my name."

The woman looks at her coolly. "So what do you want me to do?'

"For what I have, there's nothing you can do," Mom says.

I can hear the emotion catch my mother's voice, just as I can hear a self-pity that makes me sad. Mom has been facing the woman, with her back to me, so only now do I see that she has begun to cry. I am nearly hijacked. "You are a top-notch bureaucrat," I inform the woman. "My mother is exhausted and she has cancer and that's a lot more important than your rules. Don't talk to her again."

Mom will write: *My son takes over and tells her in no uncertain terms what he thinks of her and her sour attitude.* This is as much as I think I can say without going supernova. If I become attached to persuading the woman to change her mind, I'll feel anxious about a possible "no," which in turn will make me want to stuff her in a well, and stack her husband on top for insulation.

Then Julio, in Spanish, says many words, Mom will add. *I stumble off to find the dormitory before I collapse, led by my son.* Mom is just trying to escape, it seems to me, so I help her upstairs and leave Julio to deal with the Belgian. We can hear him laying into her for some time, apparently without result, for he comes upstairs, agitated, and in Spanish recounts to Marie Anne his agitation. He ends with a single word.

"Bruja!"

Witch!

It takes him some time to calm down.

"I ask her," he says, "'Where is your broom?'"

We all laugh at that, and a few minutes later I hear Julio singing Caruso-style in the shower.

The Mourning Tenor on the Camino de Santiago

In Los Arcos there is a church of extraordinary size and beauty. The Iglesia Parroquial de Santa María de la Asunción, built over a period of 600 years, betrays a mélange of styles, from Mannerist (~1530s to 1600) and Baroque (late 1500s to early 1700s) to Churrigueresque (late 1600s to early 1700s) and Rococo (1700s). After we rest up a bit, that's where we decide to go, minus Carrie, who wants to talk to her family online at the albergue.

We open the heavy, ornate door, Mom will write, *and I sit speechless in front of the golden splendor and beauty. Gold, carvings, painted walls, and stunning decoration. As we stand to gaze at some statues, Cameron puts his hand on my lower back, where the tumor resides. I feel the energy, and I am choked up and can't speak.*

We walk through all of it, trying to take in the dizzying detail of each of the competing architectural styles. At the top of a curving stone stairway is the choir, and next to that a room full of artifacts.

I light five candles, for four of my loved ones who have passed, Mom will write. Back downstairs, we four sit down near the back of the church. It is quiet. There are perhaps eight people inside.

Suddenly, from the choir behind and above us, we hear a voice. It is a magnificent voice, and it is full of feelings one is rarely privileged to hear. We turn and look up to see a small, white-haired man in a blue shirt and blue-and-white shorts in a swim-trunk pattern, with his arms spread before him, perhaps toward Mary herself, seated at the opposite end of the church, high up in the retablo. He is singing Schubert's "Ave Maria."

I turn on the video of my camera.

We look up in surprise, Mom will write, *and I see a lone man with both hands stretched before him. His voice is brimming with emotion, and I start to cry. I am remembering how violinists played "Ave Maria" at my brother Gunter's wedding to Elfriede, when they were so beautiful and young.*

Looking over at Marie Anne, I see her crying too. Everyone has stopped to listen. Then the singer pauses, and after a moment, he starts another version of "Ave Maria". His voice carries, and the acoustics are phenomenal. By this time, I am no longer thinking that he is singing from religious devotion, but from some other emotion.

Julio sits on the pew behind me, and Mom sits at the other end of it, wiping away tears and batting away the camera's gaze when it falls on her. Slowly, I get up and walk with my camera upstairs to the choir. Again and again the old man reaches his hands out over the bannister at which he stands, imploring whatever idea of an implorable consciousness he has in mind. For ten minutes, he sings three haunting versions of "Ave Maria"—Schubert's, Gounod's, and one no one in our group recognizes—as we sit motionless. When he reaches the end of his last "Ave Maria," he turns around, drained, and makes his way to a pew where two of his friends sit. He sits down briefly, and then they all stand up and walk past me. "*Grazie,*" I say. He nods at me and walks out the door.

He comes down and I shake his hand to thank him for his beautiful gift, Mom will write. *He says something in French, which I don't understand. I just place my hand over my heart.* "My heart was beating so fast," Julio murmurs to me. Our group goes outside into the quiet of the sunny cloister, still emotional, and then he is there too, as irresistible to our eyes as a magnet to metal filings, but also looking frail, spent, and awkward, with tears in his eyes. Seeing Mom's own tears, he leans toward her and says, in Italian that Marie Anne translates, "I sang to remember my son."

I am still wiping my face when I find out his son died a short time ago, and that today would have been his son's birthday. I look at him as tears stream down his face, and there is such deep pain. I cry as I write this. I fold him into my arms and he sobs, in English, "My son, my son." Then I can only touch my heart in silent communication. Everyone—Cameron, Julio, Marie Anne, and a few others— is openly weeping now.

Back at the albergue, Julio says he wants to get up at 5 a.m. For a moment, I think I might start to sob again. "Julio," I say, "At

5 a.m. I still have three hours of REM sleep left. I wouldn't ask a dog to get up at 5."

Day 13: To Viana: The Wasp and Veins of Coca-Cola

I may as well have gotten up at 5. Between the pilgrim noises in the night, the Rioja that Julio forced down my throat, and my worsening cold, I sleep fitfully. I wake up feeling at least as sick as yesterday, but I am determined not to take the bus again.

"I hated seeing Inge sad last night," Carrie writes in the morning. "But her spirits have lifted back up. Today we wake up and leave early, it is so dark but the stars are so beautiful I can't believe they are still out so late in the morning. We get to watch the sunrise too."

We're underway at 6:45. We walk under the stars, toward Venus—as close to romance as the Camino gets when you're with your mom and a girl who is assumed to be your daughter. It is still dark when the grieving tenor and his two friends pass us on the trail. His friends walk on either side of him, and one step back.

After an hour or so the sun yawns and stretches tentative orange fingers from east to west. The dawn light is something to behold, draping soft warm tones over the ploughed brown of the furrowed fields, the yellow grasses, the dozens of greens of the olive trees, the vineyards, and, later, the pines and almond trees. We are walking through nineteenth-century landscape paintings. We eat almonds from the trees and blackberries from their bushes.

The physical pains are mostly receding for me, but most days, the walking still hurts in some place or another. We're hoping we may soon all be enjoying ourselves as Julio does. Today I experience moments of real enjoyment in the rhythm of stick-stick-sticking my way across the landscape, taking in the smells and the light and shadow. I often wonder how much physical, to say nothing of emotional, pain comes from our resistance to doing exactly what we're doing.

Outside a café-bar where we stop, Mom gets stung by a wasp, twice, on her big toe. She cries out and hops around and we find her a chair and some ice. "You're going to have to suck it out," she says to me, joking, I think, and pointing to her leathery big toe. My sister and I still have nightmares from when we were kids and Mom asked us to massage her toe callouses from the too-small shoes she'd worn as a girl.

"You're thinking of snakes, Mom. You get bit by a poisonous snake, I'll be there."

"Then she keeps on walking," Carrie writes, "like a real trooper, 'the opposite of a victim,' Cameron says. Inge inspires me so much, and I think that's where I got all my energy today, from her and a mix of orange juice."

The way of the Camino is such that everyone, Mom writes, regardless of nationality or religion, is immediately helping. They don't ask your interpretation of the Bible before they're willing to help. No one holds himself above another. Sometimes the aid is as small as a band-aid. Other times, people stop and dig through their entire backpack to find what you may need. People call out a friendly "Hola!" when they pass, and everyone wishes you "Buen Camino". When I rest for a minute to catch my breath, the ones who pass always ask if I'm okay.

Julio tells me more about what he said to the Belgian *bruja* the night before. "I tol' hair, 'Why are you here? You don' speak the language, and in your veins there is no blood, only Coca-Cola.'"

"You said Coca-Cola?"

"Yes. To *do* this job you must have some *dyna*mism, not be there with your *lists* and your *forms*."

"Did she understand you?"

"Of *course* not!" he cries. "I had to re*peat* myself."

CHAPTER 12:
INTO THE WINE FIELDS OF RIOJA

Day 14: Viana to Logroño and the Mysterious Hospitalera Pregnancy

Mom has taken to repeating, in Spanish, what the mourning tenor kept saying: my son, my son. "*Mi hijo*," she says to me, playing with the sound of it. "*Mi hiiiiiijo.*" If I knew one thing as a boy, as a young man, it was the absolute boundlessness of my mother's love—I never once doubted it, or her.

The 10 km road from Viana to Logroño has little to recommend it. It passes by some small farms in disrepair, and more than the usual pilgrim trash along the road. At all times we can see the industrial buildings and warehouses of Logroño in the distance. Mom is suffering from several ailments that make walking painful, but she will not quit.

In a trailside shop I discover ventero, a soft cheese reminiscent of freshly made parmesan. I give a chunk to Mom. She savors its aroma and then bites into it. "They have some really wonderful cheeses here," she says. "Carrie?" Carrie wrinkles her nose, takes several atoms' worth of the cheese from Mom's hand.

An elderly woman has set up shop outside her tumbledown house. She is selling Camino pins and the like, but Mom and I are captivated by the five or six mutts straining to be petted. Mom agrees we'd have given her ten euros per dog if she would just promise to get them each a chain longer than 3 or 4 feet.

Farther down the trail, at the hostel in Logroño (165 km), a very pregnant *hospitalera* explains that the front doors will close at 9:30 p.m. The kitchen's stovetops have been removed and replaced with a countertop, which annoys Julio to no end. "You will see this in most of the *albergues* for the rest of the Camino," he says. "It's terrible." In disbelief he looks around at the useless kitchen. "We once had a *great* party in here."

Mom sits to write in her journal. *The 10 kilometers were so easy, but I am still tired. We buy tomatoes, cucumbers, cheese, chorizo, and bread, of course. I haven't eaten so many carbs in a long time. But there's absolutely no choice. I wonder if the veggies are sprayed. I am so far off my diet, I don't even see it anymore. My energy level is down, and I would even consider eating meat just to get something of substance into my stomach. I buy two large, lovely red peppers to eat on the way tomorrow in case the only options are the uncovered mayo tuna tapas.*

The women go out to get Marie Anne's lip waxed, and Carrie is excited to see her first person with sparkly tights, a dress, a lovely purse, and a beard. Back at the *albergue*, Julio is still exercised. "The *last* time I was here," he says, "an eighty-year-old man gave the best *service* on all the Camino. Now there is *these* people. I do not understand how the *hospitalera* got *preg*nant. To be *hon*est."

Day 15: El Notario, Fiesta in Navarette, and a Bowl of Soup

The next morning, Mom writes, *Marie Anne, Carrie, and I leave Logroño while it is still cool. Cameron and Julio are once again dealing with the notary, who Cameron tried to convince yesterday after-noon to notarize papers for selling his house in Bend. The landscape changes back to being hilly, with lots of vineyards. We stop at a bar and have our morning café con leche. I have to take two blisters off my right foot. We're in a beautiful spot by a pond, surrounded by green hills. Everywhere the harvesting of grapes has begun.*

We walk along the highway, next to a chain-link fence. Every link has a handmade cross in it, some made of wood, others of plastic bottles. I fashion one from yellow flowers and place it there as well. I remember my visit to Oklahoma City, where people did the same thing. I try to explain to Marie Anne that the bombing had hit the sacre de coeur of the people of Oklahoma City, and she understands.

I think about the ancient pilgrims, and their hardships. How they were often robbed, and if they didn't have enough to make the robbery worthwhile, they might be beaten and thrown into the river. So in spite of all my issues, they were much worse off.

It's a crisp morning in Logroño. Julio and I sit in a café-bar called Ibiza and consume *bocadillos* and *café con leche* (me) and hot chocolate (Julio). We're waiting for the notary office to finish complicatedly notarizing the documents from the title company handling my house sale, as agreed after protracted international negotiations yesterday afternoon. Julio now reads *El Pais*, one of the national papers, and translates for me the occasional outrage. Julio often sounds outraged, but it's more of a stance, like performance art. Then it's time to return to the notary. This will be our third trip.

El Notario is a very sober man. Small, neat, with a short-sleeved white shirt and a tie so modest as to border on immodesty, he exudes authority and self-assurance. A notary in Spain, I learned yesterday, occupies an economic role somewhere between a property lawyer and a machine that prints money. El Notario places before me the impressively extraneous documents that his assistant, Eva, has drawn up so beautifully and bound so extravagantly. Once my mortgage company is done with the codex I think they should give it to the Smithsonian.

Julio makes sure to legitimate me as a lawyer and fellow traveler right away.

"*El es un abogado de Princeton,*" he says.

"Harvard," I say.

And El Notario does grin.

El Notario verifies Julio's identity as witness and translator and makes him swear to translate faithfully, an injunction Julio violates repeatedly by saying "blah blah blah" over extensive portions of the document. I sign, stuff the papers into an overnight mail envelope, and we hit the trail.

We arrive in Navarette [180 km] early, Mom writes, meanwhile, *and the albergue is still closed. We wait at a nearby café, and we doze in the warm noon sun. Carrie has been sick, so she sleeps on a low wall, like a hobo. Soon, we see Cameron and Julio. They made the 13-kilometer trek in 2 hours!*

"Cheesus Crise!" Julio says as he sits down. "Jour son ees trying to *keel* me."

"Oh!" Mom cries, turning toward the plaza. "Do you hear that?"

I hear the piercing sound of an instrument that operates, like a hacksaw, on the region between the ear canal and the spinal column.

"It sounds like music from an ancient time," she says, standing up.

"It sounds," I say, "like it was designed by the court jester of some Navarran king to disable the king's enemies." We go to investigate the horrible sound. I am afraid of finding old women splayed about in the square, stockinged feet pedaling at the air in sensible black shoes, hands flailing to cover their ears.

"I think it might be a—oh, what is it in English?—a dulcimer," Mom says.

In the plaza, cheek by jowl with the local *iglesia* and in the shade of some very old trees, we find a stage rife with small children, mostly girls. To the right of the stage, Javier and the Earcrushers ply their trade on, yes, dulcimers. There are old women watching the spectacle, but they are still upright before the onslaught, their ears wholly unprotected.

"Oh, it's folk dances!" Mom says. "Look at their shy glances at their beaming parents." Delighted, she begins to clap along. I look at Carrie and see that, like me, she is watching Mom watching the girls dance, and I realize we share more than Powell blood. We are both here not so much to experience the Camino as to experience my mother experiencing the Camino.

The girls are dressed in the local traditional dress: starched snow-white dresses with flowers of fabric sewn on every hand's length. They wear white tights under shoes with red straps that wind up their calves. They kick at the music uncertainly. Nearby, a pride of women and teenage girls, similarly dressed, is showing them how it's done.

"Theese dance ees *la Jota Riojana*," Marie Anne shouts. The dancers hop and tap like a slow Irish jig, then turn this way and that as in a waltz. Most of them are smiling beatifically. A few are twirling humorlessly, *please save me* painted across their faces.

"Many parts of Spain have their own La Jota dances," Julio says. "Sevilla does flamenco. Madrid and Barcelona does something else. Barcelona's is very boring. *Very* boring. Catalans are a little like—no, I can't say that."

"'e ees rassist," Marie Anne says to me, in a fierce conspiratorial whisper.

"No," Julio says, temperately, "not racist. Just a—bwell, nevermind."

"I'm starving," Mom says. "But what's new?"

"Everything closed for the fiesta," Julio says.

"I read about locals coming with water or food to greet the pilgrims," Mom says. "I don't know how long ago this was supposedly happening, but we haven't seen anyone except feral cats and they're as hungry as we are."

The fiesta is a pleasant surprise, probably because *fiesta* and *siesta* share the same root, *iesta*, which is Latin for "let's stop working again." I drink Rioja and eat two bowls of *migas*. A live band plays Spanish tunes, along with a few traditional English-language folk songs from Lady Gaga, Tom Jones, and Spongebob Squarepants. Mom and I begin singing along to "Delilah." Marie Anne soon joins us. Carrie stays at a safe distance, for there is nothing so terrifying to a teenager as an adult body animated by music. Small children chase one another through the crowd. Mom has discovered soup that she loves so much she has two bowls. She is beyond happy about this. Carrie will write, "I loved seeing the little Spanish dancers and most of all, watching Inge enjoy the show. Her face was filled with happiness, she danced and sang and all I could think was I hope I can be half the woman she is one day."

Day 16: The Rioja Harvest: Navarette to Azofra

They're harvesting the Rioja grapes. It had rained for over a month straight by the time we'd arrived, and it's been sunny for the full two weeks of our stay, a combination that is expected to produce a good grape vintage. Julio is convinced Mom made a good-weather pact with St. Peter, and they keep up a running joke about the status of the arrangement. We run across a few vineyard workers who have made a fire out of dead vines and are about to roast an impressive array of sausage and chorizo over the flames. Mom tries to invite herself over for a bite, but the men don't understand her self-invitations, or pretend not to, and she gives up.

Mom has soldiered on to tiny Azofra (203 km), in spite of a good deal of pain and discomfort. *It is a 21-km hike to Azofra*, she writes there. *It is miserable for me, between this constant runny nose and the blisters on my toes. (This rhymes.) I try to ignore it, but snot runs down as if I am still getting chemo and don't have any of my nose hairs. My kidneys are hurting too, and I don't know whether I can walk 15 km tomorrow.*

Azofra's albergue has a cozy enclosed courtyard and a fountain in which pilgrims cool their feet. The exterior consists of a modern design of stone and wood slats. It even offers double rooms for everyone—so far unheard of on the Camino.

"I am *really* freezing," Mom says, wrapping her arms around her torso. "I'm going to go lie down."

"Okay, Mom." I go to my room and take a rare siesta. When

I find Mom afterward, in the kitchen, she says, "I was in bed and couldn't even get up." She sighs.

"Julio," she says, as he walks into the kitchen, "you have shaving cream on your cheek."

As a matter of principle, or something, Julio doesn't shave while he's on a walk. But his upper lip got sunburnt a few days ago, so he shaved it, but nothing else. I told him then that the result made him look Amish. I think he got self-conscious about looking Amish, so he shaved the sides off.

"Now you're back to looking merely Chinese again," I say approvingly.

"I'll make crepes for breakfast," Mom says. "Tired of all this white bread."

She goes to sleep early.

Day 17: To the Self-Resurrecting Chickens of Santo Domingo de la Calzado

Mom is still sick in the morning, but she's up early and cooking *pfannenkuchen*. These German-style crepes were once sliced and tossed into a tasty broth to become one of my boyhood's favorite foods, *pfannenkuchen suppe*. Mom invites Steffi to share. Kiernan, a young Irishman, wanders in and scores some too.

Mom and Carrie jump in a taxi to Santo Domingo. Julio, Marie Anne, and I walk. Marie Anne's suffering from an inflamed Achilles tendon, so we set a slow pace over the 15 kilometers. Happily, I had left my pack in the taxi: 27 pounds lighter, I move like Gene Kelly, wielding my poles like swords.

The air is noticeably colder. Vineyards stretch across the countryside, which grows drier by the kilometer. Abandoned cement aqueducts, elevated a few feet above the ground, run along the fields. We stop at a rest area with the following: a water fountain with potable water; three stone lounge chairs; a bench; and, near a fence leading into what is presumably private property, a sign saying, beneath the somewhat dynamic figure of a man:

Prohibido Defecar

The Spanish version means something very close to "Defecation Prohibited"—"As if there's an enforcing body involved," I say to Julio—but the English translation below it—"Don't Shit"—is merely hopeful. In the many clumps of white tissue nearby we see ample evidence of violation. On the other hand, as a German pilgrim points out, the graphic, which shows a man leaning forward with one arm bent high in front of him and the other bent high behind, if strictly interpreted, really only prohibits defecation *while sprinting*.

One colorful panorama stuns me with its beauty. The corduroy golds and browns of fallow fields all helter-skelter of angle, fields of green or yellow, parallel lines sketched in them by ploughs, copses of trees, and finally the hills beyond, from the evening blue nearest us to the charcoal beyond to the light grey in the far distance. I worry that at any moment I will thrust my walking stick in front of me and tear right through the canvas.

We stop at the club of the first golf course we've seen on the Camino, the Rioja Alta Golf Club, and where there are golf clubs there will be yellow Porsche Caymans and unsuccessful plastic surgery. But their *bocadillos* are *delicioso*. And by and by, we reach Santo Domingo.

Santo Domingo (218.3 km) is named for a local monk who so failed at his monk studies that he was sacked. Domingo spent the rest of his life building the area into a way station for pilgrims and won royal support and funding for his efforts, which just goes to show you. Eventually Domingo was canonized, becoming Santo Domingo.

There's a legend of the Hanged Innocent that repeats itself in various places in Europe. Most take place in Toulouse, a French city that has also laid claim to the bones of St. James, but the town of Santo Domingo has its own version. A woman, a man, and their son, all from Germany, arrive in Santo Domingo and stay at an inn. The innkeeper's daughter propositions the son, who is just not feeling it, so the little bitch arranges to have his pack filled with silver from the church. Though the innkeeper's daughter is clearly the most interesting person in the story, the legend drops her to follow our boring, spurning boy. Of course, the authorities catch him with the silver in his pack, and because fingerprint technologies and due process haven't been invented yet, he is hanged.

His parents, we are to believe, then looked at each other until one of them said, "Well. I suppose that's that. Why don't we walk to Santiago now?" to which the other responded, "Lemonade from lemons and all that." Because they leave their son hanging and walk all the way to Santiago. When they return a month later, they hear their son, still hanging from the gibbet. "Santo Domingo supported my weight all month," he tells them. (In ultra-competitive Toulouse, it's St. James himself who supports the little man-virgin.) The parents do not ask why Santo Domingo can't just use a knife to cut the rope, place a ladder under the boy, or display some useful superpower other than holding up a human body for a month. No, and for reasons that must also remain unexplained, the parents now leave the boy hanging *again* and run to tell the mayor, who is roasting chickens, as mayors will, and could really not give a shit. The mayor laughs, saying, "Your son is no more alive than these chickens."

Whereupon the mayor's chickens spring to life, grow back their feathers, and run, or fly, away.

The town still cares for two chickens, supposedly descendants of the original resurrected roasters. Purely by coincidence, Julio and Marie Anne buy about two chickens' worth of chicken breasts for lunch today, and they add scrambled eggs just to work in the entire poultry life cycle. Mom eats to her heart's content. After her nap, she writes, *We all leave to wander around town. I'm not sure if I am ready and well enough to walk 24 kilometers tomorrow, but I am willing to try.*

Day 18: Hard Road to Belorado. The Taciturn Waiter at the Café León

Mom, a serious snorer in her own right, is running a manufacturing facility in her sleep. When she stops, one of the Japanese takes over, turning in an impressive performance on behalf of his countrymen. I definitely see him in the medals when all this is over, certainly on the podium.

Up at oh-God-thirty, just ahead of the Japanese. Mom eats half a red pepper, bread, and coffee. We walk in the dark, beneath starry skies. "But we can still see our yellow arrow," Mom says. It feels good to be underway. It is chilly, though, and a slight wind makes it colder. I put on my wool cap and gloves. We pass a herd of sheep, fenced in. Their sheep dog eventually barks at our intrusion, but by then I have given the erstwhile lamb chops detailed escape instructions.

"Did you get your computer?" Carrie asks me. There wasn't an outlet near my bed and I had been charging it under hers.

"Are you kidding?" Mom says. "He'd forget his mother before he'd forget his computer."

"That's going in the blog!" I say.

For some reason Julio begins to tell me about Marie Anne's son.

"He seems to be a very bad son," I say, after a while.

"*Come se dice?*" Marie Anne says.

"Jour son is lazy," Julio translates for her, still in English. "Eet ees because 'e ees French." She smacks him.

The beautiful landscapes are behind us, and the vineyards have been replaced by fields of what used to be wheat, now cut down to 8-inch stalks. The land is growing drier with every step.

Mom is hurting. I can see it in her face and in her every step.

The toes of her right foot are painful to look at. *The skin of my foot is hanging off my little toe. The other one is raw hamburger. My H's are in an uproar, and there is a lot of blood, which creates another problem.* Her kidneys even hurt. During an emergency trip into the weeds to relieve herself she cries out, "I'm a bloody mess!"

"You can always take a taxi or bus from the next town," I tell her, when she is finished. Julio has now come back to check on her too, and we stand there, the three of us.

Mom's eyes well up. "I don't want to ride everywhere," she says. "I want to walk this."

I put a hand on her shoulder. "Whatever you decide, Mom. What about your ibuprofen?" I ask. "Have you had any today?"

"Oh!" she says, now hopeful. "I could try that."

The ibuprofen doesn't reduce her pain much. *By the time we stop to rest at a café-bar, in Grañon (226.2 km), Mom will write, I am in a lot of pain and just start crying. I can't breathe for all the snot! Cameron comes over to rub my back and give me some of his good energy. I tape up my toes and go to the bathroom and at least take care of that problem. They ask if I want to take the bus, but I don't want to. I want to walk. I just want to slow down, so that I can tend to things and not be run to the next place.*

Sitting at a table, she looks disconsolate. "There's no rule about how much we have to walk, or how fast," I say to her. "You're probably walking through more pain than anyone here."

She nods miserably.

We have our morning *desayuno*—coffees, teas, drinkable yogurt for me—and I work on Mom's back, near her kidneys, imagining I'm drawing out the negative *qi*, or energy, sending forth loving *qi*. Carrie then gives Mom a foot rub and reapplies the petroleum jelly that, I learn, she's been putting on Mom's feet every morning. Mom asks how far it is to the next village. "4.4 kilometers," Julio says, consulting the chart they give you in St. Jean. Mom decides to press on, but not before exchanging her too-small boots for the light sandals she's worn for most of the trip. I put the boots in my pack.

"We're gonna get rid of those sonsabitches soon," she says. "You can put that in the blog."

As we leave the restaurant, she is still in pain. "It's just something different every day," she says, sounding defeated. And then she points a finger upward: "Oh, look at those roses in that balcony, so pretty!"

Between the jettison of her boots, the ibuprofen, and her appreciation of beauty, her pain recedes, and she keeps a respectable pace for the next 10 km. It is Marie Anne whose Achilles tendon and other pain now keep her far in the back of our entourage.

We stop for a snack at the Café León, in Redecilla del Camino (230.4 km). It is a very beautifully done up place, inside and out. The passage to the bathrooms smells of lilacs, and the bathrooms themselves are spotless. The caballeros' walls are painted with wide vertical stripes of glistening white and blue. One thing I like about Spain is that, if you're a man and you're going to the bathroom, you get to call yourself a *caballero*.

A *horseman*. A knight, a chevallier, a cowboy.

Unfortunately, we appear to have interrupted the waiter-proprietor in the middle of a funeral rite, perhaps his own. As we approach, the only customers there, he eyes us without welcome, *hola*, or smile. "You can't bring your backpacks inside," are his first words, in Spanish. Eeyore will not look any of us in the eyes. We sit outside.

He brings some bread to our table. "I hope you choke on this," I'm pretty sure he says, as he sets the basket in front of me, "and your friends put the pictures on Facebook." I gnaw on my bread while he hovers. He asks Julio where we are from, and also if we Americans drink the tears of small children, as he has heard. He complains to Julio, in Spanish, that tourists to Spain don't speak enough Spanish. He himself had once been to Turkey, but had a bad experience when he couldn't understand anyone, so he decided never to leave the country again. Imprisoned within such tortured logic, by which he had put himself in the position of arguing that non-Spanish-speaking tourists should keep their money away from his restaurant, I thought I could see why he was so unhappy.

"Teepical Castillano," Julio says to us, after the man has gone back inside. Marie Anne cackles.

"That made me feel a little bit bad," Carrie says.

Julio turns to her. "Kindness," he says, "is an international language."

A party of Russians arrives. The waiter materializes to chastise them for some shortcoming that I can't make out. He doesn't look at the Russians, either, nor the Koreans, nor any of the other customers who come in over time. He serves us all entirely without pleasantry or comment.

As we stand up to leave, and I see his shoes, I understand at last. If the collected works of Don Elvis Presley have taught us anything, it is that the primary anxiety of a *camarero* wearing blue suede shoes is that, while in theory you can knock him down and step in his face, slander his name all over the place, you should lay offa his blue suede shoes.

We continue on. The sun beats down, having no alternative, on the nothing new, and we march over the graveled road, parallel to the highway, that has characterized the last 40 kilometers. The food has re-animated Mom and Marie Anne alike. They push on to Belorado (242.4 km). Mom has made it. Over 13 miles! The Albergue Santiago beckons, our first private albergue. With a price of five euros, flags of twenty nations colorfully flying outside, a *menu peregrino*, a bar, a "mini-market", washing machines, and even the promise of a swimming pool, it is terribly inviting, even if the American flag has been left out. The skin of Mom's little toe is hanging loose and pus is seeping out. *I wonder what possible function this little toe has,* she writes, *other than making my life miserable.*

CHAPTER 13:
HASTA LA VISTA, AMIGOS

Day 19: Belorado, Jamón, and Burgos

The onomatopoeic German word for snorer, *schnarcher*, best captures the enthusiasm of the night's symphony. Mom begins it. I had lost one of my semi-effective earplugs, so I have to use my iPod's new Anti-Snore Mix. It works a little better at keeping out sound, but against the woman who takes over from Mom, there is no defense. In the middle of the night, in the dormitory made humid by the exhalations of others, I awake feeling sick again.

Mom's right pinky toe looks like a particularly lurid crime scene, so she's not able to walk without pain and discomfort. We walk to catch the 9:30 a.m. bus to Burgos, which will eventually leave at 10:05 sharp. On top of one of the village's two small churches are four enormous storks' nests. We'd seen three of the graceful birds flying overhead a few days ago.

"Climb up there with my camera," I say to Julio.

He eyes me skeptically.

"I want to see," I go on, "if storks are the kind of birds that will violently defend their nests."

He chuckles drily. "They wan' more meat than there ees on *me*. I am good only for a *soup*."

A white van labeled *Carneceria* and *Charcuterie* pulls up right in front of us. "Carrie," says Julio, "turn *away*. You don' want to look at thees." Without a word she turns away. In each of three trips the driver walks by with half a pig, cut length-wise, draped over his shoulder, and then unloads a white plastic bucket full of pig's heads. Carrie inevitably sees how the *jamón* gets to her plate, and she declares herself a vegetarian. "I saw the most horrifying thing," she will confide in her journal later. "It was the worst thing I've ever laid my eyes on."

,   Two days ago as we were walking we found ourselves overwhelmed by the foulest stench. "This is where they produce all the shit made in Spain," I had said to Carrie, gesturing with one of my walking sticks, "up ahead." She nodded cautiously. She is required to produce a report when she gets back to school, and I try to be helpful. But once she heard the oinking she had known what we were smelling: the nostril-scouring excretions of pre-*jamón*.

In Burgos (293.4 km), we disembark from the bus not far from the Rio Arlanzón, a river framed by high, wide banks and grassy wetlands. Small, white columnar banisters rise on both sides of the river, up to the street level where we are sitting. On the old-town side of the river, there is a wide promenade bounded by giant statues and ancient trees and tall shrubbery cut in geometric shapes. This is where we decide to go walking. Burgos was once the commercial center of central Spain, the ally and favorite of Isabella the Catholic, who, with her soul mate, Ferdinand the Catholic, would start the Inquisition and send Columbus to loot the Americas. For half a millennium Burgos served as the capital of the Kingdom of Castile. Napoleon occupied it for three years, and during the Spanish Civil War Franco based his operations here.

We promenade along the promenade until Julio returns from a *jamón*-and-cheese-finding expedition. *He presents them like treasures,* Mom writes in her notebook. We eat on a bench overlooking the river. Julio and Marie Anne explain that there are about a half dozen types of *jamón*, ranging from the *jamón de bodega*, grown in humid climes like Julio's own Bilbao, which is "only good enough for frying or casseroles", to *paletilla* and *jamón iberico*, which "melt in your mouth." Julio has bought *paletilla* for us, opting for the forty-seven euro per kilo variety rather than the 120-euro *jamón*. Even the forty-seven-euro *paletilla* does melt in the mouth.

Mom loves the ham and the regional cheeses Julio has bought too. Carrie refuses to touch the *jamón*. She refuses even to make eye contact with it. After her graduation from high school, she will adopt a baby pig, name her Opal, and get a tattoo on her ankle of a miniature pig wearing a red bow and kicking up her heels.

Then it is time to check in to the albergue. There is already a short line.

"Always Koreans at the front," Julio says to the leaders. "*Ju* are the *best*!"

Burgos and the Inquisition

"Burgos is absolutely lovely," Mom says. She loves the old town center, with its helter-skelter of squares and shops, cafés and bars.

"This is *amazing*," Carrie says. Her eyes are open wide. The cathedral is by far the most monumental building she's ever seen, to say nothing of its sheer beauty. "Look at the gargoyles!" she says, pointing at the demons clutching the cathedral's tallest spires. "They're so intricate."

On the way in, I see on a placard the word "*fachada*" and I guess out loud that it refers to "*façade*." Marie Anne shows surprise. "You know zees word?"

"Sure," I say. "It's English." I like to toy with Marie Anne, who is both a good sport and as expressive as a child. Her English is only slightly better than my Spanish, which is itself an abomination.

"No," she says, shaking her head, like the language teacher she is. "Eet's French."

"We liked it, so we took it."

"Wis ze F-A and ze C wis ze"—and here she draws with her finger in the air the little hammer and sickle that hangs from the c in façade—"?"

"Yes," I say. "That's it, exactly. Wis ze—" and I draw the same thing in the air and stab at it with a Gallic nose. "Massage and chauffeur are also American. Also French fries and carabiner. Also *le weekend*."

"Zey are French!" she says. "But not French fry and weekend."

"Americain," I say. "We took zem. Zey are ours now." Mom is laughing.

Then we are inside. I take a lot of pictures.

"My goodness," Mom says, "all that *gold*!"

"When I think about Spain," I say to Mom and Julio, "I think about the Inquisition." An unholy alliance between the ideology of church and the killing machinery of state, the Inquisition squats in a dark tunnel in my mind, right next to the Holocaust. I don't want to look and I can't look away.

The Inquisition at first was content with forcing the "conversions" of Jews and Muslims into Christians. But by the late fifteenth century, Christians in Spain decided they were deeply unhappy about their belief that the *conversos* were not really sincere in their hearts about their love for the Good News of Christ, a typical bit of fundamentalist victimology that is rather like complaining that the person you have just raped did not sufficiently enjoy it. In 1492, the torture, killing, and expulsions of Jews and Muslims began in earnest.

"Other rich civilizations, too," Julio says now, "like the Inca and Aztec."

Ferdinand el Católico and Isabella el Católica—as they insisted on being called—walked part of the Camino themselves. Once they took Spain back from the Moors in 1492, the ideology of the Reconquista (Spain for Christians alone) was easily lent to the Crusades (Jerusalem for Christians alone), early and late western slavery (rights and freedoms for Christians, and then whites, alone), and then the Holocaust (Europe for Christians alone).

In 1574, the village of Santiago de Compostela—the endpoint of our Camino—was granted a permanent inquisitorial tribunal, which in Spain was, like the office of notary, a license to print money.

Without its own budget, the Inquisition depended exclusively on confiscating the wealth of the denounced. This is what we now call a perverse incentive. The inquisitors overwhelmingly targeted wealthy Jews and Muslims, whose wealth, upon their predestined conviction, flowed into the hands of the inquisitors, who in turn built the cathedrals along the Camino, like this one, full of gold and portraits of Mary cradling her dead Jewish son, the bloody wounds to his feet, hands, and side lovingly painted in by the artists.

"Ju notice," Julio says to Mom, "some of these gold artifacts, where eet says 'Origin', they say only 'Mexico'."

"No explanation for how it got into Spanish hands," Mom says.

History tells us it involved a great deal of blood. The night before, I had found, online, the Aztecs' own chronicles. In 1519, in the patio of the main temple in the grand city of Tenochtitlan, Aztec people were celebrating a great fiesta. Suddenly, the Spanish Conquistadors, "seized with an urge to kill the celebrants," closed all escape routes from the temple and, "when the dance was love-liest and song was linked to song," burst into the sacred patio.

> They attacked the man who was drumming and cut off his arms. Then they cut off his head, and it rolled across the floor. They attacked all the celebrants, stabbing them, spearing them, striking them with their swords. They attacked some of them from behind, and these fell instantly to the ground with their entrails hanging out. Others they beheaded: they cut off their heads, or split their heads to pieces. Some attempted to run away, but their intestines dragged as they ran; they seemed to tangle their feet in their own entrails.

I paraphrase this for our little group. "What," Marie Anne asks, "ees entrails?"

"It's French!" Mom says, which is true.

Thanksgiving at the Casa Babylon

Burgos will mark the end of our Camino together. Julio has business to do in Madrid. In the evening, Mom takes a shower, puts on makeup, and waits for everyone to get ready for dinner. When we've all met up in the lobby, she says, "We will buy dinner for Julio and Marie Anne, to thank them from the bottom of our hearts for all their love and friendship."

"Sanksgiving?" Marie Anne asks.

"That's right," Mom says. "Thanksgiving."

We go to the Plaza Santo Domingo de Guzmána and a restaurant called Casa Babylon, which promises *"Sabores del Mundo"*, or "Flavors of the World." The menu doesn't disappoint us. "Oh," Mom says. "My cells are a-hoppin'. So many interesting dishes here." Julio examines the wine list.

"Inge," he says, "if I can ask you one favor, please let me pay for the—"

"Okay," I say.

"—wine."

Marie Anne, the thespian, laughs, now red as her hair. "Zis is so good timing!"

I raise my glass of water. "To our wonderful new friends! May we see them in Colorado soon!" I clink Julio's glass with my own.

Julio raises his glass. "To Inge, my heroine, and Cinderella." We clink, we drink. "It's unbelievable to me how can Inge manage every day a fantastic sense of humor," Julio says. "I never heard one complaint, other than the logical ones, like, 'Can I have a glass of water'."

"Your mother ees very strong," Marie Anne says to me.

Julio addresses the waiter who has come to hover over him. He points at the wine list and the waiter withdraws.

"The Camino is like life," Mom says to Carrie. "You might get someone who goes through the day at the same rhythm or somebody is always going too fast or too slow. It's a good way to know if you can share your life with someone."

"I can't believe all the crosses and flowers and pictures for people who *died* on the Camino," Carrie says.

"Some people aren't used to walking," Julio said. "Or they don't understand the heat, or that you need a lot of water. One Japanese man was walking in winter for hours and hours. He sat down to rest under a tree and died."

"You remember ze French man who come to ze Camino wiss no money?" Marie Anne says.

"The gentleman weeth the cape!" Julio says.

"You invite him to join us in a restaurant."

Julio nods and looks at us. "Whatever you get from the Camino, you supposed to give back." To Marie Anne he says, "The next day you put twenty euros in his hand."

"He refuse," Marie Anne says. "I say, yes, take it. In ze evening, I find ze money again in my pocket."

"He could walk 60 to 70 kilometers in a day," Julio says. "Slept in the grass, outside."

"Why was he on the Camino?" Mom asks.

"He had been sexually abused," Julio says. "I think he found on the Camino the pure peace he was looking for."

A lull slips into the conversation. I am wondering if pure peace is possible.

"Some people," Marie Anne says, "zey go on ze Camino after zey lose zeir jobs. Albergues not charge a pilgrim who have no money."

"One thousand euros a month it costs on the Camino," says Julio. "Fifteen hundred if you are a beer drinker." Bereft now of beer, he drinks his wine. Carrie orders a spicy Devil's Spaghetti and, for dessert, we both order white chocolate soup like a pond into which chunks of brownies have been tossed.

Marie Anne tells us about one German *hospitalero*, 2 meters tall. She had been having a problem with her knees for many days. Julio translates. "She say she was in Palencia. After coming over the Via Romana, she say, 'I can't walk anymore.' Her feet are also in terrible shape. So. This handsome young German, mid-twenties, very tall, he ask Mariana if he can help. He touch her feet for a few minutes. I am eating my bocadillo. Bwell, I realize the massage is going a bit long, but I am just 2 meters away. Afterward, I ask her, are you better now? And she say—"

Marie Anne interrupts. "'Julio, my feet are okay, but I think I had one or two orgasms.'" She cackles. Mom snorts with laughter and her face is luminous. She hugs Marie Anne again.

"I'm going to miss you two."

"Me too," says Carrie. She has tears in her eyes. "Whenever I'm feeling down, your encouragement just lifts me back up."

"One more thing," Julio says, standing up. In his hands is his favorite Camino guidebook. He hands it to my mother. "For you, my heroine." He bows ostentatiously and Marie Anne begins to clap. On the first inside page, he'd written, *Para Inge, una peregrina con mucho corazón. Julio.* For Inge, a pilgrim with a lot of heart.

Now Julio says, "I will remember how Meester Cameron was *very* concerned about how all the *gold* got into the cat*hed*ral."

"He always rooted for the underdog," Mom says. "Always." She smiles. "I remember there was this old man on a game show and Cameron thought the host was making fun of him. He was five. He was so upset, and he felt so badly for that old man. Another time, there was a beauty pageant on. One of the contestants came out and Jimmy said, 'She's ugly!' And Cameron said, 'She's not ugly, she's just not beautiful!'"

"I think you've told me that one before," I say.

"Do you remember when we picked out Squeaky?"

I do not. I would have been four or five at the time.

"You went straight to him. He was the runt of the litter, the only one who didn't crowd forward in the basket. I asked you why you wanted that one, and you said, 'Because he needs the most love.'" She looks at me. "That's the same little boy who came on this Camino with me."

Day 20: Marie Anne and Julio Leave Us

I wake up at 4 a.m., Mom writes the next morning, *and after lying there for a while, I get my book and use my little light under the covers to read. Later, Julio is awake, and we go downstairs for some automated coffee. He then gets the hospitalero to look at my toe.*

The *hospitalero,* a kindly man in his late seventies, is actually a doctor, and early this morning he drains Mom's toe of pus, leaving in a thread so it won't close up. He wraps it in Betadine and what little gauze and tape Mom has. He also tells Mom not to walk on her foot *for a few days.*

He makes sure, Mom writes, *that I understand how vital it is to take care of this at once in the next albergue, in León. My toe hurts worse and I am limping. We go to have breakfast near the cathedral, and it is another gorgeous day. Then we go to the bus station to see off Julio and Marie Anne and to say goodbye.*

Julio tries to shake my hand. "*Cheesus Crise!*" I cry. "Come here." I give him a big hug. He's shorter than me, standing on the fatless muscular legs of a trekker, but the slight potbelly of the beer aficionado and gourmand lends him a surprising sturdiness. "Let us hope for the best," he says, quietly, growing emotional. Julio and Marie Anne had both really enjoyed my mother. Because they were morning people, too, they'd both spent more time with her than I had. Julio had been as solicitous as a butler, or a good son, giving Mom invaluable help and me the breathing room I needed. Carrie hugs him next, thanking him, so happy to have met him.

"You've become such a big part of my life," she says. "Like family."

"Buen' Camino," he says. "Don't let anyone take jour smile, Cinderella. Or jour eagerness to *challenge* yourself."

In the not-too-distant future, Carrie will get another tattoo, this one on her foot, of a hiking boot nestled on a tasseled pillow. Below the pillow, the word *Cinderella.*

Mom and Marie Anne are embraced in a long goodbye. "I'm

going to miss you," Mom says. "Thank you for everything." When she steps back, they are both crying, which gets Carrie going, and I am about to be next.

"Let's vamoose," I say, moving in to hug Marie Anne.

"That's why I don't do goodbyes," Mom says, wiping her nose. "I always just drop 'em off at the airport curb."

And so, with the heartfelt talk of "next time" that takes some of the sting out of parting—New York, Colorado, the Dolomites next year?—we leave our friends at the bus station. We know the color and texture of our journey won't be the same.

We haven't been able to sustain the average of 16 miles a day that traveling 500 miles in thirty days would require, and Mom's foot is aflame. We decide to leave out the *meseta* between Burgos and León, missing the hot, dry, flat, grasshopper-infested land-scape of the Castilian Plain. By Santiago we'll still have walked close to 400 miles. Besides, the writer James Hitt walked the *meseta* so we wouldn't have to. "I had been warned about the plains (by people) who said that they were frightening and hot," he wrote, in what remains one of the best Camino travelogues, *Off the Road*, from 2005. "There are no towns up here. No bars. No shed. Not even shade. The farmers drive here in their tractors to tend their wheat fields, and the occasional shepherd visits his flock. Otherwise, there is no one." Mom will write, *The bus trip covers two hours and boring landscape, hot, land, sand, nothingness.*

CHAPTER 14:
TOWARD THE IRON
CROSS OF LETTING GO

We arrive at the albergue in León at around 7 p.m., then hurry across the street to have dinner, which is a piece of frozen lasagna, heated on one side, with laboratory cheese, for 10 euros. Then I have heartburn.

—Mom

Day 20 cont'd – Day 21: León's Hospitalero and Brilliant Cathedral

It's tempting to think León (476.5 km) is named for a lion, but in fact the name comes from the Roman 7th Legion, which founded a camp on the site in the year 70 CE. The Romans came to protect the Galician gold mines from the grubby hands of the locals. It was also from a base in León that the Romans worked tirelessly, for 350 years, to conquer the "barbarians" of northwest Spain, otherwise known as the Celts. It was for naught, of course, because the Roman Empire would fall and León would see a succession of Visigothic, Muslim, and Christian rulers.

The Santa María de Carbajal albergue is connected to a convent, but when we arrive the nuns are, habitually, not in evidence. Since the original convent, founded in 1152, separated men's and women's dormitories, today's male and female pilgrims are also separated. According to an ancient document cited in my guidebook, "it is a dishonest thing to have women and men in a single dormitory," and the "people who come to the hospice are not of high caliber."

Nonetheless, a few hours after we arrive, I find Mom holding court with five German men in a covered section of the albergue courtyard. One of them, a pastor, is taking notes. He had run for his notebook when Mom began to tell him of her original rules for Carrie: up early, no whining, no hair-fussing, no makeup, no going off alone. Another German says, "The pastor will use the material for his Sunday sermon."

The pastor asks Carrie what was the most beautiful stage on the Camino and what was the hardest. "The Pyrenees, for both," she says. Did she regret coming? "No! This has been a wonderful experience. Best time of my life." The pastor says she is very brave.

León is a charming city. Its many pedestrian streets are a riot of color and sound: shops, café-bars, brightly painted two-story build-ings with contrasting shutters, pots of flowers in every window. We come upon a Mercado Medieval, a street fair with a medieval theme, and perhaps a hundred different hawkers of crafts and food dressed in medieval garb. Burros give children rides around a park. Eight birds of prey sit on display, and a Boreal Lynx prowls on its 10-foot leash. Octopodes slither in vats. Mom will write of the *families with their kids and/or dogs all around. Old, young, vis-iting, laughing, and enjoying their fiesta. It's a nice way to see your neighbor, in a different setting, other than court*. Carrie has found tapas of bacon and cheese on baked potato skins that causes her to forget her vegetarianism entirely.

Drawback is, walking so much, Mom will write. *My toe hurts something fierce. Stinging like mad.* She sits on a bench to unwrap it and discovers that the thread has now cut off the circulation. *I am so sick and tired of pain. Cameron is frustrated not knowing how to help me.*

* * *

The cathedral in León, copied at two-thirds scale from the Rheims Cathedral in France, is a purer example of thirteenth-century Gothic than the one in Burgos, whose fifteenth-century Flemish-Gothic additions apparently complicate matters. León's is less elaborate, arguably less gaudy, its interior more understated. But what distinguishes León's cathedral is the exorbitant number and grandeur of its stained-glass windows. From the outside, the windows look daubed in soot and dirt: they are entirely an opaque tan color, more than a bit disappointing. But when we walk inside to the transporting sounds of a man, or a recording of a man, singing Gregorian chants, we can see, to our surprise, the stained-glass windows in all their peacock splendor. We walk farther in, right through the mote-filled beams of light they're refracting. *We sit down and listen*, Mom will write, *being still and in the moment, while looking at the many gorgeous stained-glass windows in brilliant colors. Cameron sits beside me, holding "the spot" on my back.*

* * *

The award for best *hospitalero* on the Camino will be hard to wrest from the gentle hands of Thomas Schlitt-Krebs of Heidelberg, Germany. *One of the nicest and most accommodating of the Camino so far*, Mom writes. *Smiling, too!* Thomas seems to be everywhere, at all times, speaking English, Spanish, and German. I see him pouring coffee for people, mixing their milk in. He leads pilgrims to their bunks. He gives out numbers for taxis. He gives advice on what to see and do, marking directions on maps in his careful engineer's hand. And always he has that brilliant smile, and an infectious lovingkindness.

When we decide to stay an extra night at the *albergue*, he gives Mom and Carrie a room to themselves. For this he gets grief from the French *hospitalera*, spiritual cousin of the Belgian Bruja in Los

Arcos. Like any proper fundamentalist, she insists on the rules: people must fill up space in the proper order, so Mom should be slotted into the dorm room that still has vacancies. Thomas says, "I will take the matter up with the sisters if I must." The woman relents.

Thomas asks Mom if the Camino is, for her, a religious pilgrimage. "I was born, baptized, and raised a Catholic, but I didn't keep it up," Mom says. "Too many things I didn't agree with. My father, a Lutheran, was disowned by his family for marrying my mother, who was Catholic," she says. "I had some unhappy experiences in my Catholic school. I have a lot of issues with that Church. I tried the Presbyterians for a while, and then the Lutherans." She laughs.

He nods. "I understand completely. You must believe in something, though, or you wouldn't be here."

"Yes," she says. "I do. I felt the Camino wasn't even my decision, but that it called me. I would say I'm more spiritual than religious. I like Buddhist sayings and philosophy, I admire Native American spirituality and its love of nature. If you're good, that's good enough for me, I don't care what color, what you believe."

"Mom's a bit of a Pagan," I say. Thomas laughs. Mom is nodding, with a *what are you gonna do?* look on her face.

With Julio and Marie Anne gone, we find ourselves meeting and talking to more people than before. In the afternoon a French student and a wily Basque offer me some wine. The Basque had earlier played Elvis' "Can't Help Falling in Love" on his cell phone while taking a shower. I started to sing it, he joined in, and then we were blood brothers. I give my map to a departing older Irishman. An unnervingly beautiful young Scottish woman, an art student, is at a loss either to explain why she speaks with a plummy English accent or to provide a convincing rationale for why she is not twenty years older.

Sometimes my old anxiety that I don't know how to find the fun resurfaces. But then, in the night, about thirty of us pilgrims follow a nun, sixtyish and diminutive, to the sisters' modest little chapel, which nevertheless boasts a brilliant-gold *retablo*, above the altar, that would have dominated any church in the U.S. Before we are permitted to enter, the nun, in Spanish, says something to the effect that we are not tourists, but seekers of God. Then she leads us through a singing of some verse. I can hear Mom's strong, sweet timbre next to me. "*Muy bueno*," the nun says of our singing. She pauses for a beat. "*Mas o menos.*" More or less. Everyone laughs. Then we enter the church itself, and there they are, arrayed in the choir, a baker's dozen of nuns. A pilgrim's cell phone rings four or five times. The head nun claps loudly at her. Mom turns to me.

"See?"

Day 22: On to Astorga, City of Chocolate

"I prayed for you last night," Thomas tells Mom. At breakfast, he takes me aside. "When there is a sickness in the family," he says, "everyone is affected. Everyone has it, in a way. I know this. So there may be times when you need to say, 'Mom, I must go my own way for a bit, I must be for myself now.'"

Well, yes. I don't blame her for having been a very human, young, single parent, but since I began to observe the patterns in my own relationships, in college, I've understood that her reliance on me, and the responsibility I undertook for her, had long-term consequences. As I've gotten older I've learned to wrestle into submission the guilt I feel from having to protect myself from my mother's instinctive incursions. Without that protection, I wouldn't have the wherewithal to help her with the important things.

We take a short bus ride from León to Astorga (526.3 km) because we need to give Mom's toe more time to heal. Astorga is a pleasant little town. There is an embarrassing wealth of cathedrals and churches for such a small town, and a Museum of Chocolate, which Carrie is determined to see.

Astorga was originally a Celtic settlement. Then it was conquered by successive waves of Romans, Visigoths, then Moors, after which the city was abandoned until the eleventh century, when it became a major stop on the Camino. But today its cathedrals, and the neo-Gothic, fairytale Bishop's Palace designed by Antonio Gaudi, are all closed. *Fantastic-looking Gaudi house*, Mom will write, *almost like Hogwarts or some wizard's home.*

Legend has it that both St. James and St. Paul found time to travel to and preach in Astorga. The two Jews would have done well to stay clear of Spain. "A Franciscan inquisitor once confided to King Philip IV of France," the historian Cullen Murphy writes, in his fantastic *God's Jury: The Inquisition and the Making of the Modern World*, "in the early fourteenth century, that if Saints Peter and Paul had appeared before his tribunal, he had no doubt that the techniques he employed would be able to secure their convictions." This is why we have due process.

Mom is utterly delighted with the albergue's kitchen, which leads to a patio with a view for miles. She immediately goes shopping for lunch. *Carrie and I buy hamburger at a nice carniceria*, she writes, *so I can make German hamburgers. I add sautéed onions, German potato salad, white asparagus, raw red peppers, banana slices, and grapes. We eat on the terrace, which has a beautiful view, and a vast landscape with church towers, houses, poplar trees, and nice, nice weather.* We get a small room with a view, which we share with Barbara, a woman of a certain age from near Munich. Her daughter, she tells me, was once a satisfied exchange student in Iowa. Her Bavarian accent reminds me of my relatives, and occasional childhood, in Bavaria.

As we walk around town later one proud native informs us that Astorga was the site of the first chocolate maker in Europe. (He also says the first chocolate *shop* was in Aachen, Germany). We tour the underwhelming Museo de Chocolate, which appears to be the home of someone who hoarded chocolate-making tools and chocolate advertisements from the late nineteenth and early twentieth centuries.

It was the Aztecs who first perfected chocolate. Montezuma drank Xocolatl! eight times a day, believing it was the key to good health. But what didn't he consume? On a typical night he ate chicken and turkey, songbirds and doves, ducks and rabbits, pheasants, partridges, and quail. For dessert, according to secondhand reports, he had an adolescent boy, and sometimes two, which seems a bit indulgent. He finished with Second Dessert of tortillas and hot Xocolatl! When Hernán Cortés broke into Montezuma's palace, in 1519, to steal what he was sure would be all the continent's gold and silver, he was astonished to find only a vast store of cocoa beans. But Cortés brought Xocolatl! to Spain, where the bitter stuff was made more palatable to European tastes by mixing the ground roasted beans with sugar and vanilla. When more and more sugar was added, it became palatable to *norteamericanos*.

Day 23: New Shoes to Rabanal del Camino

I don't get to sleep until nearly 11, and between Mom's snoring, Barbara's (according to Mom), and apparently my own (per Carrie), the morning hours come far too quickly. Mom gets up much earlier than we do and goes to the kitchen to make some German-style potatoes.

On the road before 8 a.m. we walk surrounded by the wonderful aroma of fennel. It is like walking through a licorice factory. The blue of the dawning sky is beyond description. The power lines sizzle and buzz overhead—something I've heard only in Spain.

It is cool enough for two layers of wool. Unlike in days past, when, after thirty or sixty minutes I'd take off the top layer, I wear both layers the whole 22 kilometers. In fact, after my hands stop functioning in any way but to hold my poles, I add gloves. And my five-toed wool socks. My nose runs the entire way.

Mom is pleased with the new Salomon trekking shoes she bought yesterday in Astorga. "Oh," she had said, dancing a jig in the store. "I'm going to sleep in these! These shoes are heaven." For the first time since we began the Camino, she will walk an entire stage in one pair of footwear. In Murias de Rechivaldo, we stop for Second Breakfast at a small but cozy café run by a woman named Pilar. Pilar is playing Tibetan mantras on the stereo. "For patience," she says, pronouncing it *pot-ience*. "And for compassion."

The countryside between Astorga and Rabanal is sparsely populated. As the earth's population climbs, I hope that people will keep northern Spain in mind. The semi-arid terrain reminds me of the land in and around the Great Basin of the western United States: yellow grasses and light-green shrubs like little explosions, heather, broom, wild thyme, desert flowers, and a few types of dominant trees, none of them very tall, such as scrub oak. In the distance I see a few copses of aspens. The soil is now red, too, reminding me that the Spanish named Colorado after a Spanish word for *red* or *ruddy*.

El Ganso has a Cowboy Museum.

"Would you like to see it?" I ask Carrie.

She shakes her head. "Not after the chocolate museum."

We stop for First Lunch and I check my email. Carrie goes out to walk around the tiny village. Mom feeds bread to stray cats. The town has unique stone-walled corrals for sheep and cows. The houses all have walls of stone. Roofs are made of mined slate or even thatch. In the distance, hills, the ridgelines of which are covered with modern windmills far too tall for Don Quixote to tilt at.

We come upon a tree under which a young man has set up a table. He had been to Santiago and is now making his way back by foot. For a donation, he is offering coffee, chai, hummus, and cake. Nearby, and more interestingly, a slender, raven-haired Spanish woman plays a haunting flying-saucer-like instrument called a *hang*. Invented by a Swiss, the hang has small dimples spaced around its perimeter, and by tapping the places in between, the sloe-eyed Spaniardess is causing it to make different notes, *making it emit*, Mom will observe, *a Tibetan-like melody*.

I walk with the younger Dutchman, Hank, who is on the Camino to prove, as he put it, "that I can finish something." Shin splints had led to his early departure from the Dutch army, and it seems he lost his mojo. He tells me about a man he met who is carrying his daughter's ashes on the Camino. The man walks an astonishing 75 kilometers a day, fueled, I suppose, by a towering grief in need of exhaustion. I try to imagine that. I could have walked a long way after my cousin Mike died, of lupus, when he was only 23. Instead, soon after I learned the news, in my third year of law school, I began writing his eulogy, and after I delivered it a week later, I began writing a book, which I abandoned several years later, about our childhood together.

The *albergue* in Rabanal (547.2 km) is utterly charming. Stone walls, wooden beams, an outdoor bar and patio, and flowering bushes scattered about. The proprietress doesn't speak anything other than Spanish, but she is all smiles, as is her mother, who must be in her eighties.

I have a big plate of pasta with oily sauce (tomato?), which promptly gives me heartburn, Mom writes. *We meet Barbara from Bavaria again, Rainer from Cologne, and Hans from Switzerland, who has walked all the way from there. His Swiss dialect reminds me very much of my brother, Horst.*

Rainer had a hard day of walking after having had too much of a local spirit the night before. Rainer says he is on the Camino because he had a rough two to three years, and he wants to stop thinking about all his problems.

"Is it working?" I ask.

He shrugs.

Barbara beat cancer four years earlier. She initially wanted to walk the Camino in order to spend some time by herself, but now, she says, she is feeling *dankbarkeit*, thankfulness, for her life. While away from her normal life, she's realizing how good she has it. She has been married 26 years, she says, and she and her husband are still in as much love as the day they met. She has wonderful daughters. She wants everything, she says, to stay just the same. There, I think, is a dangerous thought to attach oneself to.

After a shower, Mom puts curlers in her hair. "I want to look nice for my visit to the cross tomorrow," she says. "You always look nice," Carrie says.

We go to a crumbling and rustic *iglesia* for a Vespers mass. *The church is sad and dilapidated,* Mom will write. *In most places, they would have closed it for fear the ceiling would fall down.* We attempt, in Latin, that odd reading-singing-without-a-clear-melody that Catholics are somehow able to do. *The priest sings and the congregation answers,* Mom will write. *I know it's all a ritual, but it isn't bad, and I love hearing Cameron with that sing-song.* We read a Psalm encouraging the Lord to crush our enemies, and then we read from Romans about how we should always be doing things to please our neighbors.

As we exit the church, another group of worshippers is waiting outside. Across a narrow road from a hotel that has free wi-fi, I sit down with my computer in the cold. A cat sits across the road from me, near the door of the hotel's restaurant. We exchange a knowing glance, we two scavengers.

Day 24: A Prayer at El Cruz de Ferro

At 7 a.m. begins the second, pre-dawn movement of the night's orchestral maneuvers in the dark. At first, one tentative soul glides around, quiet as can be. He is soon joined by another pilgrim or two. There is rustling, but it's still tentative.

With each new person, and each new noise, comes more permission for the next person to be louder. Soon the rustling turns into a manic stuffing, and then a loud zipping, and *sotto voce* voices turn into whispers fit for artillerymen, and eventually, no matter how many bleary-eyed people are still enclosed in sleeping bags, the same seemingly normal, well-adjusted pilgrims we met the night before start calling out to one another, stomping about in heavy boots, letting doors slam, singing "Happy Birthday" and the "Marseillaise."

Mom tells me Rainer was sawing away in his sleep because he'd drunk two bottles of wine the night before. At breakfast, I see him nursing a *café con leche* in one hand and a Coke in the other. He says he feels awful, doesn't know why.

"Alcohol?" I suggest.

"Could be," he says.

"I really liked staying at the albergue there," Mom says, as we resume our walk.

Today, we will finally reach the Cruz de Ferro, the highest point on the Camino and, by tradition, the place where pilgrims leave something behind. What will I leave behind? I hadn't bothered to think about it. *Crisp and cold, but walking is good*, Mom will write. *We go past old stone houses in tiny villages, stepping back through centuries.*

We stop near the top of a ridge to watch the sunrise, a brilliant orange orb sending its warm light over the cold landscape and illuminating my mother, who is wearing her glasses and a white scarf over her head. For nearly the entire day, we will walk high up on the other side of the valley, for long stretches on the ridgeline, and I will walk behind her, imagining myself willing her upward. *We see gorgeous green hills, unspoiled, untouched, and more windmills. So much space, it seems to go on for hundreds of miles and one can see to the end. Here comes a mountain, and up we go. Not as steep as the Pyrenees, but pretty close. The scenery more than makes up for it, and at times this beauty takes my breath away. I try not to concentrate too hard on the cross and what I will do.*

"I need to believe that what I'm doing is what's making them get smaller," Mom says to us, referring to her tumors. "That's what's getting me through."

Yes, and I've been cheering her on, because her belief will make her live longer.

ORDINARY MAGIC

For Second Breakfast we stop in crumbling-down Foncebadón (552.8 km). Of the few stone homes, about half are abandoned, their roofs stove in, the rocks in their walls straining to fall out like an old man's teeth. As we leave I ask Mom if she wants me to dial up Beethoven's "Ode to Joy" for her, on my smartphone, when we reach the cross.

"No," she says. "I'm going to be emotional enough. I've got all sorts of emotions going on."

"Such as?"

"Well, first, I'm just grateful I'm here. It still boggles my mind. And I feel hope. I see that tumor just hanging by a thread, and maybe when we reach the cross it'll just fall off. All the research I've done says fresh air is very important in helping to cure cancer. And exercise. We're getting a lot of that."

We begin to descend now and Mom focuses on the narrow trail. "And no sugar. I should have already starved it by now. But I'm trying not to have expectations. Just drop the analysis and let it be. And then sometimes I get a frog that comes and sits in my throat. He's there so often that I've given him a name."

Mom is climbing now, huffing. Carrie and I wait.

"Well?" I say. "The name?"

More huffing. "Timothy," she says.

Carrie and I laugh.

I sense that Cameron is getting emotional too, Mom will write, *because he keeps cheering me on. I am afraid to turn around for fear of starting to cry.* We keep going up rocky single-track trail, scanning the horizon for a tall cross. Carrie moves ahead. Mom lists all the family members she intends to pray for once we reach it. "And I'll pray for you," she says, at the end, "to have peace and contentment and to let go of anything from childhood that may still be with you."

I think I know what she means. She has implied before that I am holding on to resentments toward her parenting from when I was a kid. Maybe that's what she really believes, or needs to. I *have had to let go of all that regret of not being able to do a do-over with my children*, she will write. What I haven't been able to get across to her is probably just too painful for her to accept: when I get irritated, it's not just because of mistakes she may have made in the past, which she hasn't fully let go of anyway, or even my Tourette's and character flaws, but because she's not listening or taking responsibility now, which she can't even see.

Cameron asks me if I remember what he'd written down in an assignment about the person he admired most, and I say yes, happily recounting that memory. This was in fourth grade and most of the other children had chosen to write Luke Skywalker or something. Under My Hero is...Cameron had written "My Mom."

I sing to her a bit of singsong that she used to sing to me in the car when I was a boy, when we drove with my grandparents through Germany and Austria on the seemingly endless trip to Onkel Horst and Tante Rösli in Braunwald, Switzerland. *"We're almost there, we're almost there."*

She nods. *"Schiab'st a bissl', schiab'st a bissl',"* she repeats, with a train-like rhythm. This was my Oma's Nieder-Bayerisch way of saying "push a li'l". "Oma's here," Mom says. "That just came right into my head."

"Yes. She's been here all along."

"Yes, she has. They're all lining up now, all of them, from the past."

Her Tante Rosa was taken by breast cancer at sixty-eight. Her Tante Katarina died of a rare stomach cancer. Next was Opa, dead, at seventy-nine, of prostate cancer, in 1991. Mom and I attended his funeral. We flew to Germany again before Oma died, in 1997, of cancer of the esophagus. She was eighty-four. When we arrived at Onkel Victor's hospice bed, once again like two of horsemen of the apocalypse, he turned to my Tante Christa and asked, "Am I dying?" Indeed he was: a few months later, of lung cancer. He was just fifty-five. Whereas I shed copious tears in front of my dying relatives, Mom's composure and nurse-like competence were a thing to behold.

Mom's oldest brother, Gunter, was aware he was dying of stomach cancer when we showed up, in the fall of 2000. Mom, Gunter's wife, Elfriede, and I held his head and hands as he took his last breaths, as we whispered our love for the indulgent, childless uncle who'd stood in the street and wept like he was losing a son when Mom and Jimmy and I left for our flight to Alabama. Mom now urged Gunter to go ahead, told him we'd all be all right, just go on, where there'd be no more pain. Until the end, he had gripped my hand mightily, in his beefy hand with its missing middle finger.

* * *

Scrub oak, yellowing, growing brown. The trees are short, a sign of harsh winters on unprotected slopes. Some pilgrims say they've heard it sometimes snows here in summer. Heather lines the path, some of it already dying in the autumn cool. My toes are cold. My nose is running. The path goes up. It's all single-track now, and rocky. We gain 1000 feet of elevation in five miles. "I'm going to have a heart attack before I even get to that stupid cross," Mom says.

Stony path and much steeper, Mom will write. *A hard way to walk. Cameron walks behind me, urging me on, giving me some of his energy again. Then some way off, I see it.* About 200 yards ahead, the cross stands atop a 15-foot pile of rocks. Mom is forging ahead as if pulled by a magnet. *Timothy has taken up residence in my throat. At the cross, I see dots of colors: red, blue, yellow, white, and green. Bicyclists stand at the foot of this cross. I slow a bit, not wanting to have a whole audience. We arrive at the bottom of the stone pile. The cross is tall, into the blue sky. The first third is covered with stuff that people have attached to it all the way around. T-shirts in all colors, a bicycle helmet, and plastic flowers. Buttons, ribbons, pictures, and cards.*

By the time Mom has removed her pack and gotten out her Black Canyon rock and the rumpled copy of her PET scan, all the other pilgrims have disappeared from the rock pile, save two who stand a few feet uphill from us. Mom makes her way unsteadily up through the rocks. One thing Catholics really understand is ritual, a mindful creation of a sacred space. It is clear that Mom, even as a lapsed Catholic, has thought about how she will create such a space. *I walk up*, she will write. *I fall to my knees and offer the tumor.*

From the bottom of the rubble I turn on the video of my camera and watch her kneel down, a small figure next to the tall wooden cross. I can feel Timothy has now leapt into my own throat. The two pilgrims take their time leaving, perhaps magnetized by the sight of a grown man, weeping, holding a camera on an old woman kneeling at the foot of a cross. For several minutes she kneels there, hands in prayer, offering her rock and her PET scan, the tumor circled in red.

I remember the pilgrim I met the day before, she will write. *For just a few minutes, not speaking any language in common, but he'd said, insha'Allah, which is Arabic for 'as God wills'. And that's what I am thinking as I lift the tumor up over my head. Not in English, not anything Catholic, just insha'Allah. I am not going to demand, but to ask with grace. Then I just start to cry. I cover my face, and get up. I am still struggling to formulate prayers for all the other people in my life.*

I hand the camera to Carrie and walk up the rock pile toward Mom as she gets to her feet. I put my hand on her lower back, over the tumor. I incline my head to touch hers and now we're both crying. *Thus we stand*, Mom will write. *As we walk off the hill, there stands Carrie, crying too. And then she goes up and leaves her own stone. When she comes down and stands before me, with tears running down her face, I fold her up in a big hug. We spend a little more time, quiet, solemn, and then walk on.*

In the end, I do not perform a ritual for myself at the Cruz de Ferro. Sometimes I can't even tell that I am holding on to something, or that it is heavy.

The path away from the cross is really nice, Mom will write.

Wide and smooth, and I remark that it could be indicative of our "new beginning." I had visualized the tumor just hanging by the kind of thread a spider would make, and as we walk I now see the tumor fall, lying on the ground as a dried-up mass.

CHAPTER 15:
DESCENT

Day 24: High Up in El Acebo, A Heart on a Platter

At first the terrain leading away from the Cruz de Ferro is easy—a slight downhill slope on compacted white sand bounded by milled lumber. Before long, though, we enter an all-downhill, punishing, rocky, single-track trail, some of it without switchbacks. *On we go*, Mom will write, *through more beautiful, vast, and green countryside. Up a long hill, down the same long hill, and I am sure they moved El Acebo another 10 kilometers. This is the middle of nowhere, and nothing, except hills and a wide expanse of land.*

It's interesting that as my mother kneeled at the cross, into her mind came *insh'Allah*—as God wills—an expression of embracing uncertainty. The Judeo-Christian tradition that led to the Lord's Prayer, with its "thy will be done", arrived at the same conclusion. It will unfold as it will. This isn't fate, or destiny, or G-d, it's just what happens. If we agree that we should not resist the reality of what happens to us, then what happens to us is, perforce, exactly what, in a sense, is supposed to happen to us. That is, by not resisting, you can achieve the same effect of surrender that a belief in God is designed to bestow. And thus do we arrive at the lessons of both Buddhist psychology and recent science.

Tiny El Acebo (564.3 km) sits on a small mountain and is so isolated that for the first time on the trip the Vodafone USB I plug into my laptop gets no reception at all.

We choose the Meson restaurant and *albergue*. Mom is ready

to eat. *We are soooo hungry. Immediately, we get our credentials stamped and order lunch. Me: bean soup, and some sort of meat dish.* Carrie and I both order the Botilla del Bierzo, a specialty of the Bierzo area, which on the menu is translated as "pork with Paprika". I give Carrie a look, she knows I mean the pigs' heads in Belorado, and she shrugs. "I like spicy food," she says, "and everything else on here scares me."

When the waitress sets down our plates, Carrie and I study our boiled cabbage, chickpeas, chorizo, and a beating, pulsating, human heart, covered in paprika. Mom will write, *Cameron and Carrie get an odd-looking concoction, a little sack filled with odds and ends— bones and cartilage?* Tentatively I begin to saw at it with my knife. It parts in two, yielding unrecognizable chunks of white shards of pig bone, and something that is like, but is not quite, meat.

I turn to Mom, the expert, and say, quietly, so that Carrie does not hear, "Could this be organ meat?"

She peers at it. "I have no idea," she murmurs. "I've never seen anything like it. Try it."

"You'll probably really love it," I say to Carrie.

She shakes her head. "I'm not touching it."

I catch the waitress' attention. *"Perdon,"* I say, politely, holding up a single, graceful finger. *"Una pregunta."* A question. She nods.

"Um, *Que es eso?*" What is this?

She points to the casing of the meaty sack. "Thees is the tripe," she says, "and *thees*"—now she's pointing at the white stuff in the middle, "ees from *here.*" She puts her hand on her back. "Eet ees the goats."

"The goats?"

"Jes," she says. Her own face a question mark, she watches my face to see if I am satisfied.

I smile enormously. "Thank you so much," I say. The waitress departs.

"What did she say it was?" Carrie says.

I turn back to the table, still smiling.

"Stomach lining and guts," I say.

Carrie's mouth bulges.

In the afternoon, Carrie loses one of her money purses. Luckily she has taken Mom's advice not to put all her money in the same place, so she loses only about fifteen euros. At dinner a few hours later, I ask Mom if she still wants wine, as she'd mentioned earlier, to celebrate the Day of the Cruz.

"Yes!" Carrie answers, a little too enthusiastically.

"*You* want wine?" we both ask her. She's never once taken us up on our prior offers.

"I *need* it," she says.

We laugh at that, and when I later point out that I've lost my love handles with all this walking, Carrie says, "All *I* lost was my *wall*et."

That evening, Carrie has more to say in her journal. "I've learned that it's important to stand up for things such as Inge does, and also that I'm always beautiful so at the cross I left the opposite of those two things, not feeling beautiful, and not standing up for what I believe in."

$$* \quad * \quad *$$

Both of my mother's parents were from Bavaria. At the atomic level, they were Fränkisch, which meant they spoke with a dialect you could only penetrate with bunker-busting bombs. Christina Denk (Oma to me) was a loving, hard-working, and generous woman who often saved up her money to send to my sister and me. She was also a Catholic. When Christoph Pfannenmüller married her, his Lutheran family disowned him. I met only one member of Opa's family, an elderly peasant woman who, with her husband and a few adult kids, ran a small milk and pig farm and lived in a squalor I found depressing. Opa had been an excellent student in his youth, had excelled at both math and the mysteries of German grammar, but only the rich, my mother said, went to university in late 1920s Germany. Opa was still in his *Wanderschaft* as a butcher's apprentice when he was drafted into the German Army and sent to fight in France. He never spoke of the war, but we knew he'd traded his apprentice's white coat for an infantry uniform and then the plain threads of a prisoner of war.

From one perspective you could say Opa was lucky. The fascists who'd sent him to war managed to kill an astonishing 5 to 7 million German men, quite apart from the even greater toll in other countries, or from the Holocaust itself. Hundreds of thousands of German soldiers were captured, and if by the Soviets, brutalized, tortured, or simply murdered. My mother's Uncle Josef, an officer in the German Army, was shot in the head for refusing the order to take a group of Jews out to the fence and nail them up by their tongues. He lived with the bullet and brain damage for the rest of his life.

But maybe Opa didn't feel lucky at all. Maybe he felt shat on by life. He was born one of a baker's dozen of children, into a cold and rigid family that seemed to have survived the First World War, the Weimar Republic, and the Great Depression largely to have the chance to tell him to fuck off some day, on religious grounds. He married the woman he loved, lost his family of origin, and got someone else's kid—Gunter. Maybe he compared his life with the one he *wanted*, rather than with the one where he's not shot in the head by the SS or worked to death in a Siberian labor camp by vengeful Russians.

Into this world my mother was born, on May 31, 1944—as a Gemini, she would inform you. She joined three other children: Gunter, eight, who did not resemble Opa; Christa, six, already with impeccable manners; Horst, four, the quiet one. Oma christened my mother Ingeborg Amanda and baptized her a Catholic. Young Inge had three years, by my reckoning, of a good-enough childhood. Then came the day her father, freed from a POW camp in France, finally knocked at the door of their third-floor apartment on Feldstrasse. *I remember that my mom had gone somewhere for a few minutes,* Mom once wrote in her blog. *The chain was attached to the door and when the doorbell rang, I opened it to its allowed space. There stood a man, in uniform. He was 35 years old, but looked like an old man. He said to open the door, that he was my father, but I had been*

*admonished by mom not to open the door for strangers, many times, and so
I didn't. Left him standing there. Tired and hungry.*

What she didn't write about, or talk about in general, was the darkness
in him. Every bus driver and barista knew about my mother's health
issues, but even her best friends did not know how much she had been
beaten. I think her feelings of shame never went away—what says you
are bad, wrong, nothing, better than unprovoked beatings? What's
more, the man beating her falsely insisted her real father was a Russian
soldier—"*Dein Vater ist ein russischer Soldat!*" He told her she was a
"furlough child", the term used for the child of a German woman who
had committed adultery with the hated enemy. "This was ongoing," she
told me. "Not just here and there." Christa was the only one not beaten.

He praised Christa for looking like his own mother. He went out
of his way to enumerate the ways Christa was the perfect child and
to compare his creative, intelligent, unconventional youngest child to
her unfavorably. My mother told me about once walking home from
school with Christa, who was good and whom my mother did love,
when Opa met them half-way, opening his arms wide to Christa: "*Ja,
ja, mei' mausele, mei' mädle,*" he cooed (loosely: oh, oh, my little mouse,
my little maiden). "He didn't touch me," my mother told me. "I stood
there, waiting. Nothing."

Their father beat Gunter and Horst mercilessly. My mother would
run to hide in a closet so she couldn't hear the blows raining down. At
times the boys begged their father to let them go to the bathroom before
the beatings, before they shit themselves. "The way he *advanced,*" my
mother said to me years later. "It was like a cannon shot. You couldn't
even duck." Gunter left home as soon as he could, and Christa soon after
married Viktor and moved out. Horst, at seventeen, fled to Switzerland,
where he became an apprentice chef. After that, Inge, fourteen, bore
the sole brunt of her father's fury. "You weren't even safe at the dinner
table," she once told me. "Whack! And you're on the floor."

My mother did not stop fearing her father, even across an ocean and
2,000 more miles of America, until he died, in 1991. A few years before
that, in an assignment from her psychotherapist, she was to write a letter,

never to be sent, to her father. "It got so hard after the first little bit that I just fell apart," she once told me. "To write from the point of view of me as a little girl, with that brutal man. That was a bad experience."

When she was fourteen she finished three years of schooling in one year. Her options were to test for the Oberschule, or high school, that led to university, or to attend a trade school for three years. But university was still for people with money, my mother told me. Maybe she also believed, against her will, in her father, whose response to her dream of being a foreign correspondent was to sneer—she mimicked his viciousness and his Fränkisch accent—"You can't do *that*. You're too *stupid*." And the trades available—beautician, secretary—did not interest her. Besides, she wanted to leave, and soon.

Her father had recently knocked her to the ground with a punch to the ear, which bled. Even more recently, her *mother* had smacked her for some imagined slight or comment. "Of course these people never say they're sorry," she told me. "That was the day I said to myself, 'I'm leaving. I'm not staying here.'" Well into her adulthood, Mom seemed to believe Opa had acted alone. I remember it as something of a revelation for her when she recalled how every Christmas she had bought her mother a new wooden cutting board, because every year her mother had broken the previous year's board while beating her. "Can you believe that?" she'd cried, laughing at the thought of it. When she left home, all of fifteen years old, Opa didn't even shake her hand. "He turned around and walked back in the kitchen," she told me. When he died, in 1991, the words *ich liebe dich* were still stuck in his craw. At Opa's funeral, Mom asked her mother about Opa. "I don't know why he didn't like you," Oma replied. Mom shook her head and laughed when she told me that.

She fled Erlangen and the nuns at the schools (who, like Opa, swung for the bleachers), and went farther south into Bavaria, to a castle near Munich, Schloss Elkhofen, where she became an *au pair* for the Countess Rose Marie von Rechberg. In quick succession she became the *au pair* for a housewife and barrister in Hartfordshire, England, a student at the Cordon Bleu school of cooking in Paris, an *au pair* for a book publishing

CEO on Long Island, and a Scandinavian Airlines flight attendant based in New York City.

I was a teenager, at my grandparents' third-floor apartment in Erlangen, when Opa became upset at something. I heard his usual murmur mounting toward a train-like rumble, and I realized that, for the first time in my experience, he was really angry. Even threatening. Toward me! "Just try that shit, old man," I said. "You just *try* what you did to my mother." He understood but ten words of English, but "shit", "old man", "you", and "mother" must have been among them, and he must have registered my tone. He simmered down, and I did love him, but in my righteous anger on my mother's behalf I later found a parallel in Frank Sinatra's weird token of love to Shirley McLaine. "Oh, I just wish someone would try to hurt you so I could kill them for you."

Day 25: To Ponferrada, on a Sunday

In the morning the banging, clanging, zipping pilgrims are at it again. Sometimes it's good that I don't know which languages particular pilgrims are speaking, or how to speak them. A man climbs down from the top bunk, and then, as Carrie becomes increasingly paralyzed below, he drops his underwear, lingers awhile to put his clothes on the top bunk, and saunters to the shower: her introduction, as it happens, to man parts. "The last twenty-four hours have been an emotional roller coaster," she'll write.

When we get on the trail, we can see the lights of Ponferrada and its neighboring communities far below. Today will be one long descent.

Nice walk, Mom will write, *with pastel skies, and I feel good and capable. Carrie says, 'You're hoofing it this morning!' I say I am like a horse out of the chute. Then come the hills. Up a rocky one, hard, and down steep, long rocks.*

We walk opposite a line of hills to our left that look like enlarged versions of smoothly sloping stones bearing green,

147   *ORDINARY MAGIC*

orange, and yellow lichen. Patches of trees interrupted by open spaces give the hills the look of worn suede. In between these hills, many miles away, and us, the land is scoured out by velvety arroyos, folds in the earth, ablaze with fall colors.

We pass through a tiny village where I engage in a call and response with several roosters. In the town square Mom sits down to work on her toe bandages. "I really don't like feet," she says. She will later deny saying this.

There comes a time during every day's walk when we are ready to be done with walking. And yet the irrefutable reality is that we are not. So what we want, as Eckhart Tolle would put it, is *more future*. When we want the walk to be over, we want to be in the future, not right here and right now. And as soon as we want to be somewhere, or somewhen, else, there we are, outside of ourselves, and away from the only time there is, which is right now.

So when my feet are sore, I stay with them. I watch the pain with detachment, almost curiosity, as if the pain and I are separate. I don't push it away. I feel the roll of my foot, the pressure on the heel to the mid-sole to the ball. I note the soreness in my hips from carrying the pack. And, strangely, by acknowledging the pain instead of trying to hold it at bay, the pain doesn't hurt as much. It's just a signal from my body to my mind, but my mind is capable of hearing the signal, as a parent might hear the cry of a child, and deciding when it warrants concern and when it does not.

Carrie and I walk together for a spell. We talk about her being perhaps an older soul, about how she likes old movies, and likes to be around people two or three times her age. She also says, "I can't believe the trip is half over. I'm ready to see my family, but I'm not ready to leave the Camino."

In Ponferrada (580.9 km), it is Sunday and therefore no restaurants are open and all we can find to eat are the jamón bocadillos that have plagued us like Inspector Javert of *Les Miserables*, that have pursued us with the fanaticism of Ahab after Moby Dick, since the Basque Country. Jamón with queso. Jamón with asparagus.

Jamón with octopus. Jamón with eggs. Jamón with comic books. Jamón with tuna. Jamón with jamón. I wonder how many Spaniards per year name their sons Jamón. I would not be surprised by any answer but this one: "Fewer than sixty". That would surprise me.

Finding a place that's open, a Telepizza®, seems as providential as finding St. James' bones, but Mom's pasta turns out to be warmed up from frozen. "It doesn't matter," she says, shrugging. "I'm starving. As Oma used to say, *'Der Hunger treibt's hinein.'*" The hunger'll chase it in.

On a hill above the river that runs through town is a castle that once belonged to the Knights Templar, the medieval Catholic military order whose HQ sat right atop the Temple Mount in Jerusalem. Across from the castle we find the Hostal de San Miguel, and we spring for a single and a double room, with wi-fi. I see an email from Julio and read it to Mom and Carrie: "And Inge, how is she doing? Her body is in better conditions now, after a few days 'relax', green diet and not hurry? I wish you lovely weekend, enjoying every single minute of your stage, learning a few new words in Spanish, feeling like real pilgrims, sharing with the other walkers the good and bad stories of the Camino."

"Tell him thank you," Mom says. "We wish he were here with us."

The private room is just what I need. I carry a heavy pack during the day, and at night I sleep on mattresses that bow beneath me. I miss going to sleep only when I want to, and sleeping as long as I wish. I miss waking up in the morning to silence, and not having to get up immediately, or to rush, or to listen to fierce zippings and bellowing in the dark. But now I don't care that the bed is so hard my frame doesn't even dent its surface, or that my feet hang off it, or that there is no trash can or shower curtain. I don't even turn on the TV.

CHAPTER 16:
INTO THE KALE OR CABBAGE GROVES OF GALICIA

Day 30: From Sarria, Officially the Least You Can Do

It's in Sarria that all roads to Santiago converge. The Camino from Sarria to Santiago de Compostela is, in fact, the minimum distance pilgrims must walk to receive their "Compostela", or certificate of achievement. We leave Sarria (680.3 km now, having taken a few days' break from blogging) in the dark, and once we get into the countryside of Galicia, the poetry re-enters our language. "I woke up today," Carrie will write, "knowing that it was going to be a good day. We started walking and I just felt the forest making my heart sing and 'making my cells happy' as Inge would say. There are such big trees here, gigantic actually, and mist just falling all around us, it has to be one of the most beautiful things I've ever seen." Mom will write, *The countryside is exquisite. Green meadows with dew and tall trees. The enchanted forest. And around a corner, guess what? A steep climb. This one is for Fiona, I say to myself. My niece. Up I pant, past a huge, strange-shaped tree, and finally reach the top of the hill in time to watch a glorious sunrise. I sing, "Oh, what a beautiful morning / Oh, what a beautiful day." And it truly is. What a magnificent jewel—Galicia.*

To us, Mom says, "I read that pilgrims walk more slowly in Galicia, perhaps because it's so beautiful and they don't want it to end."

Then we are back in the trees, and we wind our way through

one small green farm plot after another. Mist rises from the fields, seemingly without source, for we can see no rivers or ponds nearby. We cross quaint stone bridges spanning tiny trickling creeks. And the smells! Every inhalation in Galicia brings with it a surprise. Wood smoke and sorghum, fall leaves and grass, soil, eucalyptus trees, an aroma of oranges (but there are no orange trees), hay that smells like chamomile. We breathe in not just astringent, bracing cow dung but loam and the leaves of autumn, and then, without warning, we smell pig farms capable of being detected by measuring devices installed in universes parallel to our own. Kale, or cabbage, is manufactured in what can only be called kale (or cabbage) trees—6-foot stalks with the eating end at the very top.

The sky is deep blue, the berries are red, Mom will write, *like in Colorado, and we are amazed and grateful for our good weather this whole trip. My toes are down to a mere little whimper, and I really enjoy this walk today.*

"It warms my heart," Mom says.

"The whole trip warms mine," Carrie says.

Soon we begin to climb, and the landscape becomes even more storybook. The small farms spread across gently undulating hills, with ever more hills in the distance, and are bounded by mile upon mile of walls made of carefully stacked stones taken from the fields. The houses themselves are made of the same stones. We see corncribs, or *hórreos*, standing on foundations about five feet off the ground. They are 6 feet tall, 10 feet long, 3 feet wide, and they're meant to deter corn-eatin' varmints. Mile after mile we can smell the sorghum. German Shepherds can be seen in most farms. Roosters crow nearby.

"The sky! The sky!" I can hear Mom saying to herself. "My cells are loving this!" she says.

I put my hand on Mom's lower back. Carrie decides to take a picture of Mom and me walking side by side like this.

"Are you in there?" Mom says. "I don't feel you." I understand what she means, and I visualize light flowing from my chest, down my arm, and out my palm into her back. "Oh!" she says. "I see a big blue light! It's like a...what's the word? An aureole."

I don't know what to make of this. I can't say I *believe* it in the sense that such a belief would matter—belief matters only when and to the extent it affects behavior. If I really *believed* what some people have said about my energy then I suppose I'd spend all my time healing people, starting with Mom. Which I don't do, obviously.

At the magnificentish La Bodeguina del Mercadoiro (697.6 km) albergue, Mom writes, *I feel a great sense of well-being. I say so, and Cameron takes a picture. I read that at 100 kilometers, people start to get emotional. I start to be emotional. I find myself in tears at any given moment. But the latest may be due to this wonderful music, played by two Catalans. Love this spot.*

Day 31: Walking Angry, Tonglen

In the morning I get an email from Melissa. She tells me she has just done something that is against my financial interests, contradicts my earlier guidance, and is not compliant with federal law. Just for starters. We pack up and hit the trail in the dark.

Sometimes the mind just wants to be angry. Something wants to resent or even hate, to be right, to have been harmed and, finally, as a result, to be owed something. I want an apology, of course, but when the feeling strikes me really hard, an apology alone won't feed me. (I may even resist it: *You aren't really sorry*). I want your compassion, your regret, your soothing of my hurt feelings. It hurts, and someone needs to soothe it. Someone other than me. So the words unfurl, the sentences spool through my head, the arguments gather, again and again and again. They are so seductive. So persuasive. *She doesn't care! Stubborn. So illogical! So unreasonable.* I tell myself not to give in to this. There is a struggle, reactive mind versus new intention. Will I hate or love? Who will win?

The wolf you feed.

When I was in Bend and pissed off, I would sometimes look at an old picture of a little girl in pigtails and a blue-and-white calico dress, about four years old. I would imagine she had gotten lost, as Melissa had told me she sometimes did; she was alone and afraid, and crying. I knew this little girl, or who she became. Following a thousand-year-old Tibetan Buddhist practice called Tonglen, I would breathe into my chest the fear and loneliness she's felt, the pain she's felt as a result of my own words and actions, the pain that even now expresses itself in ways that hurt me. It's not difficult, this practice of Tonglen, because it simply invites us to perceive in others pain we have felt ourselves. That, in fact, is the secret to its power.

And yet the pain I breathed in, curiously enough, did not really hurt. I would be reminded once again that what really hurts is not so much a feeling, like sadness or anger, but the resistance to feeling it. *It's the resistance that hurts.* I would then breathe out, thinking *love love love,* intending compassion for her suffering, and then I'd imagine her little head leaning against my chest and her tears on my shirt and I would stroke her hair, saying, *It's okay. It's okay. You're all right.* And then the anger I'd felt would dissipate and I'd sit down on the carpet of my office and cry.

I think of the man who is walking with his daughter's ashes. Now there is a purpose. Hank, the Shinsplint Dutchman, had said the man covered 75 kilometers a day, which, even at the punishing pace Julio and I have set on a few occasions, would require over ten hours of hard walking per day, not counting breaks for water, food, or equipment. Twelve hours a day is probably a more realistic minimum.

I'm not a father, but I wonder if, when he walks, he imagines, like the phantom memory of an amputated limb, a slight weight on his shoulders, imagines holding in his hands the buckled leather shoes of, say, a little girl as she squeals with delight and wraps her arms around his head. And I wonder if that is what fuels him, if his walking is the physical expression of all the grief he has within him, which is one measure of his love.

Now I note the moon, nearly full overhead, and Venus next to it, and the mist rising off the farmland, and the shadows of the trees around us. Every day we walk almost due west, and mostly we walk before noon. If the sun is behind us or slightly to our left, we are on the right path: my farmer's tan is darker on my neck and left side. If the sun is more to our left, then we are either late or we are off-course, going too far to the south.

Galicia has few towns and fewer cities. There are no grand churches to duck into. There are no water fountains. Most albergues here have no Internet, nor blankets. The Galicians even seem to have concealed their grocery stores from our prying eyes. Galicia is just a different ball game. Galicia was depopulated during the twentieth century, and the countryside is in a state of disrepair. The guidebooks don't often mention that, until less than forty years ago, Spain was isolated from the rest of the world and in long decline under the right-wing dictatorship of General Francisco Franco.

Mom tries to buy bread this morning, in a small shop, and is told it has been reserved. "All of it?" she asks, incredulous, pointing to the array of bread. Yes. All. Reserved. She shakes her head and makes the face that says *This would never ever happen in Germany.*

A Spiritual Once-over from Rene the Eagle

We walk for many kilometers with Rene, a German massage therapist who hails from near Leipzig, Germany. With dark hair, fierce, dark eyes, and a thin, noble nose, he reminds me of an eagle. I ask him why he is on the Camino. "Because," he says, in German, "I have a goal but I don't have the way." His goal, he explains, is to open a therapy center that employs massage, shiatsu, music, and crystals.

We cross the river into Portomarín over a high modern bridge and find a shortcut that doesn't take us through town. At times we come upon smells that would have decimated Napoleon's armies. After about nine kilometers we stop at a stone picnic table for Second Breakfast: bread, butter, jam, cookies, apple, red pepper, water, chocolate milk. "I'm going to miss these red peppers," Mom says. "They're sweet, as juicy as a fruit, and big. Lots of vitamins. It's going to be hard to go back to those pale imitations we get from Mexico or California." I save my slices for dessert, eating them after the cookies.

At the *albergue* in Ventas de Narón (717 km), Mom and I sit at an outdoor table, reading in the late afternoon light. She's hungry again. She wants to know how to ask our *hospitalera*, in Spanish, what time dinner is. I tell her. She practices it a few times before she pulls out her notebook and pen. "This is an important sentence," she explains, writing it down. She gets up with her book to go to the café, then stops after a few steps and turns to me. "And if she says 7:30, I'm going to slap her."

Day 32: The Smells of Galicia

The next morning, we leave so early that we navigate through the fog by moonlight, the shrouded trees silhouetted at the end of our visibility. There is a corona around the moon, like a small rainbow. From the hills we're in, we can see fog blanketing the valley below. When we enter the fog, the air is so thick with water that our packs grow wet, and the trees rain water down on us as we pass. We pass a cemetery—

Cimetario de Peregrinos

—evidently for pilgrims who fell between the 80th and 60th kilometers. "Was this *recently?*" Mom says. We are still navigating by moonlight, and when we enter the trees and the moonlight can't penetrate, we navigate by pilgrim litter, far more reliably ever-present than the Camino's fabled yellow arrow.

We stop at a store and I buy fruit and my beloved Spanish pepper, Mom will write. *My whole body gets hot as I am still wearing two pairs of socks. We stop at one little bar and have a fresh and natural raspberry drink. Oh, my, that was so good! Mainly we walk through sunlit forests, but we're still going up. One particular steep hill—I dedicate this one to my cousin Renate. Another for my sister, Christa, brother, Horst, and close friends. There are enough hills here for half the people in Montrose.*

The 18 kilometers is almost too much for her. "I wish we were already there," she says, with a few kilometers to go. I have noticed the same thought in myself. "Sometimes it's better not to resist," I say, "not to want to be in the future."

"I'm *not* resisting," Mom says, resisting even talk of resistance. "It was just kind of a little *hope.*"

Now I'm sitting under an old gnarly apple tree, she will write during a break, *looking out at hilly landscape, and wide swatches of fall colors. Birds are singing, and it's another peaceful spot.*

Mom Cannot Wait to Eat in Casanova Mato

The *albergue* in Casanova Mato (735 km) sports an ominous sign whose English translation assures us that the *albergue* has the right to "throw away" any "infractors" of the rules of the *albergue*. I tell Carrie that the fine print says infractors can be thrown into either a culvert or the trough of a pig, "at the proprietor's sole discretion". Here I make air quotes.

There are only five houses here, Mom observes in her journal. *The woman at the albergue talks very rapidly in answer to my questions.*

It's nice and clean and has a kitchen. This was put in as a joke, since there's no store here. Carrie and I take a nap. It is probably my second nap of the trip. I'm finding that naptime is an excellent time to get sleep without snorers around. Daytime has always been for me an illicit time to sleep, a hedonistic indulgence, so it's doubly delicious. In fact, it's downright—

"Wake up," Mom is saying. "It's 5:30. Time to eat."

She's perched on the edge of her bed, shoes tied smartly.

"We just ate a few hours ago," I say, stifling a sob.

"No, we ate at 3," she says, Mom-like.

Mom's gusto for food has reached a fever pitch. I point out that I'm not yet hungry, and that known laws of physics prevent anything from being cooked in Spain before 6:30. In fact, I say, delivering the *coup de grace*, the woman downstairs *already told me* that the albergue a kilometer to the east opens at 7:30, and the one 1.5 kilometers to the west opens at *precisely* 6:30 or 7.

"I'm bored," she says, trying a new tack.

"Why don't you arrange the *mochilas* for tomorrow?" *That will get rid of her,* I think, but all I accomplish is to get myself involved in her *mochila.*

Eventually we call the nearby Casa Bolboreta, and after a short taxi ride we are blown away by the great meal we get for eight euros. Meatballs, fries, lentil stew, wine—Mom says it is the second-best meal she's had here, after the two dreamy servings of soup she got during the festival in Navarette. "I'm such a happy camper!" she says, on the drive back, and to Carrie, "I could purr like a cat now."

I wonder sometimes if there is some deeper level of subconscious, one to which I have no access, in which I already live in constant fear of my mother dying. At various times since her cancer's return, death strides silently into the room and this kind of conversation happens.

I'm not ready to lose my mother.

No one is ever ready.

But look at how much Mom still misses Oma. Nearly twenty years later, she can't even watch the old videos. I'm not ready to start that.

Let go of the expectation that it's ever possible to be ready to suffer.

I can't bear the idea of her suffering.

And yet you must.

She didn't have a happy enough life. It would be too sad.

Even she would not agree with you. Your pity may be as much about you, *and what you worry about in* your *life.*

Day 33: Selling My House Out from Under Myself: On to Arzúa

It is cold when we start. After thirty or so minutes, it's warm, and I have to take off my windbreaker and cap, leaving my two wool layers and gloves. Then, without any change in altitude, as we walk across an invisible line, the temperature suddenly drops.

"Did you feel that?" I cry.

"Yes!" Carrie says. "It got cold again!" Mom says. We walk on for a bit, and suddenly it's like we're walking into a warm house, again.

Mom has a pain that feels like a band across her stomach. "Perhaps it's the lentils," she says. But she says she no longer feels pain in her back, where the tumor sits. She says that Barbara of Bavaria told her about a woman with cancer who walked the Camino. The woman visualized the cancer as a ball of wool, and every day saw herself pulling a strand from it. When she went back for her tests, the cancer was gone.

We are all starving, and need a break from walking in the near darkness. *After 4-plus kilometers, I share the last bit of chocolate,* Mom will write, *which only makes us more hungry. Cameron figures we'll have to walk about 9 km before reaching a larger place. I am thinking of all these refugees who walk for days without food.*

I am just commenting on the dearth of places to eat when, up ahead, I see it. It's like a shining city on a hill. A castle. One with a grail.

"Is it a mirage?" Mom says.

No. It is, in fact, a place to eat, and rest.

We fall upon the restaurant as castaways do toasted bagels with cream cheese.

"We can have pizza and sandwiches," Mom says. "And there's Internet! And *café con leche*! Almost paradise."

Carrie and I order medium pizzas. Then we all go to computer terminals. I get on the Internet and I click a few buttons to close on the sale of my house in Oregon, for a loss I try not to think about. In August, when we signed the sale agreement, I had staggered, briefly, under the weight of the loss, then I told myself to let it go, and myself, having no real choice, listened pretty well.

At 9:30 in the morning Carrie and I are each hoovering up a medium pizza. "This is the best day," she announces. "I haven't been happier about food in my whole life."

We walk out of the Little Magic Morning-Pizza Restaurant and are nearly run over by a small herd of cattle. Closest to me is a feisty little bull whose head has been tied to his right leg, so that he runs with a misleadingly submissive ducking motion. Then we are into the eucalyptus trees, and we come upon another hill. Mom has not yet seen a hill that didn't elicit a groan from her.

I feel my pack pulled backward. I look behind me to see that an old woman has grabbed a loop of my pack with one of her walking sticks. "Come on," my mother says. "I carried you around *every*where for nine *months*." Carrie and I both laugh at that.

"Buen Camino!" we say to some bikers.

"Good way!" they cry back, in English, much as the human-heart-bearing waitress in El Acebo, when thanked, had translated directly from the Spanish *de nada* to sing, "Nothing!"

My legs are bone-tired. But Mom is worse off. There are more hills. In Arzúa (758.8 of 798.6 km), we opt for another hostel, so we can have our own rooms and get some sleep—and just *rest* even when not sleeping. The Camino's loud, crowded dormitories are hardest, of course, on introverts, but our instinctive ability to walk without needing someone to entertain us does offer some evolutionary advantage. Mom and Carrie find a grocery store whose produce section makes my mother *almost weep with joy. Everything is here, and my wonderful red peppers too. I buy grapes and cheese, bread, yogurt, tomatoes, salad, and dressing. We come back and have a sumptuous picnic right on the bed. Then Carrie and I watch some Spanish soap opera, and since we don't understand the dialogue, we make up our own.* In my own room that night, as I write in my journal, I fall asleep on the bed with my laptop still open on my belly, something about as common, for me, as fainting.

Day 34: Next to Last Day: Arzúa to Pedrouzo

I awake to the sound of a complete set of scuba gear, with all the oxygen tanks, being dumped into the showers in the room above. A body dragged across the floor. By a man with one leg 17 inches shorter than the other, and made of wood. An entire roomful of furniture being moved across, scraped over, and finally dropped onto the tiled floor above. Then everything moved back again. The body propped up in a chair.

Once again we walk a long way in darkness, lit only by Carrie's windup light. The going is slow. We are very hungry, and Mom needs to rest. But there are no places to sit, other than on boulders along the trail. We keep walking. At about 7 kilometers, we see it. Is it a mirage? Or a site for Second Breakfast? Yes! Yes, it is—a place to eat, to sit. I begin to whistle "Ode to Joy".

We sate ourselves on the sample menu, and I decide to stay at the café a while. I find that I prefer to start from behind and then catch up. I feel better at 5 to 7 kilometers per hour. I don't get sore, and my bones, legs, and feet don't hurt as much. I thought

I'd finally gotten the hang of this walking business, but yesterday all the bones and tendons in my legs hurt. And today the bottoms of my feet. We just rested for hours and they're still sore. Maybe I'll only be in shape for the Camino *after* we've finished it.

The Albergue Porta de Santiago, in Pedrouzo (777.8 of 798.6 km), is one of the most modern and attractive we've seen, with well-constructed wooden bunks in place of rickety aluminum, and wooden slats in place of squealing springs. Rene the Eagle is already in a bunk, resting his sore bones, which he had told us he must do every day, for two to three hours, inside his sleeping bag. He's right next to the feng shuiiest area, naturally, a skylight-to-floor enclosure full of plants and trees. He grins at me every time I pass, probably because I am using my laptop and he had told me a few days earlier that for spiritual reasons I should not be. The *hospitalero* behind the desk gravely informs me that the password to the wi-fi is "*un secreto*," and only he can type it in. Carrie gets to talk to her mom and dad and she is really glad to, but, she says, "I'm not ready to leave Spain."

We're at about kilometer 21—or just over four hours' walk from Santiago, which we'll reach tomorrow, our last day on the Camino.

CHAPTER 17:
WHAT A TRIP THAT WAS

Day 35: The End of this Way

Sure enough, the rustling of the bathroom-goers starts at 5 a.m., Mom writes. *I get up at 6 a.m., Carrie does too. I go to the coffee machine to have a cup. It makes such a racket that I walk away so no one will know it was me!*

Carrie and I leave and make our way, looking for our yellow arrow. Here comes the forest...deeeep and dark. Carrie and I agree that we'd never have done this at home. We actually feel safe here.

Finally, a different path, then forest again. Then small hamlets start to appear. Same slate-stone houses, with corncribs. By now, we know that if there are six houses, two to three will be in ruins. After an hour or so we see our first bar. Stop for café con leche. Carrie has a fresh OJ. We wait twenty minutes, then move on. I tell her that Cameron will catch up, probably singing like he did the other day: "She's a lady, woh woh woh, she's a lady."

About forty-five minutes after Mom and Carrie have gone, I leave Pedrouzo at a fast pace and find myself in a dark wood, where two roads diverge, and I, well, I wait for some pilgrims who haven't lost their headlamps. It's so dark I can't even make out the ubiquitous Pilgrim Litter Navigation System. Once a group of ten of us have bunched up, murmuring in three or four different languages, we conclude via groupthink or crowdsourcing to take the wider path, a decision that works out pretty well. I catch Mom and Carrie about an hour later, pouring sweat and singing. *"I can hear the sound of violins..."*

We walk three abreast at a leisurely pace, putting me in mind of the pilgrims to Canterbury, England, who once rode their horses and donkeys toward their destination at neither a slow trot nor a fast gallop, but somewhere in between, which is why we now have the word *canter*. We're in no hurry today.

We see graffiti under a bridge. *The most important things in life aren't actually things*, one reads. Carrie's journal will not fail to note what my mother says to her about that: "The hardest journey is only eighteen inches, from your head to your heart." A Spaniard on a bike asks us if we've seen a group of four men, including one with a beard. No, we haven't. Why? Well, the bearded guy and a woman fell in love some stages back, and then they got separated. The gallant biker is trying to find the man to deliver a letter from the woman. Godspeed, man.

For Second Breakfast, we walk up to the ordering window at a café-bar. I ask for the Espaguetti a la Carbonara. Based on my *bolonaise* experience thus far on the Camino, I know this is risky; my *espaguetti* could arrive with octopus draped on top and in a peanut butter pesto sauce dotted with maraschino cherries. Mom, feeling lucky, says she'll have one too. But the man at the bar informs us that, sadly, there is only one. Mom looks at the man, then at me.

"What did they do with the other one?"

After the early forests and bits of farmland in ruin, we walk on back roads bordered by aggressively ugly houses, through sparsely settled suburbs, and on a road bordering an active firing range where the local suburban warriors are belting out double-taps. Santiago's outskirts seem to go on and on.

"I won't feel I've arrived until I see the cathedral," Mom says. "The absolute finishing point of the Camino."

I am thinking of Julio's words to me. "In Santiago the towns-people weel greet you and take you to their homes. You'll have dinner weeth them and stay the night. Eet is tradition."

I can see it now. People will line the streets of Santiago like fans of the Tour de France, holding out bunches of wildflowers they've picked themselves, and large-bill cash. Small children wearing the Spanish child-abuse equivalent of *lederhosen* will ride on their fathers' shoulders, and teenage boys will cluster high on the first-floor ledges of buildings, or hang from fire escapes and drain pipes, and try to look uninterested. The people will cry out huzzahs and hosannas. Old women will clutch at their rosaries. Señoritas will blow kisses and crowd the streets, and the cars will crawl along sidewalks. Carrie, who is hungry and moody and tired right now, will smile again, as Julio had once pointed out she always did. I'll jog around the plaza in a victory lap, but the people's joy will not be so easily contained, oh no. They will lift us up on their shoulders, parading us around the plaza, singing traditional Galician songs, songs so old they were once sung by pagans, by druids come from Stonehenge.

The cathedral, as it turns out, is well-hidden on the far side of Santiago. Also hidden are the townspeople, their comfy homes, and the huzzahs of the women, young and old. Just a few hundred meters from the cathedral, we come upon a café and sit down. Carrie inserts calories in the form of a bar of chocolate. I take off my trail-running shoes and discover my first blisters, including a 2" x 2" bubble on my big toe. With a pair of scissors I do the kind of surgery that makes fifteen-year-old girls make faces, and then I put on my glove-like footwear. They've done almost all the work that got me here, and I will not, as God did Moses, deny them the Promised Land right on the verge of it.

After a small respite, Mom will write, *on we go, through the historical section. There are lots of people walking around the small, cobblestone streets. We stop to say hi to an American couple from Santa Rosa, Marina and Craig. Did I have expectations? No. Did I have any regrets? None whatsoever. Will I be disappointed if the cancer test results turn out different? No, not really. It has been a fantastic journey, in many more ways than one.*

"You guys have really accomplished something," Craig says, as we turn once again back toward the cathedral.

The Cathedral: Camino's End

I focus on Mom, walking ahead of me. To my right and a bit behind, Carrie is doing the same thing. Our eyes meet. We nod. I surprise myself by getting choked up. Mom is feeling it, too. *Through grueling mountains and long, hot hiking, sunburn, toe injuries, hunger, thirst, and blisters on top of blisters. Santiago de Compostela. I remember a sign we saw in Roncesvalles which said 792 km to Santiago and I remember how I thought what a LONG way away that was. Now, I'm here and tears come.*

The cathedral is situated, much as heaven is reported to be, to prevent anyone from getting a full view of it all at once. We saw only the cathedral's spires as we approached from across the city, and now, as we draw closer, the cathedral rudely shows its back and side. We pass through an archway into the square over which the cathedral presides, and even now we are still facing the college opposite the cathedral, so that the cathedral still can't be seen entire, but must be inhaled with over-the-shoulder glances as you walk away from it. *Timothy comes back once more,* Mom will write, *lodging in my throat. There it is. The End. I have absolutely made it.*

We walk farther into the square, the Praza do Obradoiro, Galician for "Square of the Workshop". It's a wonderful space, filled with colorful pilgrims juggling cameras and phones, resting or sleeping against their backpacks, singing songs, hugging friend and stranger alike. Mom's hand is on her chest, in gratitude and disbelief.

"Oh, we're *here!*" she says. "*Look at this!*" Her voice high like crying. She shakes her arms with excitement, poles waving in and out, the rivers clap their hands, the hills dance like yearling sheep. The Spanish word *duende* refers to a climactic show of spirit in a performance or work of art, such as at the end of a flamenco dance or bullfight. A right proper *duende* is what Mom now does, quivering with feeling, torn between her glances at the cathedral and the sobs each one elicits from her. Carrie can't look away. On the

165   *ORDINARY MAGIC*

video you can hear my own Timothy making a throaty laugh. With one hand Mom shields her eyes for a quick look at the cathedral, then staggers back and into a near cry, "*Ahhh-ha-ha*," her voice planted deep with emotion. She's walking away, a little off-balance, toward the center of the plaza, to get a still better view— "You did it!" I say— and now she turns back to me, nodding, laughing. She cry-laughs and wipes her cheek. A few more steps and she turns and looks up again, shields her eyes, takes in the cathedral —"Ohhh, goodness!" she cries. She puts a hand to her mouth and turns away again, *verklempt*.

She turns back to me with something to express, but she's unable to talk. She walks on, turns around again. "What a trip that was, huh?" she says. "What a trip." She laughs out loud and comes in for a hug. In an even higher voice she says, "*What a trip that was!*"

She turns toward Carrie, who, as far as I can tell, has still not bothered to look at the cathedral. "Seeing the cathedral was great," she'd tell me later, "but seeing Inge see the cathedral was better."

"Come here, sweetie!" Mom says, and Carrie goes to her and they cry and hug for a long time as Mom rocks Carrie back and forth. All of us stand and look at the *massif* of the granite cathedral, based on a Romanesque cathedral in Toulouse, in the center of which is the Pórtico da Gloria, the Portal of Glory. Children chatter, bikes clatter by. Mom backs up and up and up to get a better view, then she turns and walks even farther, nearly to the college at the plaza's far end. Carrie and I stand together and watch her. I'm filming her again now. I hand Carrie the camera and walk to Mom, and when I set down my backpack she backs up and lifts her camera. *Then, Cameron reaches into his backpack*, she will write, *and comes out with red carnations. Like a magician*. She doubles over with a burst of joyous laughter. *He had carried those two flowers for a while. That really opens the water works...*I draw her in and hug her, and I'm crying too. After a day in my pack, one of the stems has been reduced to a stub, but she still reaches for it.

I'm sooooo happy to have arrived. Happy shock!

We sightsee in the cobblestone streets. Old, ornate buildings, street musicians, beggars, souvenir shops. It's just how I imagined it. Carrie and I go back to the cathedral to just sit and look. The sun is setting and it is a peaceful, beautiful moment.

The Way is finished.

Photo by Marina Chang
Harrison

CHAPTER 18:
RE-ENTRY

In Santiago, we spent two nights bathing in our endorphins. Mom had a tearful reunion with Barbara—and we met her husband, who'd flown from Germany to surprise her a few stages back. Then we took the train into Portugal and the marvel of Porto, where we bought civilian clothes and toured the Port wineries along the Duoro River. For our final prize, we rode the bus to the extraordinary city of Lisbon, whose setting and beauty called to mind San Francisco. On the bus ride along the ocean Mom was like a little girl. "Look at that! It's crashing! Do you hear it?!"

In Lisbon, as Carrie wrote later on Facebook, they "got all pretty and celebrated their achievements with shopping and seeing the city and wearing makeup! And the opera, which Inge explained was 'ancient rap music', and the Indian restaurant and the magnificent beach!" At the beach, near the former royalist resort of Sintra, she added, "it was the most wonderful day anyone could've asked for." *Carrie and I took our shoes and socks off and ran yoohooing and laughing down to the water's edge,* Mom wrote. *Breathing deep the tangy air and watching the waves ride in.* "Inge and I lay in the sand," Carrie added, "and I played in the cold water. I drew pictures in the sand, and a thank-you note to Inge for giving me the opportunity to come on this trip."

On our third visit to our favorite Indian restaurant, I asked Carrie, "What else did you learn?" She smiled and whipped out her notebook, a mix of drawings, pressed flowers de Julio, and diary entries.

"I learned you should encourage people in whatever they try to do. I learned you can always have something to look forward to. From Julio I learned kindness is understandable in every language. And then this." She shows me her notebook, where I read, *You're the product of all your influences, until you choose not to be.* She laughs. "That was you."

Back home in the States, throughout November, each of us, Mom at the grocery store or Black Canyon, I walking around Manhattan or Jersey City, Carrie between classes, found ourselves subject to spontaneous sadness. What is sadness but an abrupt end to flow? *I feel disjointed, sad that it is over*, Mom wrote. In my mother's personal cosmology, our Camino trip became one of the brightest stars in the firmament.

"Do you remember when you and Cameron ate the human heart in El Acebo?" she'd write on Carrie's Facebook page. Or, "Do you remember how Julio kept giving you stolen nuts and berries?" On her bookcase were framed pictures of our moment with the carnations in the plaza in Santiago, courtesy of Marina, the woman from Santa Rosa. And with her blogging, Mom had made Facebook friends hailing from all over the world, some of whom would later send her funds to help pay for her treatments. She acquired a following, as well, in Facebook groups like German Girls Living in America, and The Teal Warriors, a community for ovarian cancer survivors and their caregivers.

Mom and Carrie were interviewed by three TV stations and Grand Junction's newspaper, *The Daily Sentinel.* "I look at the bigger picture now," Carrie told one reporter. "I learned communication, planning. I've learned a lot about appreciation and conserving resources. And you can't be afraid to live." She began to decorate and sell cell phone cases, and she would soon sign up for seminars at a leadership institute. "I'm pretty glad I have people doubting me," she said, in one Facebook post that caught my eye. "Cause it just motivates the hell outta me to prove everyone wrong."

"I'm going to have to start wearing sunglasses," Mom told me, implausibly. "Everyone recognizes me from the news."

At home in Montrose, Mom fell back into her rhythm. *I spend a lot of time in my backyard*, she wrote. *Now that my Medicine Wheel Garden is finished and so lovely, it gives me such pleasure.* She grew thyme, basil, rosemary, cactus, and dozens more plants and flowers. In the center of the wheel she had erected a white wooden post. On each of its four sides, in four different languages, she had painted, in black letters, MAY PEACE PREVAIL ON EARTH. Through the fence she sweet-talked

Cassie, the neighbor's border collie. She chatted people up in the post office and at the bank and in city hall, and her friends (here defined as anyone she saw in public on a regular, or irregular, basis) told her she looked great. "Glowing," the flower lady at the southern City Market said. "Picture of health," said the northern City Market butchers she'd long before trained to slice beef for her rouladen.

She bought fresh, organic food daily, and a few more red peppers than before. She preached the virtues of raw or fermented fruits and vegetables, epsom salt baths, black raspberries, and alkalizing, "lemon-loaded" water. She recommended dirt, walks, sunshine, and especially love and gratitude. She cooked five-star meals for friends like Peggie and Pat, Bonnie and Berle, Silke and Gordon, and the Shannon family: Lynne; Paul; Annika, thirteen; and Gregory, 10. She watched cooking shows, in both English and German: *Chopped, Anthony Bourdain, Das Perfekte Dinner*. She had no patience for Gordon Ramsay, so nasty, British, and short. She read every night, right before going to bed, sprinkles of mass-market and dollops of chick lit. Her sister, Christa, sent care packages of books in German, along with Knorr bouillon cubes and Milka chocolates.

The highlight of many days came when she got to see her "little buddy", Gregory, after school. He was a sweet, thoughtful kid, with a gap between his top front teeth and a wary, lopsided grin. It had taken me years to grasp just how much Gregory and my mother had come to mean to one another. Framed on the wall in Mom's spare bedroom, also known as Gregory's Room, was a sheet of paper that said, in multicolored crayon:

Strong
Great
   person
I love you
Inge, all the way
to Jupiter and back
     Gregory

My light, happy moments come in the form of Gregory, Mom wrote on her blog. *We do his 4th Grade homework together and then we visit. Sometimes I pick him up at school and take him to soccer practice. We've been friends for almost 11 years now. Practically since his birth. He likes to say to me that we may not be related by blood but certainly by heart. Ahh. He does my heart good.* My mother had been first a babysitter, then a nanny, and then a kind of grandmother to Gregory and Annika. "We basically went from mom asking Inge if she could babysit us kids," Annika later told me, "to us asking if we could go to Inge's to play."

Gregory was four when Mom determined to give him something entirely of his own. She chose to teach him to sing. Opera songs. In several languages. I can see her schooling him in her mock-strict fashion, the same loving tone she took with four-legged creatures. Gregory's repertoire rocked many of her own favorites: "Nessun Dorma", "Con Te Partiro", "Panis Angelicus", "Ode to Joy". "Achy Breaky Heart" squeaked into the lineup. Gregory learned the words, and their pronunciations, and at the recitals she held for him he captured the French, Italian, German, and redneck accents. "We were all astonished that she could get Gregory to commit to something," Annika told me. "I really wanted to have my parents be proud of me," Gregory once told me, "but school was not my thing." But what a bond he had with my mother.

About the greatest thing that could happen to Gregory was staying overnight at Inge's. Mom helped him collect all the pillows and blankets in the house. She got down on the floor with him and they built cozy forts that would never fall to invaders. She showed him how to cook simple meals, and how to deal with frustration. It wasn't the first time she had loved a little boy on purpose. In the 1990s, she took an abused and angry little boy under her wing, the best lemonade that could have been made from the lemon of her marriage to the boy's grandfather, Bill, aka whatsizname. Just a few years ago, the boy, now in his twenties, had made a trip to Montrose to thank her for, in essence, saving his life.

She was nervous about the next round of tests, but she wasn't as afraid as before. *Did I bring that back from the Camino?* she wrote. *I am calm. I am happy with my decisions so far.* On the day Doc told her he'd call her with the results, she went back up to her sunken cathedral, the Black Canyon, to wait. But the first tests were a great relief; her CA-125 cancer antigen markers were *down*, and the tumor had not grown in months. "It must have been something on the Camino," she told me. "I really feel great now." The end of the year also brought a fitting celebration, as Adam and I entertained Mom on a trip to a place Mom loved, in its own way, about as much as the Black Canyon: New York City.

My daughter, Candace, with my eight-year-old grandson Kaleb, came from Alabama. What a most generous present from my son, to have all of us together for the holy days. We stayed with Adam in Jersey City Heights. And we did the town. We saw the World Trade Center monument with its perpetual pools. I was in a somber mood and felt sadness there, running my fingers over the carved names of so many people who died. We went to Madame Tussaud's Wax Museum and to the Ripley's Believe It or Not Museum. We took a carriage ride around Central Park. We went to Chinatown twice. Good vegan food there. We walked up Fifth Avenue with its Christmas splendor. We took a ferry ride to the Statue of Liberty. We walked four to five hours each day. And then a special treat: we went to a movie in Greenwich Village, The Way, about a group of pilgrims on the Camino. I cried just for the recognition of what we had done and places we'd been.

I've come to a point where I will do whatever is necessary to make this cancer history. I will use meditation and visualization techniques and not keep predicting that I will get so sick. Mind over matter. My son is in a holding pattern, ready to come on a moment's notice to mop up vomit if I decide to do chemo. My daughter is helping with love and support...

But right now my heart is full.

BOOK II:
THE LAST CAMINO

*"If you want a happy ending, that depends,
of course, on where you stop your story."*

—*Orson Welles*

"We are all just walking each other home."

—**Ram Dass**

Mom met the new local oncologist in November, a few weeks after our return from the Camino. Monika went with her. Mom was so excited, she proudly told the doctor of all the improvements in her life since she'd overhauled her entire diet and committed to her goal of hiking the Camino and—

"YOU CAN'T CURE CANCER WITH FOOD!!" he interrupted, according to her blog post. According to Mom, he was rude and dismissive, he insisted that she must start doing chemotherapy immediately, and he spoke only to Monika for the last twenty minutes of the appointment. But Monika would tell me Mom was not open to anything the doctor had to say. They were using different treatments in Germany, Mom insisted. She'd done her research: why wasn't he offering them? How could "they" not do those treatments here? I suppose we shouldn't have been surprised. She was physically fit and still on top of the world from the realization of her Camino dream, and so at maximum resistance to any talk of last resorts.

Mom fired Dr. Giggles, as she dubbed him, though he was the only oncologist for 60 miles, and we spoke with other doctors in Grand Junction (63 miles away) and Germany. They agreed there was no urgency to chemo, particularly after considering two things. One, my mother's cancer had grown exceptionally slowly for over ten years. Two, she was uncommonly clear about the quality of life she wanted. Why should she endure the misery of chemotherapy for a slow-growing cancer like hers, when even the chemo that had worked before gave her only a twenty-five percent chance of a second remission—a remission that typically extended life by about eighteen months? Chances were high that she'd go through the horror and give up the quality of her life for little or nothing.

Not yet.

In May 2012, over half a year after the Camino, Julio and Marie Anne came to visit. They began in New York, where Adam showed them around Manhattan, by foot, for several days. They reached Denver by train, and Grand Junction by bus. Mom and Carrie met them with a bottle of Rioja, a bouquet of flowers, and a show of tears, then drove them through the colorful natural monuments in the surrounding desert. We showed them Ouray, with its box canyon and roaring Box Falls, and then Mom unveiled for them the Black Canyon they had heard so much about. "I never in my life seen anything *billions* of years old," Julio said. Then I drove our guests to Arches National Park, in Utah.

"The *immensity!*" Julio exclaimed, as he watched the Martian-red landscapes of western Colorado and eastern Utah stream by outside his window.

"*La immensidad!*"

Mom hadn't been able to go with us to Arches because she was feeling a mysterious abdominal pain. "It feels like an animal is inside and trying to gnaw its way out through my abdomen," she told Marie Anne. *The pain is so excruciating*, she wrote, *that on two recent nights I lay on the floor, in fetal position, just howling. I put my feather comforter over my head, so the neighbors wouldn't hear.* But with the opiates—"o-PIE-ates," she called them—the doctors prescribed her, she exercised a steely discipline: she rationed them, using them more slowly and in smaller amounts than prescribed. "I will not trade one calamity for another," she said. Aside from the danger of addiction, she knew that, for her, opiates caused bowel blockages whose terrible pain they could not alleviate.

In mid-July 2012, still in pain, Mom met Dr. Mapleton, an oncologist at St. Mary's Hospital in Grand Junction. I was by this time house sitting in San Francisco, keeping up with Mom by phone and Facebook and blog as I explored restarting my life in the Bay Area. *I felt so comfortable with this nice, kind-spoken Doctor,* Mom would write, after her first appointment, *that I told her all the things I was doing for myself. She did not even blink. No ridicule, no exclamation of "This is nothing but quackery." Oh, I like her.*

Happily, Dr. Mapleton also had some answers. She said my mother's latest scans showed stones in her urethra. "That's the most likely cause of your pain, Inge. We can get you a surgery appointment very quickly."

When we were leaving, Mom wrote, *I took her hand and thanked her for being so kind, gave her a spontaneous hug, and promptly burst into tears. If I just get to feel better, I don't want anything else. Ever. I don't care about a new house or furniture or keeping up with certain people. I don't care about sleek cars and who's got more. I just want to feel better. In that is a richness beyond compare.*

Maybe it was, in the end, a good thing that the anesthesiologist denied her request for anti-nausea medication, that she therefore vomited so violently once she got home that the metal staples in her abdomen ripped open—"dddrrrt", as she would put it—that an ambulance sped her bumpily all the way back to Grand Junction, where she had remedial surgery, and that the hospital attempted to bill her, at the full rates, for both surgeries. Because by August 2012, I'd thrown my computer, bike, and skis in my car and driven for three days from San Francisco, where I cut short a ten-week house-sitting assignment for friends, through the Great Basin Desert to Montrose.

I lived with Mom for about nine weeks, in Gregory's Room, until she got back on her feet. But even then I didn't feel I could leave her, so I moved my skis and bike to nearby Telluride, a mountain town whose matchless beauty, bountiful ways to exercise, and optimal distance from Montrose, and my mother, I knew I would need. When I ran into my father, Clark, at my brother Damon's wedding a year later, and told him where I was living and why, he said of Telluride, "That's a rotten place. A rotten place. Lesbians holding hands on the street four dogs in each hand everyone goin 5 miles an hour on goddamn bicycles." In other words, Telluride was a kind of magical kingdom for someone who loved mountains, or other people. Mom adored it, even after she could no longer come because of the altitude. The skiing and hiking were therapy for me. Nature was catharsis. The weekly karaoke with a talented and fun-loving band of regulars sustained me more than I could have imagined. I was so happy to see Mom up way past her bedtime, hollering at my singing and whooping for everyone else.

The rest of my situation was a lot less helpful to my resilience. As it had been when I grew up nearby Rangely, western Colorado was still socially and professionally isolated. My close friends all lived far away. I read about how loneliness is the new two-packs-a-day of cigarettes, so to my loneliness I added the anxiety that I was shortening my life in the living of it. I felt defeated, anxious, and just depressed enough that everything felt so much harder. I was in deepening credit card debt. I wanted a relationship, my own safe harbor. I felt low on meaning. When would my life begin again?

You know that's a false construct, your life is going on right now, before your very eyes.

I guess so.

It doesn't matter if we know we are on the path. We're on it, consciously or not. We're already and always on the path.

In late February, 2013, Dr. Mapleton told my mother that her CA-125 cancer markers had increased significantly. Equally alarming, the most dangerous tumor had resumed its deadly growth. "If you ever needed to make a decision about chemo," Dr. Mapleton said, "now is actually the time." Mom was shaken and fled to the Black Canyon. She passed a terrible night. In the morning she began to consult with me and her friends, as well as a kind and helpful Herr Doktor Professor in Germany.

We went over the facts. First, the same platinum-based chemotherapy, carboplatin, had worked for her before, helping her reach nine years of No Evidence of Disease and over two more without any symptoms. Second, I was now in Colorado and could help her, and she would likely only become less physically able to withstand chemo the longer she waited. Third, the chemo could now be administered in three smaller doses per

179   *ORDINARY MAGIC*

month, rather than in one great bucket of it, to spread out the misery. My mother was probably also unnerved by her diet's inability to ward off the cancer on its own. She decided to go through chemotherapy.

Everything went according to plan, starting with the familiar side effects. About twenty days after her first infusion, and having had three in all, her hair came out in her hands in the shower. *The toughest part of chemo*, she wrote, *tied in with the little girl brushing her dolls' hair, her friends' hair, the dog's hair.* My sister, Candy, told her not to get a blonde wig. Peggie, one of my mother's many champions, took Mom to a wig shop, where she bought a blonde wig, with hair down just to the neck in back. *Sorry, sweetheart*, Mom said in her blog, *nothing else looked decent.* The chemo was hard on her, but not as bad as the first time. Plus, she could now legally inhale marijuana smoke or vapor to instantly dispel most of the terrible nausea, to make herself want to eat, even to calm her nerves on our drives to Grand Junction.

Three times a month, I left Telluride early, picked her up an hour or so later, and drove another hour to St. Mary's. Most of the time we rode in silence through the be-shrubbed desert, whitened here and there by eruptions of alkali. On our right rose the massif of Grand Mesa, the world's largest flat-top mountain, and on our left, a broad plain fell off into red-orange-yellow striated canyons concealing two-thousand-year-old hieroglyphics before rising into low mountains in the distance. Chemo usually began around 9:30 a.m. While Mom checked in, I'd go to the cafeteria to fetch black coffee with Stevia for her and chai tea for me. Hospital officials once caught my mother using her legally prescribed, aroma-free THC vaporizer to treat her nausea and anxiety, and forbade her from using it at the hospital. After that, she added a stop in the restroom after check-in so she could inhale her medicine unmolested.

In our meetings afterward with Dr. Mapleton, Mom would careen among her themes of anxiety and blame—the ailments, the misdiagnoses, people not listening, a background hum of unfairness—and the immunity-boosting positivity of her love and gratitude, eating smart, the Camino and its memories, and marijuana as medicine. Underneath the rush of words, I heard her terror of pain, of dying. I felt it myself, the fear of her dying, of her pain not stopping. Dr. Mapleton was, we'd find, consistently sharp, alert, and compassionate. She was especially skilled at listening to my mother, who, once underway, did not want to be stopped, and if stopped, resumed with an interruption as soon as possible. I'd put my hand on her shoulder and say, "Just pause, Mom, just slow down, let her finish." Dr. Mapleton met my eyes now and then, in a shared understanding, but never in a way that disrespected my mother. She gave my mother the room she needed to feel hope, to exist with dignity, to have some say over what the future should look and feel like, and, at least as importantly, to *feel* like she was empowered. That built up her immunity.

After we left the hospital we'd go out to lunch in Grand Junction, where we might be joined by Carrie, or my half-brother Damon, or his wife, Jannilyn, along with my two-year-old nephew, Braxton, who always came in for a massive dose of love and play from my mother.

In late August 2013, Mom got a visit from an American woman, based in Dubai, who'd followed her story. Michele talked to Mom about trying some new cure and Mom started crying. I said, "Does it stress you out to talk about it?"

"I've tried so many things," she said. "I've done all the right things. But something has shifted and I'm very scared. I've dreamt of my own funeral twice."

She was distressed. And I was Clarence Fucking Darrow. I said things like, "Our dreams are not pre-cognitive, Mom. They're just an expression of what we fear."

But, she repeated, "Something has shifted. Something is different. I don't recognize me. Something doesn't feel right."

By September 2013, after eighteen separate chemotherapy infusions, we learned Mom's sense of her body may have been spot-on: tests showed her cancer antigens were still going up, right through the chemo itself. "The cancer cells have gotten smarter, Inge," Dr. Mapleton said, as we sat in her office. They had evolved. Mom was now, in fact, *platinum-resistant.*

I was silent, Mom would write. *Just thinking of the misery and wasted MONEY of these chemos.*

"We'd have to use a different chemo," Dr. Mapleton said. "Doxil. Once a month." What were the chances this one would work? No one had an answer to that question. How bad were the side effects? Pretty bad, partly because it couldn't be delivered in smaller weekly doses, but only in one enormous dose per month. As if that wasn't enough, Dr. Mapleton told Mom there was a new lesion on her liver that was 10 millimeters across and positive for cancer.

Mom was devastated. She knew she had to regroup. *Be still, think, and refill my fighter tanks*, she wrote in the blog. *That would be the Black Canyon. I'll get off the beaten path and sit and look at the awesome surroundings.*

We'd had a week of rain, gray, and I couldn't walk a lot. I drove in and parked my car. Brush and canyon walls. Beautiful view, sun, and only a gentle breeze. I was the only person. I remembered coming here right after the Camino, when I had just plowed through the places where I used to slow down or get out of breath. It had felt so good to just walk. Now, the familiar click-clack of my poles was a little slower. But there was stillness, peace. I saw tracks from all sorts of wildlife. Rabbit tracks and larger tracks, probably elk. I could almost pretend I was walking the Camino. I saw horses in a pasture and then I saw a pair of foxes. Their ears came up as I passed.

I stopped at a picnic bench, brushed off the rain, and had my lunch. I looked around and enjoyed the peacefulness. I walked up to the edge of the cliff and looked down. The Gunnison River was like a small glittering ribbon. The walls of the canyon looked like they had been dusted with powdered sugar. It is so very beautiful here. I will do the best I can. The rest is up to bigger sources.

It made sense to her to continue with chemo for a short time. The hopes she'd had—her diet, the Camino, the carboplatin—were now all dashed. She didn't think she had much to lose. Besides, she told a friend, "I see the look in Cameron's eyes, in Gregory's..."

Mom began the Doxil a few weeks later, and for a long week she became cloaked in a vast darkness of depression. But even after it passed she had *a strange feeling*, she wrote, *as if something has shifted, internally, irrevocably. As though all my cells have moved. I can't explain it any better.*

But it has given me nightmares. I have also had two dreams of my own funeral. That was weird! And upsetting. It occurred to me that this could get me. Maybe I can't outrun it. Maybe it's nipping at my heels and I can't run any faster.

I took advantage of an offer some clients had made and took my mother to an old Victorian B&B in Silverton, Colorado, a mining town even higher in altitude and more isolated than Telluride. The owner-operator was taking a vacation, so we had the whole place to ourselves. In the evening, a visiting friend, Heath, called Mom and me out onto the porch. "Check it out!" he said. I ran outside to see a double rainbow. My smartphone, with my camera, was dead, so I was forced to simply sit and watch the rainbow, uselessly, as our ancestors had. Mom came out to the porch wearing a thin black sweater and blue-and-white polka-dotted pajamas, and she was totally bald.

She moved unsteadily but with excitement. "Ohh," she said. "Wow..." I began watching her, seeing her, it seemed to me, clearly: her good nature, her good will, her spiritedness, her childlike curiosity and willingness to feel awe. I knew in that moment that I was palpably witnessing the basic goodness of my mother. Would I remember this time when she was gone? Would I miss that life in her, which I had so often taken for granted? Tears came into my eyes, but I kept watching her that way, until I judged that the distraction of the rainbows was coming to a close, and then I wiped my tears away before she could see me and become anxious I was envisioning last days.

* * *

Through two months of the second-line chemo, Mom's CA-125 numbers continued to climb. In late October 2013, she wrote, of the bright-red Doxil, *The Hawaiian Punch carried NO punch. What is our option now? Atom bomb? This had never occurred to me that chemo may not work.* Now we were scared. We called a halt to the second useless chemotherapy.

In Telluride my mood was under siege. I saw the beauty of the mountains and trees and clouds through Mom's eyes, imagining what it would be like to see such beauty after she had gone. I often cried as I skied. I think I knew even then I was already grieving what I feared might happen. But we weren't giving up yet.

* * *

Over a year earlier, Mom had read about a cannabis oil concentrate reputed to heal or improve many different conditions. The most well-known proponent of the oil was a lanky, sixty-something Canadian named Rick Simpson, who lived in Amsterdam, on account of being on the lam from Canadian Mounties. He'd written an e-book and recorded an hour-long video about the oil, which he called Phoenix Tears, that were both long on claims and short on evidence or even any recognition of the scientific method. The many anecdotal testimonials he cited were certainly not up to scientific standards. In fact, little research had been done anywhere on cannabis oil's use against cancer. In the unassailable logic of hope, that meant it could work.

We'd already seen marijuana do amazing things for her pain, anxiety, appetite, nausea, and sleep. Even if only as effective as a placebo, taking the oil would still boost her mood and immunity. In late October of 2013, even the marijuana dispensaries weren't trying to make a pound of marijuana and two gallons of Everclear (95% pure alcohol) into eight 10-gram syringes of pure THC, so, in a parking lot down in tiny Norwood, I paid a good old boy $550 in cash for the first of many syringes made, we were assured, according to Rick Simpson's recipe. This I drove to my mother.

So, I had my first cracker with oil on it, with just a little butter, Mom wrote. *The size not much larger than a half a grain of dry, short-grained rice. My son took me out for breakfast. I thought Oh, this is not so bad. I didn't feel anything. Luckily not till I got home! Then I had to sit on the couch. Fog descended. Things seemed to move much slower. I felt like I was talking very slowly.*

My son gave me a double dose for lunch.

Well, I sat there much later, still. I thought, Good Lord, I sure hope somebody comes and feeds me. Couldn't get off the couch. Fell asleep in the middle of one of my favorite programs. But I'm thinking, The world needs more of this. People won't argue, fight, kill each other.

After a few days of ingesting the oil, Mom's recurrence of plantar fasciitis disappeared. Both a new scar on her finger and one from childhood, on her chin, became smaller, less prominent. A few weeks later, she reported, *A wart on my index finger has disappeared. My blood clots are gone and Doc says I can stop taking the awful Warfarin blood thinner. Whatever type of horrible, painful bowel obstruction that was, it's nearly gone. I sleep better, have less pain, and stopped taking my thyroid medication without any problem.* These were not actually valid scientific conclusions of cause and effect, but neither of us wanted to make any argument with the end of pain. *I've increased my dose as much as I can, and take it three times a day, hoping it will kill the cancer just like Rick Simpson said it would.*

I'm still trying to figure out how to get the cannabis oil past my tastebuds. I've tried hiding it under Nutella, butter, and peanut butter. I've settled on applesauce, so I don't need to chew. I've always said I would eat dirt if it would help. Now I take my paste and sit on the couch. I have all necessary things close by. Remote control, water, meds. Since I don't function well in this state, cooking and eating have become a challenge. I have now scheduled my waking errands and chores before I take anything. Sometimes my friends attempt conversation, but most of the time, after two words, I lose the thread and have to ask constantly, "What were we talking about?" or "Where am I going with this?" It makes my friends pay excellent attention as they have to remember.

It does feel odd. No chemo. No radiation. No magic pill. Only a tiny, dark powerhouse, that looks like a mouse turd.

Mom became a marijuana partisan, and she had no patience for resistance from the unenlightened. On Facebook, she shared two or three marijuana-related posts per day. *Let's just call it a MIRACLE Plant,* she wrote, sharing a research study. *More and more and more,* she wrote, linking to a CNN article on marijuana stopping a child's seizures. She broadcast the benefits of the plant to the Teal Warriors Facebook group. *Marijuana has saved my life*, she replied to a moralizing skeptic in that group, with some ghostwriting from her son. *It's the only thing that relieves a crippling abdominal pain without constipating me and creating more pain. It eliminates my nausea, a feeling I'd not wish on my worst enemy. It gives me an appetite, so I don't die of malnutrition, like many people do on chemotherapy.*

One month later, Mom's cancer antigens were down. We could scarcely contain our hope. A month after that, in December, Dr. Mapleton said they were down again, half what they'd been when we quit Doxil!

We hollered and danced, Mom wrote, *and the nurses all had wet eyes.*

"Amazing," said Dr. Mapleton. "Just amazing. One more test, next month, and if that's lower too," she laughed, "I'll change everyone's treatment option."

"Then I'll go on a road trip to spread the cannabis miracle," Mom said. She always said it sort of Germanically as *Cuh-NAH-bis,* which confused even people in the industry.

THIS IS HUGE! she blogged afterward. *Imagine. A little plant. Natural. NO side effects. NO trauma. Just a little woozy feeling. THE NEW CANNABIS CHEMO.*

* * *

Ah, well. Whatever the cannabis oil may have accomplished in holding the emperor of all maladies at bay, by January 2014 he was unmistakably beginning to gain ground. Mom's CA-125 resumed its threatening climb. At the end of January, she wrote:

With such debilitating nausea and loss of appetite, I've lost 22 pounds in the last month. I am trying desperately to slow, halt this slide toward starvation…Cancer cells suck the protein out of the healthy cells. No matter how much you eat, it doesn't matter. You still starve to death. Being so passionate about food, I find this very cruel. Many a night I've cried with terror of this death. I fear it's cachexia, the wasting disease.

* * *

By mid-April 2014, her CA-125 had risen to 318, an increase of almost fifty percent over the previous record high, in a single month. "Something," Mom told me, "is really moving and changing inside." Alone in my Telluride condo, I wept. *Don't focus on the sadness and the fear,* I thought. *Focus on the love that animates them. Focus on the love.*

* * *

In early June, my sister, Candy, and my niece, Brianna, visited. Mom's childhood friend from Germany, Muschi, came as well, from her home in Las Vegas. Muschi, whose nom de reality is Irene, has been Mom's friend since 1948. They grew up a few houses apart on Feldstrasse in Erlangen, West Germany, and Muschi's trailblazing of the United States is what prompted my mother to come over. The next morning I got a message on Facebook from Fiona, my German cousin, about our Uncle Horst. We had understood he was successfully overcoming his own recurrence of prostate cancer, in a clinic near Zurich—but, Fiona told me, he had been ambushed, by pancreatic cancer. And he was already gone.

I dreaded telling Mom her brother was dead. I put it off all day. I was irritable all day, too, and Mom noticed. In the evening, Muschi and I sat down on the red couch with Mom, already past her bedtime. Candy and Brianna sat on the emerald couch on the other side of a glass coffee table. Muschi took Mom's hand. "We have some bad news, sweetie."

"Oh, no!" Mom cried, instantly stricken. "Horst?"

I nodded.

And my mother wailed. "*Mei kleines Horstele! Mei Horstele!*"

Muschi cradled Mom in her arms. Candy came to hug me.

Before long, my mother was talking about her brother. "He was such a quiet child," she said, "sitting and playing for hours with his own fingers. He was a pacifist." He disliked conflict and argument. Opa, she said, had contemptuously called him something that translates to a "ducker", as in someone who ducks, or cowers. "I hated that word," she said.

"But you know," she said, "I was in my Epsom bath the other day when I began singing a German hymn from childhood. Every time I start to sing that hymn, someone has died. And when Bonnie came over the other day, I had a meltdown because I just sensed something about Horst."

* * *

In early September 2014, three years after we began the Camino, Mom and I met with Dr. Tierney, a young general practitioner who had taken over after the retirement of Doc, her primary care physician. "Well," Dr. Tierney said, and that's about the extent of my memory. It was something laudably direct. Something like, "Things have gotten worse, Inge." The dangerous tumor, Dr. Tierney went on, was pressing against the something. The spine? The liver? I didn't catch it. Cancer had gotten into some of her vertebrae. *Vertebrae?* They get cancer? There were more spots on the liver, or maybe it was also the kidney. Things would keep getting worse, we understood.

Each of the words, whatever they were, a lash. Did they feel like a death sentence as they landed on my mother's ears? I saw my mother nod. She did not make a face, did not resist, did not say no, she did not resist. She absorbed the blow. I saw it land, and perhaps she rippled, for a moment, like bamboo in the wind, but then she was up again, saying, "I had a feeling it wouldn't be good news." She had known then, I think, that her struggle against the emperor was over. She wouldn't endure any more chemo, and certainly none of the useless and painful end-of-life measures offered and demanded in American medicine. But not hospice yet, either. Hospice meant you had given up. She wasn't ready to admit she was giving up.

* * *

As bad as the chemo had been, my mother suffered more from all the terrible internal pains—from the adhesions and urethra stones to diverticulosis, bowel obstructions, and whatever the hell the Warfarin blood thinner was doing to her stomach. She had also battled a blood clot in her upper leg that, by late summer, had left her unable to walk. And for months now she'd endured a biting pain from the stents placed inside her ureters. The growing tumors were pressing against her ureters, constricting them so that her kidneys could not flush. So now there were pieces of hard, sharp plastic among her internal organs. In early October 2014, they landed her in the ER. She was put on pain and nausea medication and discharged soon after. I arrived from Telluride and took her home, but at eight o'clock that night, I saw the pain creep back in. I watched her as she sat on the couch, moaning, gasping, hugging herself, rocking to and fro, tears in her eyes. I was frantic. We had to go back to the ER.

On the flagstone path in the back yard, I steadied her with one arm and carried her bags and medicine pump in the other hand. Every step or two, she would stop, then double over, sobbing from the pain. Soon I was crying too, quietly, as always, and we stood there together like that, on the moonlit path, we couldn't go on, we went on, we trudged on, one step at a time, the shortest camino stage yet. She was moaning and sobbing and even *keening* with such terrible force that I wept violently as I walked her, haltingly, along the path to the car. She was all but disabled with pain and I could not bear it. Death is natural, but pointless and unending suffering is an abomination.

It left an impression. Sitting up in her hospital bed the next day, she told Silke, one of her many German friends in Montrose, *"Das war die Grenze. Das war die absolut Grenze."* Which means, roughly, That was the border, the absolute limit. "I couldn't ever go through that again," she added. "I'd shoot a dog in that kind of pain." Instinct makes us hold on. But now she knew she would go no further. She'd drawn her line in the sand. Probably the most consequential thing she had said was this: "We're probably going to have to call hospice."

* * *

It wasn't until three weeks later, on October 27, 2014, that I felt the return of an overpowering need to write, to go tell others. That night, for the first time since shortly after the Camino, I began blogging again.

"Let everything happen to you: beauty and terror."

—Rainer Maria Rilke

October 27, 2014

I awoke to rain in the mountains. I heard the patter of drops on the balcony outside my bed. It was a little before 9 a.m., three years and one week after our last day on the Camino, and I was in Telluride. I walked out on the balcony that looked west toward the mouth of the box canyon. Fog wound through the yellow-and-white brushstrokes of the aspen trees, and fog gave birth to and swallowed whole again the silver TELLURIDE gondolas gliding up and down the mountain. *I'll go to yoga this morning*, I thought. *At the library.* I began throwing on clothes.

My iPhone buzzed. A text. From Peggie. I tapped my screen.

Hi Cameron. A hospice nurse is going to call you. Please come down today. I believe your mom is getting very close and she can't be left alone at night.

What? What?

Yes, Mom had said we'd call hospice, a few weeks earlier, but the hospital gave her an intravenous painkiller unit and lorazepam tablets against her nausea, and with help from friends like Peggie, we'd been able to manage on our own.

I felt wobbly. I left Peggie a voicemail asking if she was saying what I thought she was saying, and then I began to hurl things into bags.

I missed Peggie's return call. When I saw the notification of her voicemail, love and duty wrestled with terror. After several long moments, I finally pressed play. "When I mean she's getting close," Peggie's voice said, "I mean very close." Peggie had just watched her ex-husband die, rather suddenly, of a fast-spreading cancer, and I feared she might know what she was talking about. "She had terrible vomiting all night," Peggie added. "She couldn't eat or even drink. She was too weak to walk. She couldn't stand up safely."

I began to sob.

No! I'm not ready. Not at all ready.

You're never ready.

I thought of something Mom told me a few months ago. "When you tell me you're on your way I can feel my breathing get calmer," she'd said. "'He'll be here soon,' I tell myself, and then I'm calmer."

I drove sobbing, speeding at over 120 mph on the long, empty straightaways, and at times with a wail as long as my very long outbreath and higher in pitch than anything I'd ever heard come out of my body before.

It wasn't so sudden as losing someone in a freak accident, or, as Adam had over a year earlier, dealing with the horror and shock of a murder. Shortly before a late-April wedding date, Adam's fiancé, Violeta, was leaving her final dress fitting, with her teenage daughter, when an ex-lover discharged a shotgun at her through her car window. One could not call Mom's sickness such a terrible surprise. But I was still disoriented, stunned by the speed with which hope can evaporate, and fear and sadness take its place.

In Montrose I walked through the back gate and along the flagstone path to Mom's back door, which opened directly into the kitchen.

"Superman is here!" Peggie said. Peggie was a dog lover, horse trainer, and conservative Coloradan who, with her husband, Pat, had gone from skeptic to dedicated marijuana advocate after seeing how much the plant helped my mother. She gave me a hug.

"Your mom keeps asking for you," Berle said, hugging me as well. Curly-haired Berle spoke in a high, sweet timber that perfectly expressed her Berleness. *Thank God for Berle* ran through my mind a lot. Months before, Mom had written in her blog, *My friend Berle is a champion. She cooks and vacuums like a little dynamo. She shops and puts it away and spends time with me.* Then Monika gave me a hug. *Monika came with good soup and a few grocery items (instead of flowers)*, Mom had added, in the same post. *She usually brings* kaffee sahne *and Epsom salts, and fixes my German TV.*

I heard my mother call out to me from the living room. I pushed aside the curtain she'd hung in the doorway between the kitchen and the living and dining area and went to her. She was looking spent as she reclined on her reddish couch. Her pajamas hung like sails. Since January 2014, she'd lost over 60 pounds. I cradled her beautiful head. "I don't want to go," she said, in a near whisper. "I just want a little longer." She was relatively lucid; in recent weeks her thought and speech had often been affected, and slowed, by the cancer's progress into her brain, the anti-nausea lorazepam, and, to a lesser extent, the enormous doses of cannabis oil she'd worked up to.

"I know, Mom," I said, overcome. I kissed the top of her head. "You've been the light of my life."

I leaned down onto the couch and hugged her for a long time.

"I'm so afraid of leaving you," she said. "With your abandon-ment issues."

Well, I was too. She knew my biography better than anyone, from how I had responded, as a boy, to leaving the Germans, to being left by and then leaving Jimmy, and of course to finding out I'd been preemptively left by my real father. Maybe she had also taken note of my emotional state as I had watched three of our German relatives die, back in the 1990s. I feared I'd be like I had been in Germany, and I could not bear to be like that around my mother.

"I'll be fine, Mom," I said.

* * *

Dying is a messy affair.

My mother itched for the fight, but her arena was littered with the detritus of palliation: four pillows, the teddy bear that when microwaved for three minutes and placed on her abdomen relieved pain, a glass pipe ready with marijuana, a lighter, a short plastic bottle of indica, a pen-like THC vaporizer, a tall bottle of Smartwater, the IV unit with painkiller drip, and a small plastic orange bowl of lorazepam tablets that had been cut in two.

I held her hand as she rested, eyes closed. With the other I sifted through a pile of mail. Cards from Carrie, addressed to "My Sweet Aunt Inge." A card from Candy's oldest friend, Tanya, addressed to "My Second Mama." One from a Karin, saying, *I so appreciate that you opened the door to marijuana for my sister and me.* Mom had sent the desperate woman cannabis oil *through the mail.* At the bottom of the pile, and all over the house, stray pieces of paper bore recipes in her hand.

After a while she fell asleep and I walked back into the kitchen. The women were speaking in low tones. Peggie looked over at me. "She has been so much calmer since you got here." I sat down on a wooden chair next to a small table. I opened my laptop to cancel all my appointments for the day, and the next day, and then I began to cry.

The women gathered around. "You won't be alone, Cameron," Peggie said firmly. "We'll be here with you." I had bawled like an abandoned calf as Uncle Gunter was dying. I had done this around Uncle Viktor, too, which must have given him great comfort. Probably Oma, too. I don't know if it was my job, exactly, to cry right in front of them so that they could be confident we all thought they were dying, but if that had been my job I would have gotten bonuses, promotions, a big gold watch. And now it was my *mother*? "People get through this," Adam had said to me during a visit back in September. He'd been present when his mother had died, in 2000, of cancer. He'd cared for his mean-spirited grandfather in his last months because no one else would. But I didn't think he was even a little bit *through* Violeta's murder. "That's what they say," I'd said.

Now Mom said something from the other room. Peggie answered, "Cameron is just feeling sad, Inge."

"Come here, son," my mother said.

I went to her and leaned down to hug her, my face against hers, and kissed her head and temples and neck. She smelled like old person, and probably like cancer, to a trained dog, and she smelled, too, like marijuana salve and Vaseline and the excellent playgrounds and soccer fields of Bavaria, and King Ludwig's castles' damp walls, and pine needles on the floors of German forests.

"My little fella," she said, patting my head.

Night. I am single-mindedly here now, on a conspicuous path, with my mother. This path has the virtue of my knowing, for the first time since the Camino, and like it or not, exactly what I'm supposed to be doing. I am ferrying my mother to the other side, or at least to the *Grenze*, the border.

If there is a consciousness that persists, then all the pains of the body and ego will fade away and her conscious spirit will reflect only on the love she felt and showed and received in her last weeks. While she is alive and able to feel either the pain of meaninglessness or the joy of meaning, I will be here to influence that story. My mother's story, and inevitably my own. Can I muster the empathy? How much compassion can I bear? There will be no time to indulge in my fears.

It's just words we have now. She sleeps a lot. We walk only to the bathroom. There's no cast of characters. No flowers or cathedrals, bridges or *mochilas*. Just a very small house, no bigger than a theater stage, and the words spoken by or to my mother. I know I'll forget the things I see, and many of the things I hear. I'll forget just about everything that *happens,* excepting what I write down.

I lie down on the emerald couch opposite Mom's with the same MacBook Air I carried on the Camino, lay it across the incline of my thighs, and begin to write in my journal. I am desperate to feel less alone. In the morning, I will post my journal on our blog, for the first time in three years, and I will keep posting until there is nothing more to say.

THE FIRST WEEK

Day 1

Mom is up again in the middle of the night. She walks on her own power to the kitchen and makes herself coffee, per the recipe she'd once shared in her blog:

> I brew ONE cup of coffee. It's nearly a ritual. NO automatic drip pot for me. I boil my water, add 3 scoops of mild, non-acidic coffee from Germany, and throw in a few salt crystals and a breath of cocoa. I heat my cup, so the coffee won't turn lukewarm from hitting a cold cup. Just a dash of half-and-half. That first swallow is sooo good.

My friend Laurel eventually gets up with her. Laurel had come from Telluride yesterday afternoon, armed with Thai food, craft sodas, and her own sleeping bag, in response to an alarming text I'd sent a dozen people during my drive (Carrie, her mother, Laurel, Jannilyn, and Gregory and Annika were among many who dropped everything to come see my mother). "She was totally herself," Laurel would tell me later. "She was walking around, didn't need any help. And she was *bossy*! She said to me, 'This is my quiet time, so you can go back to sleep now.'"

I awake to the harrowing realization that yesterday was not a dream. I really am here, doing this. I also awake to a text message from Adam, who informs me, without ado, that he will be arriving at the Montrose airport tomorrow night. On Facebook he announces that he will be staying in Colorado "indefinitely". I feel immediately relieved, and grateful. Mom has known Adam for almost as long as I have, since her first visit to Harvard Law School twenty-five years earlier. Suddenly I feel a little less alone.

Day 2

Mom sleeps much of the day. Marie Anne writes me with a message given to her by Julio, who is somewhere without Internet, and Mom smiles when I read it with his accent.

Inge, you look nice in the pic.

You still my heroine, my amazon, always struggling to survive and always nice smile. Olé

Adam arrives after Mom has gone to bed. He falls asleep on the red couch as we watch TV. "I've cried for days," Mom had written, after Violeta's death. "For her, her daughters, and our good friend Adam. Instead of the wedding, there was a funeral. My problems pale immensely in light of so much pain." Mom had called Adam, and they had talked about Violeta, whose name alone my mother adored, just as they'd commiserated years earlier about Adam's loss of his mother. But Adam deals with pain unlike anyone I know, and so privately as to seem not to be suffering at all. "Poor Violeta," he would simply say. "Poor Violeta."

I stay in Mom's bed with her until almost 3 a.m., when she begins to vomit. I caress her hair and neck and help her sit up, help her hold the blue plastic vomit bag, get her a hot warm cloth to clean her face. I help her to the bathroom to brush her teeth. Back in the bed, she vomits again, and again she wants to brush her teeth. Back in her bed at last, she tells me I can go sleep in my own room.

"It's one of the few gifts I have left to give," she says.

Adam comes into her room, smiling. "Hello, beautiful."

She looks up. "Oh, hi, Adam," she says, too spent to sound either happy or surprised. "What are you doing here?"

"I came here to visit you, Inge," Adam says gently. "And Cameron. But mostly because marijuana is legal in Colorado," he says, adding, with an unconvincing naïveté, "And I've always wanted to try it."

She smiles with such sweetness, such gratitude and affection, and reaches up her arms.

Day 3

I awake to hear the commotion of Mom vomiting and Adam trying to help. I take over from him and hold the bag for her. After she has finished, she begins to cry. I lean down and, careful not to put weight on her, hug her and kiss her neck and head.

"I thought I would have more time," she says.

"I did, too," I say.

I go around the bed and crawl next to her. She puts her head on my shoulder. "My precious son," she says. "So tender with me now."

"This isn't the last time we'll meet," I say, not because I know it to be true, but because it hurts a little less afterward.

"I know," she says.

I watch her sleeping later in the morning, so vulnerable on her couch by the window, and I want to kiss her face fifty times, six hundred times. I am saddened to see how much it is possible to feel for my mother, and to know, now, a depth of emotion I've never known before. The force-field has been so strong. She was alternately prickly and needy, and the combination was like a wall I never figured out how to scale. But now I am overflowing.

She asks for some more strawberries. "And maybe a half a banana cut up in it," she calls after me. I cut the strawberries quickly and toss them into one of her tiny bowls. I get another tiny bowl and begin hacking away at the banana.

Slow down. You may never cut a banana for her again.
I slow down.
Pay attention.
I intend love into each cut, and love tumbles into the bowl.

* * *

She is more lucid in the afternoon. I enjoy having her back. I love the smooth skin of her face. I love her short grey hair. Every time I look over at her I want to kiss her.

Adam and I help her into bed at a little after nine.

In the bowl of the orange-and-vanilla glass pipe Adam and I had picked up earlier, she lights up the marijuana leaf and the more concentrated shatter hash. She inhales and closes her eyes, the pipe still clutched in her left hand, the lighter in her right. I put a hand on her head and massage her scalp and her fine, fine hair. I do that for a good while. I wonder if I will, some night, have a dream like the kind I used to have about my cousin Mike. I'm in a dream with him, at school or a football game or dragging Main in Rangely, but I'm lucid enough in the dream to know that in real life I am dreaming and he is dead, died, of lupus, at twenty-three, so that in my dream my heart is breaking. Or will I have the dream in which I am caressing Mom's head, happy as can be that she has *not* actually died, only to awaken into the sadness of a world with a Mom-sized hole in it?

Day 4

After a hot bath, before she can even get her shirt on, she begins to vomit. She reaches down for one of the blue vomit bags on the floor. "It's like a heart-retching," she says, "a stomach-heart-retching. Deep down." I bring her a clean shirt and the glass pipe filled with indica. In between her retches into the toilet,

199

I light the pipe so she can breathe in the smoke, which works with a speed I still find astonishing. Her nausea subsides.

"This could be cachexia," she says, nodding. I look at her. *Cachexia?* Over the last year, she's gone through many explanations for her weight loss, pain, and nausea—not cancer but Warfarin, not cancer but her body "flushing out" toxins, not cancer but a "healing crisis" caused by the cannabis oil, not cancer but the pain of the stents. But this is the first time since her abrupt weight loss in January that she's admitted, to another person at least, that it's the emperor of all maladies who's her primary antagonist.

* * *

"Hey, Mom," I say. "Do you want to go for a wheelchair ride?"

"Not right now," she says. She dozes or considers weightier things. Ten minutes pass. "I'm ready," she announces. She sits up to put on her shoes. Her gorge rises and she grabs a blue bag, into which she vomits.

"Oh," she says. "I hope this isn't going on all day." She begins to cry. I soothe her and hand her a warm towel.

Adam and I load her into the wheelchair. She doesn't like that it's out front, on the porch. She hadn't remembered it was there. "I saw that we have some madeleines to eat," she adds. "I wish I'd known that."

"Do you want one now?" I say.

"No, I just want to know these things."

Dan and Nancy's border collie runs up to the fence and Mom reaches her fingers through the fence to pet the squirming dog. "I know," Mom coos, "it's all so different now."

I push her for a while and then Adam takes over. I take off my sweater and give it to Mom to put on her legs, which she says are cold. She takes my hand and we go like that, Adam still pushing, to Main Street. A Halloween-themed street festival is starting up. Mom's eyes follow a tiny Latina girl whose mother has dressed her up for Halloween as a bee. "She has a very pretty dress," Mom says to the mother. We cross Main and Mom spies a new store that sells kitchen supplies. "Oh! Can we go there?" she says. Nothing could stop us. We go there. I had a sort of tradition with Mom: whenever we were in a different town, we went to a gourmet cooking store and I bought her a cookbook, or some cooking utensils and gear.

"Good afternoon!" she says as Adam wheels her across the threshold. The clerk says hello. Adam pushes her through the aisles. She points at kitchen implements.

I imagine that I am in a dream. My mother is there, touching cooking tools in a store, and I, knowing even in the dream that she is gone, am filled with the greatest happiness to see her again. Why can't I feel that now, awake? Why can't I look at her as if her presence is the rarest, most precious thing in the world? I try it, imagining I'm waking up, from a dream in which my mother is dead and I am feeling the most piercing sadness, into a real world where *here she is,* and I feel a smile taking over my face, and joy fills up my heart. Then it becomes too much, and I hide a few aisles away while I get myself under control. They're saying now that nostalgia is healthy for us, but there is no nostalgia without pain. Nostalgia means, in fact, *a return to pain.*

Day 5

Adam sleeps irregularly, so he's often up in the middle of the night—just like Mom. He makes her coffee per her instructions. He makes her breakfast and keeps her company before I'm even sentient. He goes out to fetch things she needs. This morning he was up with my mom at 4 a.m. He grated an apple for her, but her gorge sent it back.

*　*　*

Silke, Berle, Peggie, Bonnie. Afternoon. Silke tells a story about how her husband once rode a Learjet to San Francisco, where the three passengers had lunch and then turned around and flew back to Colorado.

"Someone is out there living my life," Mom says. She looks around with a hangdog expression. "And I'm living theirs."

Bonnie laughs sympathetically. It was Bonnie who had worked through her lunch hours a dozen years earlier so she could leave work and take Mom to chemo once a month. It was Bonnie who had shaved Mom's head of its last patches of hair. Mom had told me how she'd felt the warm tear drops falling on her bald head.

We're quiet for a while.

"Cameron, you're so calm," Peggie says. "Did you take some of that cannabis oil I got your mom?"

"I *thought* he'd changed," Mom says, energized. "He's been really attentive—well, he's always attentive. But—he was *patient*. I thought I must be dying."

The women laugh.

*　*　*

"I love you," she says. This is later.

"We'll always be connected, Mom."

"Always have been. I don't know how," she says, "but I always felt that. You were such a gift. A gift. But I didn't always treat it well."

"Treat what well, Mom?"

"My gift," she says. "You."

This does not feel true.

Muschi arrives and Mom cries. "Sixty-five years!" Mom says. "*Meine Ingelein*," Muschi says. They hug a good long while, Mom's face tear-streaked, and before long we have moved Mom into her bed. She is barely able to stay awake.

Just a few years earlier, Mom had visited Muschi in Las Vegas. They got tickets to the Righteous Brothers and went back in time, back to when they were young and unmarried and childless and free. After the concert, my mother spied a small, colorful tent and a "gypsy-like woman" offering to read the future. *Full of vim and vinegar*, she would write in her blog, *both of us laughed and said, 'Oh, why not?' This woman said that after a health challenge, I would live to be 96.* Back home, she'd written "96" on a piece of paper and taped it to the same TV cabinet where she'd hung the tower in Lucca.

At 9 p.m. I drive Muschi to her reservation at the saddest, seediest motel in the world, and she insists on staying there anyway because it is only three blocks from Mom. If Muschi noticed, before she left, that the "96" was still tacked up on the wall behind Mom's couch, she didn't say anything. I couldn't take it down.

Day 6

The label says lorazepam is for anxiety, but the main benefit for Mom is to help prevent nausea. It makes her very sleepy. Her thinking is slower, her speech slower, her laugh encased in amber. She is rarely alert. It's harder for her to follow conversations, difficult for her to express her thoughts. She feels too little energy to have a conversation—most of her speaking is done in sentence fragments. She makes a few jokes, but she isn't talking about food and cooking, not watching TV, not making much conversation—even the kind that used to annoy me. The chattering or the soliloquy or even some negativity would be nice.

I feel a wave of sadness come over me. Missing her already.

Mom groans and stirs on the couch.

"What is it?" I ask.

"I need something for my lung," she says, reaching a hand around her right flank.

"It hurts?"

She nods.

She begins hiccupping again. *Uhuup!* She has done this for a few months now.

"Something you ate?" Adam asks, tenderly.

"No," she says. *Uhuup!*

And then she sleeps, and sleeps, head back, mouth partially open. Her face has lost its fat. Her skin hangs more in some places, but is pulled taut now over the bones of her face.

* * *

Mom instructs Adam on how to make potato and leek soup. She has him bring a spoonful to her on the couch, where she tastes it and announces its deficiencies. Sea salt. Dill. Heavy cream.

Adam and I now keep a notebook of everything she takes and when—food, water, lip salve, pain meds, lorazepam, cannabis oil. Now we can spot trends, know when to give her the next round of meds, and make for smooth handoffs with the hospice workers and her other caregiving friends.

In the evening I stop in the doorway of her bedroom and watch her sleep. Her head is back, her mouth open. She reminds me of Oma, at the end. I step into her room and see her eyes open slightly. "Do you want the light off?" I ask. She nods and I turn off the light. I bend down and kiss her on the head and hug her and put my head and face against hers. She murmurs that she wants me to lie in the bed for a while.

I go around the bed and lie down next to her, on my back. She puts her right arm across my chest and her hand under my chin.

The fingers of my right hand clasp her skeletal upper arm. "You my sonny boy?" she murmurs. "My sonny boy."

"Always," I say. A fierce whisper.

My face is pressed up against the cloth of her pajamas and her hair. I smell the scent of her. Every now and then, our breathing follows the same rhythm. I feel tears from my right eye drip across the bridge of my nose, down the other side, and around the left side of my mouth. I feel them wet her short, grey hair. I am thinking of stopping time. Of making this moment go on forever.

I feel her other hand, lightly clasping mine on her stomach. I see the light coming through the open door from the living room. I can't believe I am even here. I am so sad, so afraid.

* * *

Later: "I'm getting dizzy. Can you come in here?" Her eyes are closed, but she is not sleeping. With my left hand I caress the back of her head.

"Mom," I say, "I want you to know that whatever you may ever think you did or didn't do, you are forgiven. I just feel love for you. Just pure love."

She nods serenely and pats my face.

"That's all I feel now," I say. "You know?" I'm close to crying. "The last ten days have changed me."

"I know," she says. "I don't know why."

"It's compassion, Mom." One memory of my early teenage years stands out. I suppose I had said or done something hardhearted or mean to someone, possibly to my mother. Was she crying? Certainly she was exasperated, defeated. She said to me, several times, "If you don't have compassion none of this intelligence matters. You have to have *compassion*."

"I just remember that I looked up at you the other day," she says now, "and you said something, and any other time it would have been some smart-assed remark, and you didn't." She's quiet for a while. "And I'm saying half-kiddingly, to myself, *Oh, he's so nice, I hope I'm not dying.*" She cries.

"I don't know any more than you do, Mom," I say, because I can't think how to address what is probably her main point. How absurd my irritability with her seems now. "It's because I see you suffer, not because I know you're dying," I add, with at least the first clause being true. "I feel compassion, and that's outweighing all the other stuff, burning it all away. Maybe for both of us."

"Do we have to prepare for it?" she says. "Hopefully."

"For what?"

"This experience."

"How do you think we should prepare?"

She does not answer.

* * *

She mostly sleeps as we watch the British TV series *Poirot*. Pumpkin, elderly orange poodle of Mom's friend, Madeline, alternates between the tummy of his favorite person and the back of the couch above her head.

Mom reaches up for my hand. I kneel down on the floor and she pulls my hand against her cheek. She begins to cry. "The pain," she says, and I can't make out the rest of it.

"What, Mom?"

She works to pull herself together. "The pain," she repeats, "losing you—I don't think I can handle it."

I see her in the cloister of the church in Los Arcos, so moved by the grieving tenor's "My son, my son!" that she took him in her arms.

"Oh, Mom," I say, and take her in my arms.

Day 7

Adam and Muschi hatch the idea of bringing in a proper hospital bed, one with air sacs to alleviate the bedsores around Mom's backside. Two of Mom's local German friends, Monika and Inge, come to talk with Mom, in German. When the hospice bed arrives, I have it installed in the living room, in place of the coffee table, so that the emerald couch is on her left and her red couch is to her right. The TV is straight ahead so Mom can watch her German TV and cooking shows.

Peggie, who is following my blogging, texts me: *Thumbs up to Adam cooking for your mom! I know how terrifying that is! :-)*

* * *

Later that evening, Mom wakes from a dozing. "Do I need to go to bed?" I tell her it is nearly 8 and she can if she wants to. She does.

I walk around the glass coffee table to help her up. But now something is different.

"I can't stand up!" she says. She has been feeling pain and discomfort in her right calf and knee for a few days. But now she can't stand at all. I stoop down and scoop her up. She whimpers as I carry her to her bed, and again as I lay her down. Then she realizes she needs to use the restroom.

She tries again to stand up, and again her legs will not obey her. I put my arms under hers and guide her into the bathroom. She isn't able to turn herself around, so I sit her down on the toilet seat and pull her legs around. By the time I get her back into her bed she is crying. Another milestone.

But I know that the more time I spend fearing the end, or fighting it, the less time I'll be spending with my mother.

* * *

Mom lights up her glass pipe filled with marijuana herb and shatter hash. "Have we talked about all my wishes?" she says.

"I don't know if you've told me everything."

"That I want to be cremated."

"Right."

"Where I want the remains to be spread," she adds.

A year earlier, even as the cannabis oil had seemed to be pushing back the cancer, she had written, *I've decided that this spring I will go to the gorgeous Black Canyon, find me a pretty spot, and when the time comes, my family can put the ashes there, among the breathtaking surroundings of the canyon and its billion-year-old rocks.*

"The Black Canyon," I say.

"Yes." She nods, slowly.

Mom, about 5 (1949), on the phone in Erlangen, West Germany.

L-R: Gunter, Christa, Horst, Mom, Oma (Christine), and Opa (Christoph) Pfannenmüller. Mid-1950s.

One of my mother's headshots, in the pre-me mid-1960s. Her natural hair color was auburn.

A sporty Inge attended the 1964-65 World's Fair, in Queens, with friends who were also a couple, including Don (pictured).

Cousin Ty supervises Mom and me at the Powell Ranch near Rangely, Colorado. Summer 1967.

Jimmy, on the floor, entertains my cousin Fiona, L, and me, as Uncle Gunter watches. Erlangen, February 12, 1969.

Mom, a cowboy, and Lumpy shortly before his untimely demise, Christmas, probably 1970, Huntsville, Alabama.

My sister joined us in May 1972. Here we are at Christmas, 1974, in Huntsville.

Mom and me before prom in Rangely. At least 1983 because in another picture I'm holding a speeding ticket.

Oma, Muschi, and Mom in our house on Cottonwood Drive, Rangely, for my high school graduation, 1985.

Mom and Candy at Mom's wedding to Whatsizname aka Bill in 1988.

Oma and I drink late-night tea at Horst and Rösli's marvelous Hotel Rubschen, Braunwald, Switzerland. 1989.

Most of the German family gathered
for Opa's funeral in 1991. Front,
L-R: Christa, Oma, Renate, Anni.
Rear, L-R: Brigitte, Elfriede, Horst,
Mom, Gunter.

With Uncle Viktor at the home he
shared with his wife, Christa, a few
weeks before his death, in 1995.

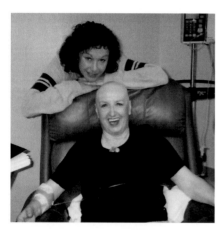

Mom during her first round of chemo, in
2001, with "heart-friend" Bonnie, who had
recently shaved off Mom's remaining hair.

Mom, in the wig she's about to toss, charges across
Cannon Beach, Oregon, after being declared NED,
No Evidence of Disease. 2001.

Mom explains finer points of cooking to one of her students. About 2005.

Adam escorts my mother at my wedding on Whidbey Island, Washington, in 2008.

Adam gives a funny extemporaneous toast at my wedding.

Mom comforts Gregory, her "little buddy", in April 2011.

Julio in a restaurant in St. Jean, France, on the afternoon before the trek began. September 2011.

Mom and Marie Anne get tangled in Mom's glasses string, hilarity ensues. St. Jean.

Julio hands Carrie contraband flowers he has relieved from their rightful owner.

Mom, Carrie, and I in Burgos before parting with Julio and Marie Anne.

Mom with one of her beloved daily
red peppers. On the Camino.

Mom exults in the plaza of the
cathedral in Santiago de Compostela.

Celebrating with Carrie and
Mom in a port winery in
Porto, Portugal.

Carrie joins Mom and me for lunch after an oncology
appointment in Grand Junction, Colorado.

In Mom's home a few weeks
before chemo, February 2013.

Mom wraps herself in Jannilyn's tresses at her party for her caregivers, September 2014.

At the end of her incandescent "Hänschen klein" or "Little Hans," Mom's knowing gaze falls on me.

Christa and Mom sing German folk songs back to back, as Carla looks on.

THE SECOND WEEK

Day 1

I suggest to Mom that she turn over on her side, so as not to put stress on her bedsore.

"Which way?" she says slowly, and a bit thickly, like a child just awakened.

"It doesn't matter, Ingelein," I say softly. She begins to roll to her right side, groaning a bit as she does so.

"You can put a pillow behind her," the hospice nurse says.

Mom turns her head toward me. "You stay here," she says.

"I'll just be your bolster," I say. I climb onto the bed and support her back with my body. The nurse is delighted. My right arm goes under the stack of pillows and my left rests on Mom's arm.

"I love you, son."

"I love you too, Mom."

"More and more," she says. "Not less and less." She is silent for a moment. "Amazing how that happens."

* * *

After she falls asleep, I go into the living room, where Adam surprises me. "Come here," he says, opening his arms. The instant we embrace my body begins to shake, and for the first time since I was maybe seven years old, I cry on a man's shoulder.

In the mid-afternoon, Mom has a hankering, she says, for steak and broccoli and zucchini. Adam goes out to buy these things and then prepares them. As a cook, Adam is very enthusiastic. The meat, though expensive, turns out not to be very good—not Adam's fault—and I'm still hungry. Adam elects to solve the matter with a nap.

"I'll fix you something," Mom says.

"You'll *what?*"

Mom hasn't been able to stand up for over a week now.

"Help me up," she says. She's in her pajamas, as usual.

So we shuffle into the kitchen together, along with her IV gear, and Mom goes to the refrigerator, bends down to rummage around, finds chicory roots and yogurt, and somehow stands up long enough to slice up the chicory and make a chicory salad with curry, sour cream in place of yogurt, olive oil, and garlic. It's surprisingly good. But to sit up, to get out of bed, to shuffle and stagger, to bend down and push and lift, to stand and wobble and cut and pound, to stretch toward a high shelf and carry, to stir, to stagger and shuffle back to bed, to get into the bed, all for another, and all without much use of one's legs—oh, *rage, rage against the dying of the light.*

Day 2

"She shouldn't leave today," Mom says, breaking into tears. She's talking about Muschi. "But I know she has to watch her grandkids."

Muschi brings Mom fried potatoes and eggs. Mom begins to eat, and then to cry. I can feel in myself her terrible sadness, and I am felled by it. How to describe such pain as I see in her and feel within myself without giving it more tenderness than God would give it? She pushes the food around on her plate. I reach out to clasp her shoulder.

"I can't do this all day," she says.

"Do what, *Ingelein?*" I say, as kindly as I'm able. I've just begun using the diminutive of my mother's name. I have felt strongly for my mother, and acted out my love in many ways, but this tenderness is new.

"Watch her leave." She looks at Muschi, and now I see thin rivulets of tears edge down her cheeks. "We've both been through this many times," Mom says to her. "We know how this goes."

"Every time I've said goodbye to you, huh," Muschi says, "I've seen you again, and this time, huh, is no different, honey."

She has that little speech tic, and a German accent as thick as a *doppelbock* beer. I remember Mom once marveling at how strong Muschi's accent still was. "She's been here longer than I have!"

Now I say to Mom, "Remember when Muschi called to you from outside the hospital?"

Eight-year-old Inge had already spent two days and nights at home in bed and then another two nights in the hospital after her appendectomy.

Muschi is happy to help me bring Mom into happier territory. "Dey took you to de Universitäts Kinderklinik in Erlangen, huh?" she says. "Do you remember?"

"I remember waking up and being very, very thirsty," Mom says, already more animated by the story to come. "I asked the nurse for some tea. She said I couldn't have any." Mom gestures with her left hand toward her own tea cup in such a way that Adam understands he is to leap up to refill it. "When the nurse left," she says, "I got up and climbed over the rails of my bed. I drank water. Lots and lots of water."

"Uh-oh," I say. "Is that when they put you in the bathtub and pumped your stomach?"

She nods. "I threw up green bile, and dreamt there were dwarves chasing me. I dreamed, or hallucinated. I was walking toward a city. The city was walled all around. There was a river running in front. A bridge led into the city. I saw turreted houses and trees. Everything was bathed in golden light. I felt I needed to go there, I felt pulled in that direction. Then I came to the bridge.

I heard my name: 'Inge! Inge!'"

Muschi is smiling. "I was a loud kid, huh." She is caressing Mom's head and stroking her hair.

"You were about seven," Mom says.

"I was too young to be let in on my own," Muschi says, "so I went around the side of Pediatrics until I was below your window, huh, and started hollering."

"I think you saved my life," Mom says.

"What was I gonna do without you?" Muschi says.

"I believe, if you hadn't called out, I would've crossed that bridge."

Now they are both smiling through tears. Muschi leans down to embrace my mother.

"I will see you soon," she says. "I love you."

"I love you," Mom says, a bit groggily.

"I love you so much," Muschi says, caressing Mom's face and hair.

"Just go," Mom says, not unkindly.

Muschi kisses her one more time, and then she is gone.

* * *

Getting to the bath, and into the bath, and out of the bath, and dressed, and back into her hospice bed, is a trial. She seems in constant pain, and it takes great effort to move in small ways. As she is getting back into her hospital bed she says to me, crying, "I don't want to do this."

"I know, Mom."

"I just wish I could go to sleep."

She curls into a fetal position and weeps quietly. Tears course down her face. There is nothing harder to watch. Nothing. I lean over the bed railing and hug her. "I feel like I'm walking into this strange place and I don't know what's going on or what to do," she says. "And I'm doing it all alone."

She vomits. I hand her the glass pipe and light the gentle herb inside it.

"When's the last time we clicked my pump?" she asks.

"It doesn't matter, you can do it whenever you want."

"Click it again," she says. "I don't want to feel anything. I don't want to feel mad, sad, glad, nothing. I just want to be nothing."

I press the button on the bolus. We consider nothingness.

* * *

My mother had passed on to me her own love of music, and dance, even song. The Righteous Brothers's "Unchained Melody" was the theme song to her courtship with my father in Bavaria. When I was a child—even after we came back to Alabama—she often sang along with her German folk records. While Jimmy was showing me how to throw a football, Mom was showing me how to waltz by standing me on her own feet. Da da da da da daaaaa dum dum dum dum. (We also did the Bump and the Hustle.) Mom and I waltzed at my wedding to Strauss's fairytale "Blue Danube," which I associate with my mother more than any other piece of music. She wore a purple dress, and you couldn't tell she was battling kidney stones. She so loved to dance.

* * *

At 8 p.m. I walk into her room. "Mom," I say. "Mom. I need you to take your lorazepam." Eyes still closed, she opens her mouth. I put the pill in her mouth and still without opening her eyes she drinks water from the bottle I hold to her lips. I stand there for a moment, watching her, and then walk around the bed. I get up on it and put my head against hers.

Look at her hands, crossed over her abdomen. Inscribe them on your memory. They are thin now, fingers slender, the left one looks older, in this light, than the right one, which looks smooth. My right hand atop hers. These are the hands that have lovingly made me many a meal. They've caressed my head. They've patted empathy onto my shoulder. See her collarbone, more prominent now, and still familiar, yet a part of her I must have seen thousands of times without registering what it looked like.

I start writing in my head, and then I think about the fact that I'm writing in my head rather than being here with my mother. I think about the little book the hospice people left us, called *Gone from My Sight*. It lists the symptoms that tell you when someone is likely to die in one to three months, when they're days to weeks away, and when they're hours to days away. Specific changes in breathing that I didn't commit to memory apparently happen near and at the end.

She's still breathing.

Day 3

Mom's old friend from Rangely, Linda Berry, has arrived to spend the day. They've been friends since shortly after we moved to Colorado, in 1976. Linda was a nurse, and they met when Mom got a job at Rangely Hospital as a nurse's aide. Linda moved to Montrose in 1983, and Mom arrived in 1987, after meeting Whatshisname aka Bill. In the early 1990s they found themselves working together again, at an elder care facility, and a decade later Linda went back to Rangely.

Linda is applying lotions to Mom's back and straightening out the folds in her shirt to minimize bedsores. She asks if Mom remembers the time both of them, and their kids, went up Dragon Road to try to cut down Christmas trees with an axe whose head fell off after every swing? Or the night, very late, when Mom had diarrhea, and neither of them had enough gas in her car to do any more than drive to work the next day, so they both set out walking and met halfway so Linda could hand my mother a roll of toilet paper? Mom laughs, then Mom complains of being cold. I lay her featherbed on top of her blanket and lean down to add the heat of my body.

"Do you need anything else, Mom?"

"What I want," she says, her voice breaking, "I can't have."

I hesitate. Would it hurt her for me to ask?

"What is it you want, Mom?"

"To get up," she says, and now she is crying.

I lean down and cradle her head in my arms and put my face against hers. "I love you so much, Mom."

"I'm sorry," she says.

"For what, Mom?"

"Always on you."

* * *

Mom says, "I keep thinking they're going to tell me what to do. I think I'm being taken away."

"By who, Mom?"

"Like kidnapping," she says.

Kidn—I absorb this.

"I'm always asking where you are," she says. "'Where's Chris?" she says. "'Where is he?' I want to know where you are."

"I'm always right here, Mom. With you."

* * *

She picks up the vaporizer pen in one hand and a lighter in the other. She seems on the verge of trying to light the pen on fire. I take the lighter out of her hand. Earlier, she had seemed unsure which end of the glass pipe to put to her mouth.

She is confused. She is irritable—is that similar to being "agitated"? The hospice book says that confusion and agitation happen when the patient has one to two weeks to live.

Day 4

"It's so surreal," Mom says, "that we're sitting here talking about death and dying." It's morning. My sister, Candy, who got in late last night, has been up with Mom for a few hours already. Mom begins to weep. I hold her head against my chest. "I know it's all been so sudden, Mom. It's happened very fast." She presses her head against me. "But you've been so brave, and you've touched and inspired so many people. What a life," I say, "for that little girl from Erlangen."

"I was always on the move," she says, waving her hand slowly. "Couldn't sit still."

Candy begins to describe some of her memories, of how Mom would let her sleep in her bed "and we would get under the covers and squeal and kick our feet", or how Mom would play German records and translate them, or how Mom taught her how to waltz, or rubbed Vicks on her chest when she was sick, and how "you would always hug and rock me and sing, just 'cause." I'm happy. I had asked Candy to share memories with Mom that might assuage Mom's anxiety that she had not been a good-enough mother.

Mom is nodding along, a faint smile on her features, the way Anthony Hopkins can do. Candy says, "Remember when I was upset about a hateful note someone wrote me in school? You told me to circle all the grammar and spelling mistakes and hand it *back*?" Candy erupts with a laugh-sob, and then a sob-laugh, and wipes her eyes. Mom smiles broadly through tears, and then she's chuckling. "I did just what you said, Mom," Candy says, "and it felt so good."

* * *

The hospice nurse practitioner arrives. Roxanne. She's formidable. Candy is on the red couch. Roxanne examines Mom's pain medication pump.

"She's used twice as much medication in the last twenty-four hours," says Roxanne.

Mom begins to cry. I go to her and put my arms around her. She looks into my eyes. "Did you hear that?" she says. "It's *double*."

"Is that why you're crying, Mom?"

"It means," she wails, "I'm going to die *sooner*."

What, in one's life, prepares a person for this?

* * *

Later, though, Mom says she thinks her unsteadiness could be due to her medication. Roxanne disputes that, gently but firmly. "It's not your medication, Inge."

"Well we don't know what the problem is," Mom says.

"Mom," I say, "we know that the cancer is spreading in your body. It's getting into organs and pressing against nerves, and it's causing such pain in you that you have to take pain medication constantly. It's making you vomit when you eat most food."

Roxanne says, "Inge, I know you're angry, and I get why. I do."

"No, I'm not angry," Mom says. "Sometimes I'm just pissed off"—she takes a breath, and then tears fill her eyes—"because I did everything *right*."

There it is. I fight the tears.

"You sure did," Candy says. "You worked and tried hard."

"You did everything right," I say.

"I just need to take some time with this," Mom says, her voice now even smaller. "Everybody is telling me what's going to happen but I need to feel inside myself and see for myself."

* * *

I'm sitting with Mom in her bed. Mom asks Candy to join us. Candy doesn't want to make Mom move over, so she gets herself into an uncomfortable position with one leg on the floor and one on the bed, so that we now sandwich our mother between us. I grasp Mom's arm with one hand and lean on her shoulder, while Candy rests an arm across Mom and holds my wrist. We lie like that in a small web until we fall asleep.

Candy is in the trial period of her new job, and if she stays beyond tomorrow morning, she'll lose it. I wish she could stay here to go through this with me, with Mom, as an *us*, reconstituting the original tiny family that was put asunder when I was fifteen.

Mom had fought off the terrible accusations for years. By the time I was 9, in Colorado, I was writing in the *Christopher* autobiography:

> But he [Jimmy] started much more trouble he made Inge go to court and Inge always won. But usually he lied.
>
> Once he said that Inge let Chris and Candy run in the streets unattended. But that was not true.

The second lawsuit to split up my sister and I came when I was thirteen and Candy was eight. I had to return to Huntsville to testify that my mother wasn't "unfit" as Jimmy had decided to claim. I can still hear my mother howling over the word.

After the trial, I stood in the upper level of the courthouse atrium and watched Candy, Jimmy, Janine, and their lawyer walk across the tiled floor below. I can remember thinking that if Tommy and his lawyer said that Candy was the source of the lies about my mother, then she must in fact have been. What I yelled at her surely hurt us both for some time: "Why don't you love us anymore?"

That lawsuit nearly bankrupted my mother, so when the next one came two years later my mother told Tommy, "Enough. I can't fight you anymore." If I had not already been a feminist, I surely was by the time my mother had to let my sister leave us. I have no memory of her departure.

Day 5

"What happened to this place?" Mom asks in the morning, not even really looking around. "It's a dump."

"What's a dump?" I ask.

"This," she says, gesturing around her. "I used to have my coffee, all my medication in the right place, everything. It used to be a high-class place. Now it's all gone to hell."

My mother's sense of humor has gotten drier by the week, and now, for the first time in my life, I can't be sure when she is joking.

"Mom," I say. "I'm going to finish the book." She'd read fifty pages or so, months earlier, and since then had occasionally asked me when it might be done. I tell her that she will one day be famous, her inspiring story spread far and wide. And there'll be a movie too, I add, absurdly.

She says, "Who will play me?"

"Meryl Streep," I say. "Smart as a whip, strong, and she could do your accent."

She looks at me very intently, a slight smile playing on her lips. Measuring each word out slowly, she says, "If you say so."

* * *

She is so light, so vulnerable in her complete trust. She reaches her hands over my shoulders and around my neck, and my arms are around her so that I am at once supporting the weight of her and gently hugging her to pick her up. As we start moving she puts the top of her head against my chest and holds on tight. We walk in a shuffling minuet.

We walk the lengthy, exhausting camino out of the hospital bed and through the living room, across her bedroom and through another too-narrow door into the bathroom. We pull her pajamas down and she sits down and I stand there because I've got the IV drip wrapped complicatedly around my neck. "Do you want me to leave you alone?" I ask. No. She is done. Coming out of the bathroom, I walk backwards, holding her medication pump, as she gamely takes small steps after me.

"Do you want to go back to your bed or out into the living room?" I ask.

"Go out," she says. "Out. In the little time I have left, I want to go out."

* * *

She stands up, with my help, and brushes her teeth. I give her half a lorazepam and her cannabis oil—which she still takes, doggedly, under applesauce on a spoon. "Do you want some of your marijuana to smoke, Mom?"

She nods. "I just don't give a shit," she says, in that quietened voice she now speaks in. "And I want something that will enhance that feeling."

"Enhance what, Mom?"

"Not giving a shit. I want to enhance that."

And so we do, Mom and I. We enhance the shit out of it.

Day 6

On the way back from the bathroom she stops to catch her breath. "I need to find some water therapy or something."

"Water therapy?"

"For my legs. I need to do something. I'm not going to just lie down here and die, no matter how [unintelligible] that would be." She is crying.

"How what, Mom?"

"How *gra-cious*," she says loudly, and now she is sobbing. I reach out to her. "Everybody keeps talking like it's a done deal," she says.

This stops me cold. A little earlier I'd found her crying and said something probably facile about going to a beautiful place. But now I realize, to my horror, that my mother has reverted to believing her cancer can be healed. I feel both sad and abashed about my presumption.

But I can't give false hope. I can't tell her that she will get better, or that we'll find a way, or that it's going to be all right. I haven't said any of these things to her. Nor have any of her friends. I'm lucky to be surrounded by a lot of grown-ups. But for me, having no solution to my mother's distress is my own private hell.

Candy texts me from Alabama, *I'm worried about you. Are you going to be okay? You're the one that will find out first. I worry about you.*

Day 7

Mom asks me to get into the hospital bed with her. She begins to cry. "I don't want to go."

"I know you don't, Mom."

"And that God the Father, I was always so afraid of him. I don't want to see him."

I've never heard her say she was afraid of God. But when the mind is going, and is contemplating death, it may be the earliest influences that win out.

"That mean God is a fairytale for scaring children, Mom."

"I know," she says, "it was just always beaten into me in Catholic school and Mass."

"Wherever we go, Mom," I say, "it's going to be to a place full of love."

* * *

"I'm not ready to go now," she says later. "I want to talk to the shaman. I want to find out what Father Sky and Mother Earth say about all this."

A little over a year earlier, after the second chemo had failed, Mom had met the shaman at a local powwow.

> For 15 years I've visited the annual powwow of local tribes. Always loved the colorful regalia. I picked out 2 necklaces for my granddaughter and her beloved. I went to the kitchen section and was greeted by one Native American woman I've seen once a year for years. She came out the side door, beaming, and enfolded me in a big hug. "How are you?" I pointed to my blond wig and said, "I'm surprised you recognized me with this on." She answered, "I would recognize your beautiful smile anywhere." She gave me a cup of mint tea, from leaves she had grown herself. When she heard I was sick, she went to find an older man.
>
> He asked me, "What was wrong?" I told him that I had cancer, now the second time. He nodded and told me, somberly, that his wife had had breast cancer and died 5 years ago. He said it was the worst but also most awesome experience he'd ever had. "Awesome?!" I said.
>
> He said it was because of their rituals and her grace, how she dealt with it. I remembered how much it bothered me, when I worked at the elder care facility, how many of the residents died alone. He handed me a long, gray feather with two smaller feathers, one yellow and one green, bundled and fastened with a leather strap. It was a "smudging feather" and meant to heal. Tears ran down my face. He took a step toward me with wide open arms. "Come here, sister." Made me cry more and I was so embarrassed. Here came a younger woman, also hugging me from the side,

and then a third one who said, "This is a healing circle." I told them that I had wanted to go to Santa Fe to find a Shaman for a long time and that it almost felt like a pull.

They took me to a shaman. He sat me down in a private area and told me that he could see my aura, the rainbow colors and also the black spots blocking me. He took my smudging feather and waved it up and down my body, chanting in his native tongue. He stopped one time, looked at me, and said, "Your chakra is way out of line on your right side and it has been that way for quite awhile. I will try to align it." On went the chanting as he moved the feather from head to knees. He said, "Oh, there is a big blockage in your leg." I said, "Yes, this where I have blood clots." (How could he know?) He told me he would now give me over to the Great Spirit, to heal me. I started crying again. He too, had tears in his eyes as he looked at me and said, "If the Great Spirit would not be filled with love for you he would have not put you in my path." He told me what a beautiful spirit I had. He asked me, if I felt the heat of his hands (which never touched me) and indeed I had. He apologized as he had had many sessions the day before and was thus weakened. I told him, that I was grateful for anything he could give me.

After about 30 min he got off his knees and asked me, if he could hug me. I totally said yes. I took the only $20 bill I had and handed it to him, saying that this was all I had but wanted him to have it. He thanked me big time and said that most people didn't even say Thank-You and that I was only the second person within those past days that had given him a GIFT. He also gave me his phone number, in case I wanted to have another session.

*I sat on the bleachers and enjoyed the rest of the program
and felt very much at peace, marveling at the many "coinci-
dences" which had brought me there that Sunday.*

I've called the shaman's number several times and each time
I get a busy signal. And he's not on the Internet.

"I'll try again," I tell her.

"The chaplain said he knew of two shamans," Mom says.

"Let's get in touch with him then," I say.

"Tell him I'm a crybaby," she says.

"Well," I say, a bit taken aback, "if you are, I am."

She is quiet for a time. Quietly, she adds, "I'd like them to come
here and make a hell of a noise."

THE THIRD WEEK

Day 1

I am so grateful that Adam came back. He'd gone to Texas for a few days, on a previously scheduled trip. I feel bad that he is spending so much time here, in this dark, crowded, cluttered little house in a town devoid of synagogues, good food, and multilingual Rubenesque exotics. As we stand in the kitchen, I give him an out.

"I think this could go on for weeks or longer," I say, quietly.

"I've got nothing else I need to do," he says, "and I can work from anywhere." He's a legal recruiter, just needs a phone and a laptop.

She sleeps until after 10, which, for her, is unheard of. When she wakes up she begins to vomit up coffee along with bile. Adam and I tend to her, wiping her mouth and nose, holding her bag, holding her up. She is shivering. She says, "I'm going to starve to death."

* * *

Bonnie comes by at 4:30 p.m. Mom has been sleeping almost continuously. Bonnie sits with her, just occupying the same room, no TV, no book, no smartphone, for almost three hours. She is extraordinary, this "heart-friend" whom my mother calls "my Bonnie".

Mom moans softly and I look to see her turning more on her side. "That's good, Mom," I say, in a voice I mean to soothe. "You move just like that." I don't know if she can hear me, but just in case.

She hiccups. It sounds different now. It's shorter, more of a sharp high *yip* or even *ip* than the throatier *uhuup* she did for months. Occasionally she will awaken to lift a hand uncertainly and murmur, "Do we need to take a pill?"

And I will say, "No, Mom, we don't need a pill yet. We just took the last one a little while ago."

Because that is what you do, with the dying. You give them every comfort you and others and circumstance denied them in their lives. Death concentrates the mind—and, I would add, the heart. Right now, I *feel* more. More than I normally do, more than I ever have. I am ablaze with feeling, and most of it is love. And finally compassion, which is the will to feel another person's fear and sadness and pain.

And when I tell my mother no, we don't need another pill, she is satisfied because she knows what's happening. She feels control over something, safe in knowing that we are doing our pills the right way, perhaps like a good girl would. And she drifts off to sleep again.

* * *

She asks for orange juice. While I massage her head, Adam hands her a coffee cup of juice and says, "I haven't filled the cup all the way up, but there's more if you want it."

She looks up at him and nods glacially. "You're my favorite son."

Adam and I both start laughing. I am delighted to see my mother's face light up with a smile.

I tuck her in and tell her I love her. She murmurs, "Don't worry. You don't have to worry."

* * *

When I was thirteen, in Rangely, my mother handed me seven typed pages with the title, "Storm Warning." She'd left Candy and me with a friend for a few nights, and I suppose she wanted me to know why. This was in 1980. She was thirty-six.

"The mighty self crumbled," her tale begins. "I felt I would die if I didn't get away." She is having a panic attack. "I tried so hard to be okay. See, world? I can do it—marriage, divorce, three custody battles, three jobs, now aren't I terrific? Helen says, 'Be human, it's O.K. to cry and let go.' But I don't know how." Her friend Jean arrives as she's putting her suitcase in the car, "so broken herself and yet by my side...misery in her eyes (one of which is black and blue)". She gets in her '76 Cutlass Supreme and starts driving. East.

"I drive and I don't see anything for the tears," she writes. "I didn't know there could be so many for so long." She can't go through anything like the nightmare of eight years ago, the divorce and first custody battle. "I lost six months of my life, can't remember anything. Sessions with the psychiatrist, probing, unveiling and pain, such pain." After an hour of driving, she arrives in tiny Buford, Colorado, where she checks into a cabin, thirsty from all the silent screaming. She goes down to the lake, where the water soothes her battered soul. But she's not ready to talk to the Lord yet.

The next morning she looks into the mirror to see swollen eyes, and she "can't feel anything", but the beauty of her surroundings continues its work on her. She walks. Wildflowers and sage sparkle from the rain. She praises the warm sun on her face, addresses the Lord now, too, but the only answer is a hissing sound. She jumps and turns. Two deer stand looking at her. She says hi, and then, though embarrassed by the spectacle of it, she has a fine time telling them of her "past years". Inside a rancher's fence she sees a "haughty, regal" camel. "I throw my head up and laugh." And finally llamas. She can't believe it. She wonders why it took her four years, living in Colorado, to find such wonderful places. "The solitude is great and I'm warming up to being by myself," she says. "I listen inside myself to find out what's happening. I look up to the sky and feel at least some of the life juices returning and an awakening of sorts. With the help of the good Lord and my friends, I will learn to reach out more, not isolate myself, give them a chance to help me, too."

About four years earlier, when we were still living in Alabama, she'd written a short story called "Christopher's Vacation." I don't recall her showing it to me then, but I stumbled on it years later. She wrote that the main character, Chris, has been missing his father "with such an intensity and fierceness that it had really worried his mom." In fact, not much good has happened to Chris in the last year. "He saw and heard [his mother] crying, even though she tried to hide it." And his mom worked such long hours. "But now it was all different," because Chris, his three-year-old sister, Renee (Candy's middle name), and their mom ("pretty," she has Chris think, "but it's a shame she's a little old, already over thirty") are going on a rare vacation—to the ocean! In the car, they sing their hearts out, they laugh and giggle. They check into a cabin near the ocean, where the next morning they all splash and squeal with delight.

The morning after that, Chris slips out while Mom and Renee sleep. He goes to the docks, where he meets a man with dark hair and twinkly blue eyes. The man, Stan, is the captain of a fishing boat. Captain Stan "sensed the loneliness in Christopher…who was much too serious for his age". They walk back to the cabin to ask Mom if Chris can go out on the fishing boat, and then Chris gets to join the crew to fish and sleep on the boat overnight. Stan talks to Chris about his life, school, and what he likes to do, and Chris beams one of his "rare smiles." It's "almost as nice as being with his father," Chris thinks. The crew tells grisly ghost stories over a crackling fire. One plays a harmonica. "Christopher felt a hard knot in his throat because it was all so beautiful and he was so very happy."

Here, in one tossed-off trifle, was my mother's rawest wish: that she not be so anxious about money and lawsuits, that she have more time for us and enough money to do fun things, and that I benefit from some kind of fatherly love. She often said a parent is only as happy as her unhappiest child. She'd witnessed and remembered all the childhood traumas I'd endured and forgotten, and then she'd held them within her, where I could feel them in her own sadness, a sadness felt twice.

It marked me. I'd long harbored a primordial sadness that my mother hadn't been happy enough. The pain my mother had suffered throughout her life was beyond reckoning. But reckon I would try. I found I could lose myself in trying to solve the unhappiness of countless women other than my mother, and sister. Our empathy was entwined, our compassion doubled, if not always skillfully. My mother knew more than anyone the depth of my disappointment during my own divorce. She'd emailed me, *Sometimes, I think I feel your pain and despair. I'm so sorry that you are still going through a difficult time.* She taped a band-aid inside one card, adding beneath it, *This is for your wounds.* In another, she let me know she was, *as ever*, in my corner.

* * *

Back in May, on a beautiful Colorado spring day, we'd driven to see Dr. Mapleton in Grand Junction. Mom was wearing the light blue capri pants and blouse we'd recently gotten her, because her clothes were all too big, and matching earrings, shaped like seashells, that I'd bought for her in Santiago.

"I was always struck by one thing the therapist told me," Mom had said to me, on our drive. "'Inge, just let go with love.'"

"I remember you mentioning that many times."

"Over time I figured out how to do that. I wrote and read a lot. I'm still working on it. I really am."

"Working on what, Mom?"

"Not to experience everything as a rejection. The things that annoy you. It's still the first, tiny sensation I have, and then I deal with it."

"Well, that's good, Mom. I think a lot of us struggle with that."

The desert sped by. How to address my own fear and sadness? I hesitated. Miles passed. Mom and I would soon be on the outskirts of Grand Junction. Suddenly, at long last, I surrendered the question. "Mom," I said. I cleared my throat. "One of the things I am finding hard to deal with is my feeling you haven't been happy enough." I had to pause. "I still really want you to be able to experience great happiness."

"Oh, son," she said, turning to look at me. She gathered her thoughts. "Since I started therapy with Whatsizname"—this was in the late 1980s—"and all that stuff around Jimmy, and my parents, I've felt very—I don't like to use the word *happy*, but content. I have been very *content*."

"Well," I said, and then had to clear my throat again. "That makes me feel a lot better."

If my mother, even my mother, insists she's had a good life, what does it mean for me to keep worrying that she didn't, or doesn't believe she did? Is that not just sentimental projection? As in: *If I were her, given what she's told me and what I've seen, I would see more suffering than happiness.* Or even more personally: *What if I feel that about me one day? That I didn't find a way to be happy enough, to do enough—because how else can you let go and die well?* What if I felt that way about myself *now*?

"Let me tell you something," she said, turning back to me. "If you ever wonder whether you've done enough, or you could have done more, let me tell you you couldn't have."

She was crying. Then I was too.

"It may be nothing," she said, meaning, *Don't cry because you think I am dying.*

"I can't bear to see you suffer," I said, instead of, *I'm afraid you're dying.*

"I can't stand to see you cry," she said.

"I feel like I need more time to love you enough," I said.

"Oh, son!" she said. She put her left hand on my right, which was gripping the gearshift. "When you were eight months old and your father had already abandoned us, I went to Denver to get another good job, so I could keep you. When I came home after a few days, you had the most beatific smile on your face, and you were just so *happy*. You didn't know how to kiss, so you puckered up your mouth and patted my cheeks with your fat little hands over and over." She patted her own cheeks with open palms. "That's when I really, really fell in love with you. Nothing in this world could have ever taken you away from me." She sniffed, tears again afoot. "Those little fat hands in my face. And you *loved* me *then*." Crying. "You see? And *that's* what's important."

I couldn't speak. Sat behind my sunglasses and drove.

"There are happy times that are like snapshots in my mind," she went on. "Those gummy little lips and no teeth! So that's one snapshot. I have snapshots from when I was a child, too. So I *do* have moments. And in spite of it all, I got fourteen years. To get that with ovarian cancer is amazing."

Day 2

Morning. Early. I hear my name.

"I need to go to the bathroom," she says.

When we return to the bed, she is exhausted. She is breathing hard. "Put your legs this way," she says, pointing at the slice of bed beside her. "Help me get warm." I sit down on the bed next to her. I pull the featherbed into her from the front and embrace her from behind.

"I always wanted to be close to you," she says. "Even when you roll your eyes at me."

"Oh, Mom, I'm sorry."

Almost imperceptibly she shakes her head. "It's all right. I do it too. It's like a pre-conditioned thing."

But it feels to me she's letting me off a bit too easily.

I think of all the love I felt and did not show, and of all the love I felt and could not show.

* * *

"I'm always here," Mom is telling Lynne, on the phone. "I'm just stuck in some crevice."

* * *

She is gazing toward the TV, which is off, and its cabinet, where she had once taped up the picture of the tower in Lucca. Her gaze is diffuse, unspecific.

"Do you see something?" I ask.

"Just for a second," she says, ever so slowly. "I saw two blips... of a Camino sign." She gestures vaguely ahead of her.

"You mean the yellow arrow?"

"Yes," she says.

Day 4

Morning. Unable to fit enough personal survival time between Mom's bedtime and my usual bedtime of midnight, I'm now going to bed at 2 a.m. every night. Adam, who has wordlessly taken the early-morning shift, comes to my room. "Your mother is pretty alert," he says. "You might want to spend some time with her." I get up and go to her.

"I need something that's going to give me hope," she says. Adam and I exchange a look. "I manufacture it at night," she says. "But now there's not any left, and I'm not getting better. Can somebody tell me something that will give me hope?"

It is excruciating not to offer her religious certainties or other false comforts when she's so clearly in despair. I tell her, "I love you so much, Mom," and I give her a long hug.

She wants to call her cousin Renate. "I just want to be able to say goodbye. Say thank you." Renate was one of my mother's best friends, and one of the most generous people I'd ever met. If you walked through Renate's house you had to be careful not to look too long at anything, lest she take it off the wall and cause you to take it home with you.

But when I try calling Germany, I'm unable to get ahold of her. Mom begins to cry.

"This wasn't supposed to happen like this," she says. "We were going to end up in Iziba"—she means Ibiza, the Spanish resort island where Renate's late millionaire brother, Hans, once had a villa—"on the Strand"—the beach—"to make up for the crappy life we had before." At this she weeps again.

I'm stunned.

Oh, Mom. Oh, Mom. What happened to being content?

The angel I'd been wrestling and once thought vanquished had returned, or had never gone, and I know now I'll have to wrestle him again and again, long after this is all over. We end, just as we burst from the womb, wrestling with our story.

Day 5

Oma and Opa's antique clock ticks away.

I am leaning down to press my face against hers. I breathe in her soft grey and white hair. In her small, girlish, trusting voice, she says, "Am I getting any better?"

"Are you what?" I say, not sure I've heard her, or not ready to go where it's going.

"Am I getting better?"

Breathe.

"No, Mom," I say. *Breathe.* "I don't think it's getting better."

Her eyes fill with tears, her face is a mirror of pain. She puts her hands over her face and begins to shake with weeping. Now she is keening, ripping the flesh of my heart. Is this not just the worst conversation I have ever had?

After a while she says. "I wish someone could tell me something. I don't know how I'm going to live without you—" She begins to shake again. "When you die too are you going to come find me?"

"Mom, you know that's the very first thing I'll do."

It's around 8 o'clock and Mom is dozing in and out, mostly out. The medication pump keeps beeping, annoying both of us. I hear her talking in her sleep. A minute later, with one eye open about twenty percent and the other ten, she spots my fancy marijuana vaporizer, and I hear a question.

"You want what?" I say.

"Weed!" she bellows.

With a pin I clean out the charred material in the bowl of her glass pipe and sprinkle in fresh indica. I put the other end to her lips and pass the lighter back and forth over the herb in the bowl, keeping but the tiniest bit lit up so her draw doesn't get too hot or too smoky. She inhales. And once more. And without further ado she says, "Good night, my beloved son," and closes her eyes.

Day 6

At about 6 a.m., Adam is awake. I get up to go to the bathroom and he says she cried a lot in the night. "She was sobbing," he tells me. "She said, 'There are so many books I haven't read.'"

She's in the hospice bed in the living room. She looks around her without comprehension.

"I keep being puzzled by all my stuff," she says.

"What puzzles you?" I say.

"That it's here. Because I don't know how it all got here. I don't know how I got here."

"From where?"

She shrugs. "From hospice, wherever."

"Well your stuff is here because you're in your home. Your little house. You're where you want to be."

"How long have I been here?"

"You've been here the whole time," I say, an answer without sting.

"I'm hungry," she says. "If we're this close to Erlangen," she says, slowly, "why can't I have *sauerbraten*?"

"That's a damned good question, Mom."

* * *

Berle and Silke rub Mom's feet and reassure her. She cries, as she has been crying since I told her she was not getting better.

What to do? How to make the most of her time? Should I be reading to her? Making her laugh? Reminiscing? I'm afraid I provide no entertainment, no comfort other than the constant attention I give her. I can't keep my hands off her head, her shoulder, her face. I kiss her every other time I pass by. I fly to her when she cries. All things she'd done for me for the forty-seven years that ended last week, in the kitchen, as she made me the last meal she'd ever make.

* * *

She cries about leaving us.

"We'll always be connected, Mom. Always be together." This is the only thing that makes it feel a little better. "We'll be together in no time. I'll come and find you."

She emerges from the frozenness of her sadness. "You better bring some good Camino shoes."

Berle and I laugh. Mom's smile lifts like the rising sun.

"Look at that smile," I say, and I kiss her cheek and her forehead.

"You take such good care of me."

Soon seven words just like this will be all I have. I would not trade this for anything else I might have chosen to do. When I decided to move to Telluride to stay near my mother, over two years earlier, I wrote in my journal, *Whenever she leaves this world, the last thing in her consciousness will be months, weeks, days, hours of love, honoring, acceptance. I won't allow the burden of unlovability on top of the supermassive black holes of her pain and despair. My mother once told me that her father had beaten into her that—and*

235

I remember her exact words —"You're ugly and stupid and no man will ever love you." So, who else, and what other man, would, by his presence alone, say to her: You do matter. You are worthy of love? And now she has two of us.

"That's because you've always taken such good care of me, Mom."

* * *

The rivers of sadness that pound through my mornings continue to fade to a trickle by the evenings. Now Mom sleeps. Adam sleeps. Oma and Opa's ancient wooden clock sits atop the heirloom buffet and audibly counts down the seconds, just as it did for Opa and Oma, and Oma's parents before that. The seconds will slip away, 3,600 every hour, for several hundred more hours. They will be up before I know it. The heaters blow white noise. It's not even 8.

Day 7

In the morning she has some confusion but is feisty. Adam is up early with her and gets her coffee, canned (!) peaches, tea, bone broth, and a quarter of a slice of toast. He gives her the lorazepam on schedule. Muschi calls and I give the phone to Mom.

"I can't believe this is how it ends," Mom says to her, "after stealing potatoes and pears." Their families had gone hungry throughout the 40s and 50s. Sometimes they could afford only chunks of fat in place of meat, though for the ladling of guilt, in Mom's household, Muschi once told me, there was still the heirloom family porcelain.

Later, Mom is concerned about what will happen to some of her things. She has me take a picture from the wall and look for the name written on the back. There is no name. She tells me to write "Inherited from Ingeborg Amanda Cheatham" on it.

"Who do you want to give it to?" I ask.

"You!" she says. She looks up at the shelves to her left. "If Oma's Madonna doesn't stay in the family," she says, "you'll all be cursed." She looks at another figurine below it. "That black Madonna," she murmurs. "Pretty much the same." Adam laughs. "Giving away, losing, stealing—nothing bad should happen to those Madonnas."

* * *

At half past noon it's time to pick up Melissa. "It's been a long time!" she says, as we hug on the airport sidewalk. "How are you doing? Never mind," she adds, "I know how you're doing. I read your blog." It has been three and a half years since we last saw one another, negotiating our settlement agreement in the Barnes & Noble in Bend, Oregon. She is still beautiful, hasn't seemed to age, and she's very smartly dressed. I had never once held the desire that we resume, but I did hold too long to the wish that she would, in a sense, return as recognizably the person I thought I knew. But we can't always choose whom we recognize after a breach.

At the house she goes to Mom and hugs her. They are both crying. Then Melissa sits for awhile and chats amiably with my mother. She has brought a wave of positivity into the house.

I listen in and watch them talk for a while, and then I think it would be good to let Mom sleep and let Melissa be alone with her. I explain to her the workings of Mom's world —the pain pump and lorazepam, her need to be on her side, her water bottle and vaporizer pen, the bed control, the marijuana salve—and Adam and I jump in Mom's Kia to go to Starbucks to get some work done. "Well that was sweet," I say to him. "I'm glad she's here to love my mother."

Mom eats some plain yogurt in the evening. Several spoonsful. Spills a good bit on her pajamas and chest, and then makes it *really* clear she doesn't want any help with all that. Melissa manages to clean it up anyway, and to put a paper towel on Mom's chest while she eats.

Adam goes to bed early. Melissa and I watch a movie, then begin a second. She is cold so I get her the heavy Afghan blanket and drape it over her. She falls asleep and now, four and a half years after the Big Bang, both my former wife and my dying mother, separated by a few feet, are asleep in the same room.

* * *

Where were my mother's male friends? I'd seen them. They'd eaten like kings at her dinner table, they'd eaten from paper plates on their laps in her backyard. I knew they existed. Do men think of being with the dying as women's work? And is that because they feel such work is beneath them—or that it's beyond their grasp?

THE FOURTH WEEK

Day 1

Sometimes she says things that are somewhere between an attempt at a joke and a slippery grip on reality. A cat with shiny pajamas—who turns out to be Adam, with hair like a prophet and in his gaudy paisley silk robe—promised her a bonbon. Really quite clever, equating the two, but the cat also told her to take oolong tea into the garden, where waterfalls sing.

"We don't have a dog, do we?"

I watch her as she falls asleep. I kiss her forehead and smell her hair and skin.

I am mostly numb from this waiting game, but at the funeral home earlier, when the woman handed me the cremation contract, I did find myself shaking between the impulse to cry and the effort to hold it in. I was surprised to find Adam wet of eye as well.

Adam has been invaluable in the kitchen and at night, and has helped me with hosting when people visit. On their way out, he thanks them for coming.

* * *

I tell Melissa it's nice to have her here. She agrees. It's both strange and very familiar. Earlier, she was washing dishes in the kitchen and I found her presence in the house surprisingly comforting, and I felt myself not wanting her to leave so soon.

Day 2

I do some work from my office atop the spare bed and then go into the living room to kiss her head and stroke her hair. "My cousin!" she says, maybe trying to make a joke. "My son," she says more softly. She pulls me down into a hug.

"You're really smiling a lot more these days," I say, responding to her smile.

She begins to cry.

"What? What is it?"

She waves her hand in front of her mouth as if to dissipate the tears. At length she says, "I have such good friends."

"Of course you do," Adam says.

"And you have friends who live in other places and have never met you who would love to be here with you," I say. "All kinds of people on Facebook are saying 'Inge has been an inspiration to me and Inge helped me immensely when I was diagnosed', or, 'I always loved Inge for her posts with beautiful photos of nature first thing in the morning.'"

"When you haven't been worth anything," she says quietly, "it's really hard to believe."

"Believe it, Mom," I say. "This is who you really are." I read a post from her Facebook page: "'Inge is that kind of woman I always wanted to be—always open minded, always kind and helping others—even her words always are kind.' It's your old way of thinking of yourself versus how everyone else does. And you know they're the ones who are right, don't you?"

"It's weird," she says. "It feels fake." But she doesn't sound as sure now.

"You did everything right. You did everything you could do. You fought the good fight. You have been a warrior in every sense. And you touched and inspired so many people."

"They used to say that when I was little," she says.

"Say what, Mom?"

"Say I inspired them. And I had no idea what they meant."

Was she referring to her old grade-school classmates in Germany? *I still see most of these kids when I go back*, she'd written in her blog once. *They wait with reunions until they know I'm coming. I am so very lucky to still have these friends in my life. They found me, a few years ago, after searching for years. I remember the letter starting with: 'Dear Inge. Finally, finally we have found you.' And I cried.*

"It's your life force, your energy, Mom," I say. "And your grace. We'll always be connected."

"I know," she says, softly.

* * *

Before she leaves, Melissa wants pictures of herself with Mom, and she applies makeup and lipstick to her. "It's a girl thing," my mother explains. When she's finished, Melissa holds her iPhone's camera toward my mother as a mirror. Mom takes the phone.

"My God," she says. "Who is that person?"

Melissa hugs Mom. Melissa is crying.

"It's not over," Mom says.

Melissa continues to say goodbye. "Just go," Mom says, not unkindly.

* * *

Carrie and her mother, Laurel, arrive. Carrie, now a high school graduate, has impulsively moved to Nebraska with her first serious boyfriend, but is back in Grand Junction for a few weeks.

Carrie and Mom are stroking one another's faces and speaking in low voices.

"Remember first meeting Julio at the airport so full of life?" Carrie says, and Mom nods, smiling. "Or our first day, 'out the door and up the hill', like you said? And being in the dark forest forever? And then in Pamplona when Julio did the bunny trick and we laughed so hard?"

"Heh, heh," Mom says.

"And remember on the way to Estella when I ate all those stolen grapes and *then* was told not to eat them?"

"And in Navarette," Mom says slowly, "you slept outside on a ledge. Like a hobo. Until the *albergue* opened."

"Yes! And in Belorado when those poor pigs were just hanging in that truck. And in Burgos where we had to say goodbye to Julio and Mary Anne. And the Iron Cross and eating the human heart in El Acebo after Cameron said he lost his love handles, and I said all I lost was my wallet?"

"We had a time, didn't we?" Mom says, smiling.

"Then we finally reached the end," Carrie says, "All I could do was see the joy on your face for how much you accomplished, and how proud I was of you."

Mom reaches out to caress Carrie's face. "My love," she says.

"And now I have this hunger to learn," Carrie says. "To experience things that people are, for some reason, scared of. I have never been so happy as when we were on the Camino."

Day 3

She repeats some words from a poem that she wants read at what she calls her "memories party", a sort of wake she wishes us to have after she dies. Having this conversation ranks, in terms of unpleasantness, just below drug-free oral surgery. I find the poem, "Do not stand at my grave and weep," online, and read it to her with a firm, measured cadence, so that she may feel the truth of it: *I am not there. I do not sleep.*

"To save a wretch like me," Mom adds.

"Amazing Grace," I say.

"I did it my way," she says.

"Elvis," I say. "Or Sinatra. Are those the songs you want us to play?"

She nods.

* * *

I look up to see her gazing at me. I look back at her and smile. She continues to look at me very intently, and then she turns her bony furry head away and begins to cry.

* * *

"Words seem to be important to me," she says, as if she has been mulling it over.

"I think it's a memory recovery that I need," she says.

"I want to know everything," she says.

* * *

"Do you have to leave tonight?" she asks.

I think my tone is at least as important as what I say. If I *sound* unworried, caring, protective, then the content that she may not understand anyway becomes less important. "No, sweetheart. I'm staying here all night, with you. I'm going to sleep right over there on that other couch so I can keep an eye on you and make sure you don't have too much pain."

And she is satisfied.

Days 4 and 5

She asks about our life together. "You were always loving to me," I say. "For forty-seven and a half years."

She regards me with amazement.

"*Really?* You're that *old*?"

"That's what *I've* been saying." I add that I've been with her for over two years, in Montrose and in Telluride. Before that I was in San Francisco and New Jersey, before that Bend, then Seattle, and before that, Portland, Austin, Washington DC, Denver, Cambridge, Boulder...

"That's quite a resume," she says. She looks at me. "How did I luck out so much?"

"You deserved every good thing that ever happened to you, Mom."

"You're a good man," she says, as if she were just deciding it.

"You raised me," I say.

She smiles.

"Do we have cows?"

* * *

At times we sound like characters in a work by Samuel Beckett, like Didi and Gogo in *Waiting for Godot*, like Mercier and Camier.

"We're not the worst, are we?"

"No, we're not the worst."

"I mean, our standards is good, right?"

"They are very good."

* * *

She comes out of another reverie. "Do I have to have assistance in dressing?"

"Do you want assistance, Inge?" Adam says, with astonishing tenderness.

"No, I want to know if I can dress myself. Am I able to."

"I think a little assistance is helpful," says Adam, ever so gently.

* * *

"Do you want to sleep?" I ask her. It's the middle of the night. I sure do.

"I don't want to sleep," she says. "Bits of my life are falling away. If I have one."

* * *

"What's the situation?" she asks me, later. "How did you react? I mean, did I fall?"

"No, you didn't fall. Your cancer has just been spreading."

"Do we have a lot of good steady friends, too?"

"Yes, very steady," I say.

"A *lot* of friends," Adam says.

She cries. "That's good to have," she says, wiping her eyes.

"It's great to have," Adam says.

"We can raise a barn," Mom says.

"Yes, we can raise a barn," Adam says.

"But I can't walk."

* * *

She opens her eyes, looks at me.

I look at her for several moments, until I can feel a real smile creep into my eyes.

"You're a great mom," I say.

"Am I a great other things, too?"

"Sure you are. A great cook—"

"A great friend," Adam says.

"A great walker," I say.

* * *

It's about 4:30 a.m. Adam will leave for the airport shortly for a brief, previously scheduled trip, so he's packing quietly as Mom

ORDINARY MAGIC

talks. Mom wants an easier way to go pee on her own, without calling to anyone else first. I can't gather what she is saying, but she seems to be designing some kind of contraption. I tell her that's not necessary.

"I'm almost always here, so you just have to ask me for help."

She brightens a bit. "Are you a gentle person?"

"Yes," I say. "Why?"

"Because I've had it so rough," she says.

* * *

She breaks the silence in the room. "Do we have a father?"

Before I can ask her about this, there's a knock at the door. It's Bonnie, come to take Adam to the airport. Mom cries as Bonnie hugs her. "I'm having a snot or identity crisis," Mom says. "One or the other." She looks at Bonnie. "I can't remember you."

"I'm Bonnie," says Bonnie.

Gesturing in my direction, Mom says to Bonnie, "I didn't know what to call him for a while there."

"You can just start with 'son'," Bonnie says.

Mom's eyebrows go up. "I wasn't sure," she says, somewhat conspiratorially.

* * *

She has been sitting in bed with her eyes closed. She stirs. "I was thinking, that as soon as I get back on my feet"—Silke and I look at each other—"maybe out of pride, I can make a walkway, an elegant one, so I can get around the house." She points at the walls and draws an imaginary railing or something. "Because," she says, as if answering an objection, "people do challenges."

* * *

"I just feel like *bits* and *pieces*," she says, sounding so sad. "Are they ever going to come back together?"

"Yes, Mom. They will come back together. And you'll be much happier."

"Soon?"

I take a breath. "Yes, soon."

* * *

Sometime after saying something, she stirs. "Is that a true thought?"

"Yes," I say. I can see that she's upset about her mind going. "You have many true thoughts."

She reaches for my hand. "My soul seems to want to find you."

* * *

I keep administering painkillers. Four pumps in a row, the most ever. I hold her hand as she falls asleep and then I sleep on the couch, waking up to her groans every so often, reaching out for the bolus, and clicking the button. The mantle clock ticks down the seconds. The air pump hums.

Day 6

I look up from my laptop at the sound of her crying pitifully. She has spilled her piping hot tea on her chest. I help her to dry it off but it still smarts for a while. A year earlier, she'd written, in her blog, *When my children were little, I always had a "Magic Tea" and "Magic Salve." They totally believed in that power.* Knowing her belief in her marijuana salve, I offer to apply it to her skin, and, with some fanfare, I rub it in.

ORDINARY MAGIC

She speaks more slowly this time, almost asleep. "I have," she says, "an advice. For Damon."

"What is your advice, Mom?"

"To be a good father," she says.

From what I have observed, I tell her, he already is. "He's a good man," I say. I tell her that at Damon's wedding, a year ago, Corky, the oldest of my three half-brothers, told me, "Damon is the best damn one of us." I add, "And I'd not have gotten to know him, or Jannilyn, Mom, if I hadn't been here with you these last two years."

She nods, satisfied. "Have we always lived here?"

* * *

"Am I an angry person?" she asks.

"No. Why?"

"I hate angry people," she says slowly. "I was beaten by angry people."

"You didn't deserve that, Mom. It wasn't your fault."

* * *

"If I had those wide-soled roller skates, do you think I can go through the house?"

How to render that tone, like a curious and humble little girl who's a little afraid to ask the question.

"No, you can just relax."

"That is so boring." In a small voice she tries again, asking very politely, "Can I not work on that little bench that Silke gave me for working outside?"

"I don't think so," I say. I'm afraid she's going to cry, or I am. "It's winter now," I hasten to add, "and the garden is starting to hibernate."

I recall one morning, a few months earlier. I'd awakened to the sound of my mother outside, in the rain, working in the dirt of her medicine wheel garden after a night of blinding pain. I could hear her digging: *oh, oh, oh*.

* * *

"Can I have a dog?" she asks.

"If you want," I say.

"What kind of dog?" Adam asks.

"Small one. I mean, nobody's sleeping with me, right?" She says this like she needs confirmation. "I'd like to sleep with somebody."

"I can sleep on the couch there again," I say.

"Yes but you don't lick my ankles," she says.

* * *

"Tell me about yourself," she says to me, with a trace of the interviewer and a hint of the stranger. "Something that's good."

"Well, I remember that just before my seventh birthday, you gave me a choice between having a birthday party with all my friends or having a seven-course dinner with you at the Brickskeller, in Huntsville. Do you remember that?"

"You chose dinner with *me*," she says, slowly. "That's when I really knew." Pause. "You were going to be a different kind of kid." She smiles. "We spent the dinner talking. Like two adults."

"You've said I talked about black holes and white dwarf stars and red giants." These had been my passions. I'd checked out all the books I could find in the school library.

"I remember the white stars," she says. "You were like a little professor. I thought, 'Who is this little person? Where did he come from?'" She pauses and rests for a moment. "That was the first time. I saw. To my *astonishment*. How smart you were." She looks like she's going to cry.

I remind her of our many trips to Germany and Switzerland, including the one with Aunt Jayne and her son, my cousin Mike, who would die ten years later, at twenty-three, of lupus. I remind her of how excited she was to attend my law school graduation. Whatzisname and Aunt Jayne came, as well as Candy with infant Brianna, Oma and Tante Renate, one of my college professors, and Clark. As Class Marshal, I spoke to the assembled guests during the commencement ceremony, and I credited my mother in front of God and everyone. Afterward I gave her a sturdy plaque with all the Harvard crests and her own name in the center as the honoree. It still hangs on her bedroom wall.

She brightens at the memory. "I could not have been prouder, happier, anything."

* * *

"What's that thing, hanging down?"

I reach for the travel pillow we've been using in her hospice bed. "This?" She nods. "This is for airplane travel." I put it around my neck and lean back on the couch. "See?"

"Did I travel with that?"

"You sure did."

Her face breaks into sadness. "Where did I *go*?" she says.

"You went all over the world, Mom. All over Europe, to Brazil, around America..."

"How did we afford all that?" she says.

"Well, you saved up money. You went on a few trips with Bill"— aka Whatsizname— "and I bought a few tickets."

"I would never go on a trip with Bill," she says.

"Well, you did back then."

She shakes her head. "Not even then."

* * *

6:40 p.m. I hear her cry out and begin sobbing. I leap up from the couch. "What's wrong, Mom? Do you have pain?"

"Nightmare," is all I can make out.

"You had a nightmare?"

She nods.

"Well it's over now."

"Are you sure?" In that voice like a three-year-old girl.

"I'm sure. It's finished now."

But only seconds later she is again in distress. "Why does my tummy hurt so much?"

"We need to get you some more medication," I say, moving around the bed to the bolus.

"I thought it was over."

"No, Ingelein. I'm sorry. But we can stop it with this medicine."

I sit with her and caress her head and hand until she seems to be asleep. Then she opens her eyes and looks at me. She reaches out her hand and strokes my cheek.

"You're the best man I've ever known," she says.

"Who raised me?" I say.

* * *

"I look like a starvation person," she says, quietly. "If you put me side-by-side with a starvation person, I would look worse." And indeed she looks like nothing so much as the concentration camp survivors photographed, in 1945, by Allied troops. That is cancer: the concentration camp of the human body.

* * *

I'm on Skype with my startup team, in Gregory's Room, when I hear Mom, loud enough to penetrate the door I've closed to let her sleep. I dash into the living room. She is heaving with sadness, great big sobs.

"Are you hurting?" I say. "Do you have pain?" I have already reached across her and pressed the painkiller bolus when I see her shake her head. "What's wrong then, Mom? Why are you crying?"

"Because," she says, each word wrapped inside a sob, "I have to die."

What could I do but hold her? I had reached the absolute nadir of my helplessness. "I don't know how to do this," she says.

That makes two of us.

I offer some variety of faux profundity.

"It's not so much the journey," she says, after a while. "It's that...I have to do it alone."

"You won't be alone, Mom."

I don't know what I'm talking about, which is why I'm agnostic. I don't have a strong belief in what happens, but I know I want to cobble together a story for my mother to hang onto. "That's what all the near-death experiences have in common, Mom. We are greeted by guides who are made of light and love. Oma will probably be waiting for you too. And your big brothers."

She weeps.

* * *

"One day we'll sit down and discuss this whole thing."

"Discuss what, Mom?"

"The story."

"What story, Mom?"

"How you and I ended up together."

"Do you remember?"

She draws a breath. "Not really. It's giving me some different..." She stares off into space.

"You gave birth to me in Rangely," I begin, "and you were living at the Powell Ranch with Grandma Powell, and my grandpa, whom I never met."

"They didn't smoke pot?"

"Um, no. Neither did you."

"How did all that marijuana start?" she says. "I didn't just go out in the middle of the street and say, 'Hey, I'm a middle-aged flower girl.'"

* * *

"I want a last hurrah before I die," she says. "I want to be happy just for one second, feel what the feeling feels like." She is near tears at the end of the sentence.

"You've been happy before." I say this hopefully.

She takes a moment to respond. "Not in material matters."

"You know that doesn't make people happy."

"I know."

"You've been happy before, right?"

"More than anyone I know," she says, "including me."

* * *

"There's an innate star of strength inside," she says later. "That's what I need to find. My star. And a dog." She is silent for a while. "And he better not die before me."

Day 7

"I can't get over that you're my son," she says. "I mean you seem familiar...But I've missed so *much*," she says, hitching a terrible sadness to that last word. "Where have I been?"

"You haven't missed anything, Mom. You were there my whole life."

"What are you, sixteen?"

"I'm forty-seven."

She is astonished.

"Forty-*seven*?" She turns her head away from me and mutters to herself, "I'm worse off than I thought." She is lost in thought for a little while. "I need some time. Can I have some coffee? It's like whiskey to me. For this shock."

* * *

"How did I meet you?" she asks later.

"Well, you gave birth to me, or so I'm told."

"But surely you must have had a house somewhere. You must have wondered where I was."

Memory is a mistress, lovely and cruel.

* * *

"How did I get here?"

"Where, Mom?"

"Here," she says, gesturing around her.

"It's your house."

"It's so frustrating, to be denied things that I need to have and to know."

"I know it is. Do you want to try some more water?"

* * *

The certified nursing assistant, Janie, tells me my mother asked her how much time she had left. "I told her I couldn't know and I wouldn't try to tell her. Some people hold on for weeks. My mother lived a week and a half with only a few sips of water. But your mother's confusion is getting worse. Your mom told me, 'They're telling me my mom and dad are dead, but I can't accept that.'"

THE FIFTH WEEK

Day 1

"I don't even know where I am."

"You're in your bed, Mom, in your living room, in your house."

"You keep saying that."

* * *

She is tetchy. Tells me I speak to her very disrespectfully, says I have an offensive tone.

"I think you are mistaken," I say.

"That's your opinion," she says. She is also peevish because I can't hear her when I'm in the kitchen. She leans over with her big mug full of coffee and I think she's trying to set it on the floor. I reach out to help her with it and she snatches it away, giving me a cold stare.

Later, she is frustrated with her nausea. "I wish I could just go away. I want to go home."

The hospice book says that with one to two weeks to live, a person begins to use the "symbolic language" of "going home".

"You want to go home?" I ask her.

"Yes."

I consider this. "Where is home?"

"Someplace not here."

Day 2

She is up at 2:30 a.m. and again at about 8 a.m. and asks for her coffee. As she drinks it I ask her to take some more lorazepam.

"What's it for?" she asks.

"It helps you not be nauseated," I say.

"I don't like not knowing what I'm taking."

"You've taken it every few hours for over four weeks."

"I want to see a piece of paper," she says, her hands miming words going across a piece of paper, "that says what it's for."

* * *

"What are we going to do today?" she says. "I'd like to go some-where. I want to go outside and read."

"It's cold outside, Mom. The last two times we took you out in your wheelchair it was warmer than today and you got cold."

"You can dress me and we'll go outside."

"You can't walk, Mom."

"I *can't*?" She struggles to absorb this.

Each discovery like a blow. My mother awakens each day into a nightmare of unremembered incapacitation.

"You're so stoical," she says to me. "It's my *life* we're talking about."

* * *

She talks of travel with friends. She speaks of "an ocean of pumpernickel".

She looks at her glass mosaic lamp. "I remember how *excited* I was to get the lamp. Through the lamp came three colors: yellow, green, green, and emerald."

She considers me for a moment. "How did you show up in my life? I didn't just show up and say hello are you my son?" She is silent a moment. "I would have never ever ever ever left you alone."

* * *

"Do I have a clear thought?"
"Sometimes you do."
She begins to cry.

* * *

Nurse Donna asks her, "Are you excited for what's next?"
"No," Mom says. "I don't even know what's next."
"You don't know where you're going next?"
"My whole life was taken overnight, not to be replaced by any-thing I know," Mom says.
"Do you know heaven?"
Mom shuts down. "I don't want to have this discussion," she says. "I'm not having this discussion. I'm sorry."
Folks in Montrose have, at various times, asked my mother if she's made peace with God. "I was never at war with him," she'd say.
"I just want to go home," she says, later. "Just get it over with."

Day 3

Another night of pain that the base level of hydromorphone drip can't handle. I call hospice to come in and increase it. Several times I awake to hear her moan and to press the button. She whim-pers. "Just make it go away," she murmurs.
We wake up at a decadent 10:20 a.m.
"Happy Thanksgiving, Mom." I kiss her head.
She brightens. "Happy Thanksgiving." A pause. "I didn't intend to forget about it."

"I know you didn't, Mom. It's okay to forget. Would you like some tea?"

Her smile is beatific.

* * *

"Can you tell me, in complete sentences, what is going to happen?"

"What is going to happen when, Mom?"

"Today. What are we going to do? Are we going to get dressed, go outside, see a movie, or the dolphins, or—I just want to know something."

* * *

"Are you a doctor?" she asks.

"No, but I'm a lawyer."

"You can't help me."

"Neither could the doctors."

Now she chuckles.

* * *

She's asleep again. Or was. If one sound can bring her out of her sleep, it's the sound of me cracking my knuckles.

In the early evenings, not long after sundown, she will fall asleep. I watch a movie or work on my laptop from the emerald couch. At around 11 or midnight I throw Mom's bedroom comforter onto the reddish couch, to which I've added a layer of foam brought by hospice. Some nights, like tonight, I hear her making sounds that might mean she's distressed, but I'm not sure.

"Are you having pain?"

Tonight, just now, she says yes and nods her head. I find the bolus and press the button. She groans a few times over several minutes and then falls asleep.

I read things on the web for a while. I hear Mom whimper. I lean off the couch and press the button.

* * *

"It feels like you're holding me here."

"No, Mom."

"I don't know what to think. I'm trying to be kind. But I don't know for what purpose."

Day 4

She mentions two things that don't seem to relate to one another. I ask her what one has to do with the other.

"I thought I might find a friend in you," she says, "but I guess not."

She has been like this today. She's a little paranoid, hears disrespect and offense in neutral or even loving statements.

Picking at the primal wound.

Day 5

"Do you want to sleep now?"

She nods. "There's nothing else to do anyway."

"Except talk or watch TV. Or we could look at the Camino pictures now if you want to."

She shakes her head. "That part of my life is over," she says.

I feel chilled.

Day 6

"I'm a very avid reader," she says, at 2 a.m, as if she were explaining her hobbies and interests on game show. Which is true. My mother was a reader. Every day. I'd have discovered the world of books without my mother's influence, but surely I stepped into it sooner and more passionately because of her.

"And an even greater writer," she adds. She has never said anything like this. "Some people may think it's not that great but I like it."

Who said it was not that great? I wonder. Other than her father?

On the book shelves that she can see from her hospice bed, I go through a number of books to find one she agrees on. I guess that she has not read Doris Kearns Goodwin's *No Ordinary Time*. "I started it once, and it was an excellent book," she says. "I'd like to start it again," she adds, with the sound of someone choosing her words carefully. I pull it out and hand it to her. I turn on the light behind her. For a few minutes she flips through some pages, stopping occasionally, because her eyes keep closing.

Day 7

I ask her, "What're you thinking?"

"Oh, son." She lifts her hand to the level of her forehead and waves it in circles for several seconds. "I don't have a coherent thought," she says.

At about 1:30 a.m., the lights are out and I'm on the couch, unable to fall asleep, needing to wait to press Mom's pain pump in any event. Mom begins crying vigorously. "Mom," I say. "Are you having a dream?" She nods. "Do you want to talk about it?"

"Oh, son," she says, and turns away.

This hurts.

* * *

"Do you want some water?"

She looks at me. "What does it matter, really?"

I have thought the same thing: why would we force food or water on her? It's not like it's going to heal her, or extend her life by weeks or months. If she drank more she might live a day or two longer.

"It's up to you, Mom," I say.

"Insha'Allah," she says.

* * *

She puts her hand on my face.
She gazes at me with so much love.
"From your very first breath," she says.

THE SIXTH WEEK

Day 3

Bonnie comes to see Mom. I'm working on my laptop in my bedroom when she appears in the doorway. "Your mother wants to talk to you," she says. "I think she's worried about all of us. All the people she raised. It's holding her back."

I recall the conversation I'd had with my mother in the hospital back in October, when the stents had achieved maximum crucifixion. Bonnie was there, too. I hadn't meant to have that conversation, not then.

* * *

We'd had the conversation many times, and I'd never really figured out a skillful way to manage it. I don't remember what she said or did this time, but I said something about listening, being heard, being seen. She said she didn't want to talk about it now. Well, I said, she never did, and would there ever be a time when she would? Thinking that Bonnie would surely come to her aid, she asked Bonnie for her opinion—and Bonnie told her to take a deep breath, not be defensive, and hear that I was saying I don't feel heard.

"Just don't, Bonnie," Mom said. She asked Bonnie to admit that she'd just witnessed me criticizing her. Bonnie also did not do this.

Mom said we needed counseling, implying that this would somehow help me to see my errors. I said we could do that, but it wouldn't turn out the way she thought because she wouldn't be able to talk over me or retreat into victimhood or blaming.

I said, more softly, "Mom, you often mistakenly believe I'm accusing you of something shaming, some horrific thing you couldn't possibly admit to, so you can't hear the emotional content of what I'm saying."

"Well," she said, "I've been garbage all my life."

"Oh, Mom," I said. "You already believe you are being torn down, even when I am *not* feeling judgmental and *not* expressing anger. I'm so sorry about all the things that have made you feel that way, but that's why you can't hear me."

Mom tried to turn things around, began talking about my failings. I said I would be happy to talk about them separately, but they were a diversion now, another way of not hearing me. She said I could read her journals some day for her side. I said I got her side all the time, and I did not doubt that I behaved unskillfully at times and I accepted that, and could, I hoped, forgive myself. Could she forgive herself?

Mom reached for her leg wraps, attached to some tubes, meant to prevent blood clots, as if she were going to leave the room. Bonnie was up and saying, "No, no, honey, we're not going to do that," and I said I would leave instead. I'd reached the door when she spoke up. "Sometimes you are really cruel," she said. "I think you love me, but I don't think you like me very much. I think my mere presence upsets you."

"It's not your mere presence, Mom. I just haven't often felt heard or seen," I said. "Look, whenever you and I are at dinner—"

"What dinner? We haven't been to dinner."

I sighed. "My point is, when we're among a group of people, no one I know would recognize me." Pause. "They wouldn't recognize me. Because I don't say anything." Longer pause. "I just want you to think about that."

I bade them goodnight. She had taken responsibility for the things she could see—her busyness, stress, the yelling—but what she couldn't see any more than a fish sees water was her inability to listen. And I knew she wouldn't be able to, and that was all right.

After I left the hospital, I'd texted her: *I love you and hope you have a good night's sleep!*

She had texted back: *I have chosen a very bad time and am not only sorry but really upset that I did not tell you that I do hear you and I will 'listen'. I don't want to leave things this way. We will sit and TALK. Yes? I love you more than I can say.*

* * *

Now I go to Mom's bedside, Bonnie on the red couch. Mom reaches for me.

"I've done a lot of wrong by you," she says.

I think that's overdoing it. "Mom, I want you to forgive yourself."

"I want *you* to forgive me," she says.

"Mom, I have already forgiven you. A long time ago. I just love you, unconditionally. We all make mistakes. It doesn't mean we're bad people."

I look at Bonnie, who regards me with a face of many feelings, and back to Mom.

"Thank you," I say, "for being my mom."

Such a grand smile creeps across her face. She opens her arms for a hug.

Day 4

I've been up for an hour with Mom. She has such pain in her abdomen that she is crying, again. I hit her pain pump, give her some morphine, renew her lorazepam.

"I've been thinking," she says, so quietly I strain at first to hear, "about comparing the good colors with the evil colors."

"What are the evil colors, Mom?"

"There are also safe colors," she says.

"What are the safe colors?"

"Yellow."

"Yellow is a safe color?"

"Well," she says, "I wouldn't say safe, but you can rest a while."

"What are some good colors?"

"Temerald green."

"Emerald green?"

"No, not emerald, temerald." She thinks for a moment. "Did I dream that?"

* * *

Yesterday she had gazed into a corner of the room and talked to her mother. I couldn't make out what she was saying, other than how she addressed the corner as *Mutti*. This talking to the deceased is typically a sign that a person has one or two weeks to go, but Mom is outliving all of our predictions. The hospice nurse asked her about her mother, in the corner. Mom did not respond.

Day 6

I take a cup out of her hand so she doesn't fall out of bed as she's trying to set it on the floor.

"Rudeness!" she cries.

Later, I offer her lorazepam.

"Who says that is good for me?" she says.

"Well, the nurses do and I do."

"Who are you?"

"I'm your son."

"You're not my son. My son would be frantic with worry. My son would be kind and compassionate. My son would offer me food."

THE SEVENTH WEEK

Day 1

This morning I show her pictures posted by her Facebook friends. She gazes at all of them with such wonder and gratitude. A picture of Carrie: "Gorgeous," Mom murmurs. A video of a dog that walks on its front legs, its body in the air, pissing all over the sidewalk. A real baby chimp clutching a stuffed-animal baby chimp. I am sitting on the emerald couch and holding the phone's screen toward her, so that I see her watching the videos with the open curiosity of a child.

I read aloud people's comments on her Facebook page. "Please give her a hug for me," says Antje. I watch Mom's face respond to that, with what one Birgit, in Germany, calls "such radiant and warm-hearted eyes." Birgit has added, "I keep looking at her pictures. She is such a strong person, and always loving." Christina writes: "Although I only knew her from Facebook, she truly found her way into my heart." Debbie: "She is more special than any of us will ever be able to fully express." Karen: "It is amazing the connection we can have with people we haven't met. Her spirit pierced the pages of Facebook." Ulrike: "She is such a courageous woman, and with such wisdom and wit. I just love her." I speak in different voices for different authors and make everything sound even better. I explain things in such a way that they all sound wonderful.

Day 4

I sleep in a bit, dehydrated from karaoke, weed, Flatliner cocktails, and altitude the night before. Last night, as I drove to Telluride—friends had insisted I join them for the weekly karaoke—I tried to run through some of my standards. What I heard surprised me. I'd lost about nine notes of my upper register. I couldn't sing most of my songs! Psychosomatic, I thought, but what was the connection between my *psyche* and this vocal *soma*?

Adam tells me that Inge, Mom's Munich-born friend in Montrose, stayed the night. "Your Mom woke up in the middle of the night and she was really obstreperous and paranoid," he says. She fought them at every turn, he says, threatened to call the police.

"It sounds like terminal restlessness," Roxanne says, when she arrives.

I let these words wash over me.

"She doesn't want to go," she adds. "She's just really bummed. The folks who usually go down kicking and screaming are strong-willed and they're usually women. Maybe because of all the obstacles they've had to overcome. Your mom definitely falls into that category."

Roxanne had more than doubled Mom's base dose of the painkiller last night. She thought Mom had crossed a line between consciousness and comfort, and she needed to be less conscious to feel less pain. Indeed, Mom hasn't been able to sit up, wake up, or say much of anything since I got back ten hours ago.

Roxanne asks if I want to talk to a social worker, a grief counselor. It's included in their services. But I don't feel like I'm having any abnormal reactions. Sometimes I cry. Most of the time, I don't. It hurts all the time. Nothing to be done.

* * *

Our evening routine has left the stage of her bedroom and moved exclusively to the stage that is her hospital bed. She now lives in the living room. Instead of walking her to the bathroom, we stand her up and turn her around about 120 degrees to sit on a portable commode next to the bed. She is able to eat fewer and fewer things, even as she complains of hunger and accuses us of not bringing her something she can eat. For about the last week, she hasn't kept down more than a spoonful of anything. She's not even drinking much water. How can a person survive for weeks on less than 6 ounces of water a day? In a dry climate? And now she sleeps without cease and breathes out through her mouth, over and over.

Sometimes there's a long pause between her breaths. Some are only five seconds, but some are seven, even ten.

Ten seconds.

* * *

"Why are you so loving to me?"

Her sole sentence of the day.

I have been touching my mother's face and hair and holding her hand more in the last few weeks than in the rest of my life together. Kissing her, calling her sweetheart.

"Because you're so lovable," I say. "Because I love you. Because you're worth loving."

She reaches an arm up. The gesture isn't clear but I have the feeling she is seeking a hug. I lean down and hug her, this woman who is often either asleep or unable to respond to questions, and she reaches up and wraps both arms around my torso *tightly*. After a long hug I stand up and caress her face and head. Her head is now something that is reminiscent, I suppose, of a skull. I think of the last line of one of Beckett's earliest short stories: *They found her caressing his wild, dead hair.*

* * *

From the bedroom I see she has awakened and is sitting on the edge of the bed. I run out to help her use the commode. She sits on it for quite a while, a vacant look on her face. She pees four or five streams, separated by several minutes each. At last I sit her on the edge of her bed and there she perches, stubbornly, falling asleep, then falling backwards until she catches herself, but refusing to lie back in the bed. "I want to go to sleep," she says, and no sooner have I stood up and repeated, "You want to go to sleep?" than she shakes her head or says no.

The emperor has taken her curiosity. The questions have largely ceased.

Day 6

Adam wakes me at 5:30 a.m because Mom is insisting on getting out on the wrong side of the bed. She spends most of the next ninety minutes sitting, as before, on the edge of the bed, like a statue, or a memory.

"This will be another indecision marathon," I say. Adam nods.

Questions about whether she is ready, or whether she wants to go back to bed, are ill-received. I understand that many dying people exhibit negativity and restlessness or agitation, but I have wondered if hers has not followed some of its old courses. The exasperation, the defensiveness and prickliness, the victimhood, the annoyance when given a suggestion.

She's also refusing to take her sublingual drops. Adam and I have been dropping them in while she sleeps, and trying not to get caught.

I've noticed that when I'm away from Mom, out of the house, I tic more. Around the neck, face, eyes.

I get into the hospice bed, squeezing myself between her

shoulder and the railing. I listen to her breathing, once even a light snore like old times, and I try to imagine not hearing any such thing ever again.

* * *

I walk into the living room at a little after midnight. Mom is on the floor between the bed and the red couch. "What are you *doing*, Mom?" Adam instantly appears out of Mom's bedroom, eyebrows up. We get her back on the bed. She talks about birds. Yesterday, she had a cat. "Need to get home," she says.

But a few hours later, I'm cracking my knuckles and she comes out of sleep and says, "Can you please not do that?"

Then she is speaking in German, and I speak German back.

She says something about one getting spanked when one gets home.

"Did this happen in Germany?" I say.

"I've really got to get home," she says.

What is this urge, this instinct, to get *home* when one is dying? We could say we want to do many things other than *going* somewhere, and we could certainly go many places, real and imagined, other than home. Why not sing? Sleep? Jump? Why not go to a forest? Heaven? The womb? Why not go to mother? Or one's birthplace? The cave? These all have a similar symbolic power. But we say *home.* Is there something the dying mind knows about what's next?

"You can go whenever you want, Mom," I keep telling her. "I'll be okay."

Day 7

Bonnie comes over. Mom asks her who I am. I kiss Mom's head over and over until she smiles. "She's smiling!" Bonnie says. I hear such joy in her voice.

Sometimes I do Tonglen, breathing my mother's fear and pain into me, breathing out only love and acceptance. If I start thinking at all, especially of my future, without her, wishing she could see and experience what I will, my eyes fill up. I'll start wishing she could be here to experience more joy, that she could have experienced more joy.

THE LAST WEEK

Day 1

Mom has been all but unable to speak all day. Her stays on the commode are getting longer. She keeps trying to get out on the wrong side of the bed, and then it's nearly impossible to persuade her to go to the other side. She fingers the railing, staring at nothing. She stiffens to the touch. "In a minute," she says, minute after minute. But I won't begrudge these minutes in which my mother is still a living being whom I can hold.

"Don't you touch me!" she says to me later, in what one could call a snarl, as Adam and I try to help her out of the bed. I haven't heard that particular voice, I think, since I was a kid. But it's not really her speaking now. "Ohhh, sugar pie honey bunch," I sing back to her. *"You* know that *I love you."*

She lifts a red box of tissues and tries to drink from it.
"Are you thirsty, Mom?"
"Very," she says, in that slight wheeze.
"I've got water right here."
"It better be water," she says.

Day 2

Adam leaves to return to New Jersey. He has taken to calling my mother "sweetheart" and "my beautiful Inge."

I would do this again. For my mother, for others. Love is healing. The more love, the more healing. If there is anything that is God's work, it's showering love upon the dying. The hospice brochure approves the wisdom of saying words to the dying that actually come from a Hawaiian prayer meant to be repeated over and over: I love you. I am sorry. I forgive you. Thank you. Hospice workers are fortunate to be able to express love and compassion five days a week.

I am enormously grateful for them. Hospice work is not the glamorous, TV-ready work where people in uniforms race about with needles and IVs, and somebody shouts "Clear!" Hospice workers want intimacy. They want to slow life down. A study by Massachusetts General Hospital shows the good hospice can do. Each of two groups of stage 4 lung cancer patients was given the standard oncology treatment, but one group had a series of conversations with a palliative care specialist. "The latter group chose fewer days in hospital," the study authors concluded, "stopped chemotherapy sooner, went in hospice earlier and suffered less." They also lived twenty-five percent longer.

Some families, I've read, ask hospice workers not to mention the word "hospice", or "cancer". Some families have not even informed the dying of their diagnosis, much less talked to them about what is happening. Which is to say, they don't give the dying a safe place for their terrors and their guilt and their sadness. It makes me unbearably sad. Is it not the least any human being deserves, to be guided, in oceans of love, through the final passage? I read that the dying often awake from nightmares—with guilt about something they've done or the fear and sadness of what has been done to them. Some family members are angry and deny what is happening.

It's been said that we know too little of life, in America, in the West, because we know too little of death. Why are we here? One of the reasons, surely: to have compassion for, to walk with, and finally to carry, our fellow human beings, to ferry them to the *Grenze*, and then bid them *aloha*. I could refuse to do my part, but I'd be cutting myself off from life. There is no keeping out the painful and ugly and scary without also building a moat and fortress against the healing and loving.

* * *

Mom is annoyed that I don't hear something she said. "I'm gonna call the police," she says. And the next time: "God, I'm going to a hotel." This time I have to laugh.

* * *

In the evening she is mostly unconscious and unresponsive. I could sleep in the bedroom without worry. But I don't want to spend so many hours apart from her. I sleep on the couch within arm's reach of her bed, getting to sleep sometime after 1 a.m.

Day 4

It's 6:30 a.m., still dark outside, but I wake up. *That sound!* She was making a gargling sound as she breathed last night, but it is now loud and ragged. It fills the house.

I get up and raise the head of her bed. I get a sponge on a stick. Three times I dip it in water and squeeze it into her mouth. When I clean her parched lips, she moves her head slightly. Her breaths are shallow and quick. Her hands are hot. Her forehead is like the outside of a cauldron.

I crack every last one of my knuckles. *Crack. Crack crack. Crack.*

In some cases two per finger. I watch her face.

Nothing.

Ten minutes pass before it hits me. This ragged sound. This must be what they call the death rattle.

Oh, boy.

* * *

Later. I climb into the hospice bed next to her. I hold her hand. I kiss her head. Her hand is limp now. Her body like a furnace against my leg. I weep, quietly, unobtrusively, as usual, in case she can still hear and understand anything: I've read sense of hearing is the last to go. I hold her hand, kiss her head and soft eyelids every so often.

For almost forty-eight years she's been as constant to me as the sun and moon.

* * *

Peggie arrives that evening armed with a Holy Bible. She talks to Mom about her strength, how she's fought bravely and hard, and now she can go, she can just let go. She reads from Psalms. I wonder if, for Mom, there are too many "praise the Lords".

"Is she crying?" Peggie asks. Peggie believes she is.

Bonnie arrives. She goes to my mother and embraces her for a long while.

Mom's breathing is barely audible. She seems much more peaceful now.

On YouTube we find "Stille Nacht", the original, German version of "Silent Night". I sing it to her as she once sang it for my sister and me. I play some of the videos I'd taken during the Camino. Here she is singing the German folk song "Hänschen klein." We're going up a slight hill and she's singing through effortful breathing. I play the video of "The Mourning Tenor of Los Arcos" and the one of the Spanish woman playing the hang. And finally the video of Mom spinning round and round in the great plaza of Santiago de

Compostela. "Can you hear yourself, Mom?" I say. "I was so proud of you. That day and always."

Bonnie leaves and Peggie stays on, encouraging me to go back to sleep. I want to write, but as I lie down on Mom's red couch I can't keep my eyes open.

* * *

Night. Mom is as responsive as I've seen her in a while. Her eyes are closed but she is conscious of my hug, squeezes my hand.

"I love you so much, Mom. I'll be okay. You go home whenever you need to." Now I am crying.

I turn off the lights at about 1:30 a.m. As I lie in bed, I notice how dry my mouth is. I haul myself back out of bed and go to her. Dab her lips and mouth with water, rub Vaseline on her lips with my thumb.

* * *

This was my last post. I wrote down what happened the next day and night only in my personal journal, which follows.

Day 5: El Duende Ultimo

Though ill-starred chance and circumstance kept beating against her...
few women have ever pursued a dream so relentlessly against such odds,
probably for that reason still always on my mind.

—Julio Angel Redondo

When I wake up again it is after 11 a.m. The house is quiet. I come out and give Mom's head a kiss. Shave, shower, eat cereal. I sing "Brown-Eyed Girl" to her, remembering to change some of the browns to greens. I sing songs to her of my own making, absurd, childlike, heartbroken. I get into bed next to her and cry.

I apologize for my irritability with her, my exasperation.

I lean down and press my chin and cheek against her face. I realize I have begun to match her breathing exactly, there is out and there is in.

In the afternoon I crawl into the hospice bed again. Sobbing. I take her hot, furry head into my arms, press my head into hers, feel on my forehead her wispy, silvery hair. Her breathing like the slow swells of water at lakeside. The in-breath clearly harder to take than the out-breath is to make. Fast, slow. Fast, slow.

"I am sorry," I say. "So sorry. I know how disappointed you are, how very disappointed. And I couldn't do *any*thing."

This wrecks me.

Her chest moves ever so slightly. Her throat with it. She has not opened her eyes in a day or so. She has not stirred. She has not moved her legs around or tried to sit up to re-situate herself on the cushions beneath her. Or moved her hands or arms. Or moved her head.

I stand up, pace around. Maybe you are on your way to dance round a fire with the druids right now. Maybe you are flying over the energy meridians of Spain right now.

My heart swells at the memory of yesterday's last, conscious embrace.

* * *

It's already after 7 pm. Where has the day gone?

I'm sitting on the sofa to her right. The room is lit only by small white Christmas lights and the Tiffany lamp that she'd recently told me emits the three colors of light: yellow, green, green, and emerald. Not to be confused with the *good* color temerald.

I look at Mom. Her heart and lungs keep pumping, lifting her chest, making her throat and chin move with every breath taken in. I think of watching a movie.

"I wish we could have just sat here and talked sometimes," I say to her. "Instead of watching movies."

* * *

Her labored breathing continues. She's been making more sound in the last half an hour than in the last twenty-four put together. Something like hiccups, or sneezes. A few brief vocalizations that don't sound like pain. I debate where to sleep. How do I want to find her? I'm afraid to go to sleep. I'm afraid to wake up if I do. Should I stay up all night?

"Just three hours and twenty-one minutes to the solstice, Mom. I'm going to miss you so much."

I lie down next to her, cramming myself between the railing and her body. I put my right hand around the far side of her head and stroke her hair. I sit up. "Mom, is it possible I am doing something that's holding you here?"

I stand up and imagine her floating above me. I wave my hands up. "Go! Go! You can go now."

I feel foolish. Then I remember I'm a little high.

*　*　*

Music, as usual. I need to have music on all the time, even when my mother is not dying. But now more than ever, to fill the silence, to buoy the mood on a river of sound. Then I hear the opening chords of "Blue Danube". Peggie is here. I start to sing out the famous notes. *Da da da da da daaaa bum-bum bum-bum...*

"Do you hear that, Mom? One of your songs!"

And my mother stirs!

"Oh, my goodness!" Peggie says.

With just the slightest movement, Mom is keeping time with her head and left arm.

I move closer to her and caress her head. She turns her head to the side, toward my voice, something she has not done in days. She lifts her head! She's not done *that* in days. She looks like she might sit up at any moment. With both of my hands, I gently pat her cheeks.

Now she moves her head again, slowly, following the sound of my voice as I walk around the head of her bed. "You did it your way, Mom," I say.

And in response my mother lifts her body away from the pillow behind her and thrusts her bone-thin arms up over her head, triumphant. Her eyes register nothing, but her face is aimed straight at my voice, at the sound, the emotion, she surely still knows comes from her son. I lean over the low railing of the hospice bed. I put my forehead against hers, hot as a kiln, my right hand holding hers, the other caressing her head. Then I take my mother's other hand as well, and begin keeping time with both of her hands, so that her arms move with mine. I hear her breathe. I feel her grip on my hands. The ever so slight roll of her head from side to side. She is here again, back again, right here, knowing it is me, knowing what we are doing. With my ear on her chest, a creaking woodwind concerto inside, I sway us to and fro, as we'd done so long ago on a living room carpet in Huntsville, me on her feet, one-two-three, one-two-three, and with the darkness visible outside her rust-colored drapes now, we dance just like that. The song ends. I begin to shake. From behind me Peggie says, That was a beautiful dance, Inge. Midnight now. It's the winter solstice and Mom is still alive. I hold her for a long time.

EPILOGUE

"One must imagine Sisyphus happy."

—*Albert Camus*

I t's just like in one of those dreams: I open my eyes, and my mother is alive. But it's not a dream.

Here, before me, she sits, on a red divan. She's dressed herself smartly in black slacks and a stylish black-and-red top, both new because she's lost so much weight.

Her older sister, Christa, and niece, Fiona, finally booked their trip to Colorado: they're here with us now, Christa for the first time in over twenty-five years. Mom and Christa are swaying to live German folk music, back to back, like the last two Spartan warriors, if Spartans ever sat on red divans, I haven't had time to look it up. Gregory and Annika bookend my mother, and another half dozen of us are clustered a few feet away: Silke and Gordon, whose home we're borrowing for my mother's celebration of her caregivers; Jannilyn and Damon, who have made my mother so happy by embracing her into their lives; and Aunts Jayne and Willa Kay, who have known her since before I was born, and in just three months will arrive at her hospice bed to tease her and paint her fingernails teal. I look at Damon. If I hadn't already fallen in love with him when he approached me at his wedding a year earlier to tell me I was *his brother*, by god, and he *loved* me, I would a few months hence, when he'd cry as he mentioned my late mother's name.

Silke and Gordon's home has a large, open living room and floor-to-ceiling views of a golf course. More distant, the sharp teeth and white flanks of the San Juan mountains rise into dark blue sky. The yellowing aspen trees remind me it is fall, early September. Just over three months before my mother will die, at two hours and thirteen minutes into the winter solstice. To my left, outside the windows, a two-story concrete fountain leaps and falls. In the right corner of the living room, Mom's eighty-four-year-old German friend Carla is sprawled in a big cozy red armchair, her cane at her knee, her smile beneficent and unflagging.

"There comes acceptance," Mom had said to me, during the drive over. "I'm going to fight the way I want to. Since I started making up my mind and quit waffling, my depression has been lifting."

My mother now dandles twenty-month-old Braxton on her knee. She holds his hands way up, puppet-like, and dances him to and fro, as Braxton's face continually expresses his utter astonishment. Damon and Jannilyn, his parents, laugh as they watch them. Everyone is watching them. Fiona is smiling as she stands behind me. We're all enchanted. Silke catches my eye and shakes her head.

Jannilyn is saying she wants to take pictures with Mom. Mom slaps her lap in invitation. Jannilyn sits with her and holds the camera at arm's length, and Mom buries her silky white-topped head in Jannilyn's long brown hair. Mom grabs a handful of it and pulls it across her face like a giant mustache. She looks over at me with a grand smile, peering out over the V of brown hair starting under her right ear and hooking under her nose before sweeping back up to her left ear. Just a few days earlier, I had called her up on FaceTime from Telluride, and she'd appeared on the screen with a towel over her head, crying. She couldn't bear how she looked, she'd said, and didn't want to be seen. She'd hung up.

In come Paul, Gregory, Annika, and Lynne, and then Berle and Madeline. Inge von Munich sweeps in soon after. Mom stands up to hug them, opens their cards, thanks them for their love and effort. Peggie arrives through the kitchen, keeps her sunglasses on. We hug. Here's Bonnie, too, and we hug. "Just about everyone is here," Bonnie says to me, with a motion of her head. "Everyone she raised."

After my mother's death we'll all stand windswept above the dizzying maw of the Black Canyon. I'll reach into the box of ash and bone in my hand and pull out the stardust most recently on loan to my mother, Inge, Mom, Oma, Ingelein, with the cancer finally baked out. Mom had said to me more than once, with a small laugh, "When I die, I want to be cremated, because I *soooo* love to travel." I'll hurl the handful into the void, into infinity, and far back in time. Then I'll hold the box for Candy, Brianna, Carrie.

I feared my grief over the death of my mother, of all people, would surely prostrate me at the bottom of depression's ocean floor, unable to work, want, or motivate. I'd been there before, at lesser relationships' ends. But grief, I was surprised and grateful to learn, was less like depression, which, while it lasts, weighs me down continually and in known ways, and more like Tourette's, so that it was often hard to make out what was grieving and what was, say, anxiety or loneliness, neediness or laziness, sadness or life.

For well over a year I avoided reading any letters she'd sent. I wouldn't look at photos of her. I couldn't watch a video of her for close to two. For the first three years after her death, my thoughts, the images of my mind's eye, even my aural memories all seemed focused on her suffering, rather than on myself, my loss, my loneliness, as if I were still worrying about her, as if she were eternally not okay. I didn't feel so much bereft of my mother as torched by every memory of her suffering.

All this seemed to be what we think of as grieving. But what of the fact that the only music I could stand to hear over and over was early soul music, from the mid-50s to the late 60s? What of my less than usual concern for taxes and bill deadlines, and what other people might think? What of the deterioration of my own body, like the lower back pain in the same spot as her tumor, or the ten pounds I added, or the cardio health and muscle mass I lost? What about being largely unmotivated to exercise, even in Boulder, Colorado, where I moved to next, or to meet people? *Other People!* is how I renamed the folder for my iPhone's social apps, as if people might be made to seem less exhausting through exciting punctuation. Was this grieving too?

Grieving, in our culture, is a little like breastfeeding: a person can know it's right and natural but still be abashed by the idea of bringing attention to oneself. I was grateful I didn't need to think about her all the time, and I was grateful I could think about her whenever I wanted to. In these returns to pain, I concentrated on the love behind the pain, and the love fed me. As a young friend of my mother's wrote on Facebook, "It's okay to feel sad. But as our dear Inge would say don't unpack & stay there."

When I bring my mother to mind with attention, it sears me still. The opening chords of Tchaikovsky's "The Waltz of the Flowers" land on my chest and take the air right out of me, and I am once again like King Lear stumbling across the heath, wracked. The sadness is engrieved on my heart, and I am irreversibly more compassionate, toward myself and others. I know that the pain does not, in fact, ever go away. That seems to be the American dream: that we never have to hurt, even and especially after having loved. We wonder why we aren't just *over it*, whatever that means. Well, it's not how we're built. Feel for yourself.

I didn't resist my sadness, and the depression I'd felt before my mother's death became not greater depression, but, through some happy alchemy, a years-long state of flow. Less than a month after Mom began chemo, in 2013, I'd been hired as a startup coach by a doctor who was building a differential diagnosis algorithm. By January 2014, I'd become co-founder and CEO of the self-funded startup company we called Physician Cognition, and for a year and a half after Mom's death, I worked on the project almost every single day. The app we called Xebra could calculate potential diagnoses from any combination of symptoms, physical signs, test results, and patient and family history. It used pattern recognition, Bayesian analysis, and other cognitive tools expert clinicians use. But the algorithm worked without the error that humans bring to any project, like a misdiagnosis rate of fifteen to twenty percent, which in turn leads to unnecessary tests, or no tests where tests should have been done, unnecessary treatments and procedures, delays in proper diagnosis, and, my strongest motivation, a lot of unnecessary suffering.

I'd seen it when my mother's excruciating adhesion pain and ovarian cancer were both misdiagnosed, back in 1999, as gas and "women's problems." No one had asked the questions or ordered the tests that were the standard of care for abdominal pain and "a cyst on my ovary." And those failures, like most misdiagnosis, were solvable problems. The Xebra app was able to identify *adhesions* as a top potential cause of her symptoms. Critically, it also recommended the pelvic ultrasound that would have confirmed the adhesions hypothesis sooner, and perhaps even revealed the growth on my mother's ovaries.

Xebra was too late for another long and painful misdiagnosis. In 2008, Mom had reported terrible back and kidney pain, her hair began falling out, she had "grainy eyes" and difficulty swallowing, and she felt heart palpitations. Her local doctor told her, she wrote, *nothing was the matter except "old age"*. An oncologist for whom Candy worked, in Alabama, made a remote diagnosis of a thyroid problem. Another Colorado doctor was confident: she had interstitial cystitis, and he recommended a medication with a cost equal to her monthly income. *I felt*, she wrote, *I was being passed around like an old shoe*. She lived in heartrending pain for eighteen months. Once again, our technology could have prevented all of it: in the same symptoms, it could spot the high probability of a *kidney stone* right away, and it could recommend the CT scan "without contrast" that would confirm it. I wanted everyone in the *world* to have this kind of technology. I felt at long last a return to the fuel of willpower, and I pitched myself bodily into work that gave me meaning. Meaningful work, like meaningful living, is healing in action.

In August 2016, I decided to begin work on this book. Mom would have appreciated that I was finally able to use her frequent flyer miles, and that I decided to start this work in Italy, where law-school-era Italian friends had invited me to join their family vacation in the Dolomites for a week. In Bavaria afterward, in Möhrendorf, which pleasingly means carrot village, I visited Christa and Fiona. At the end of Wasserwerkstrasse, we stepped onto a wide path into a forest. I was drawn to a sunlit and narrower path to the right, and sixty-eight steps later I had come abreast of the only tree as far as the eye could see with ivy hugging its trunk. I lifted a chunk of brilliant mossy green at its base and dug down into the dirt a bit, then poured in my mother's ashes. Then I folded the moss back over like a blanket and Christa laid atop the moss a handful of red berries. "*Vogelbeeren*," she said. Bird berries.

Back in Boulder, I began singing soul for the first time, publicly, before a rowdy crowd of millennials at a place called the Bohemian Biergarten. Before, I'd sung only rockers, the faster the better. Soul music slows down to put the voice, the naked self, front and center. In soul the voice has no place to run to, and may not wish to hide. In the house, car, and karaoke, now I sang Otis Redding, Ray Charles, Wilson Pickett, the Righteous Brothers. When I sang "Unchained Melody" for the first time, my hands shook the mic, and my legs became so weak I wasn't sure I could get off the stage. I edited the last pages of this book in a windstorm of waltzes.

Beyond Mom, with their backs to the windows, a man and a woman have begun to strum their zithers. A zither is a Bavarian instrument, often used to commit German folk music. A close relative of the dulcimers of Navarette, which would be an excellent name for a Jason Bourne novel, a zither looks like a piano that fell from a high window onto a guitar. Both zither strummers are in their eighties, both are Bavarian. Carla, a fiftyish Mexican-American, is the main singer. She now sits next to Mom on the divan, and they begin to pore over the songbooks.

"Mom," I say, "you're getting that come zither look again. Remember what Bill Bryson said."

"I know," Mom says. "You keep reminding me." Christa and Fiona are passing around the *been stich kuchen* (bee sting cake) they've made, with its cream filling and flakey goodness. Silke and Bonnie are offering *kaffee* to go with our *kuchen*.

"It should have been a condition of the armistice," I intone, quoting from Bryson's *Neither Here Nor There*, "that the Germans lay down their accordions." Mom adores the German folk music of her youth, but she's just enough of an outsider to laugh. Or maybe she just thinks what's funny—just hilarious—is how, afterward, and how easily, the sounds of German folk music will squeeze the air right out of me.

Yodeling happens, without so much as a by your leave. My mother nods in time and sings the occasional verse. She closes her eyes. A smile plays on her lips and around her eyes. As the next song begins, her smile widens and she nods and lifts her head in happy recognition. "Edelweiss". She begins to sing, and she gazes at Gregory while he mouths the verses she's taught him. Gregory is fidgeting, crawling in and out of his chair, not noticing her attention. He's wearing the #10 red-and-white Bayern München jersey she'd given him.

Since he was about seven, she'd arranged a half-dozen recitals for him. *International Concert!* she announced on Facebook. She pressed Lynne and Paul into buying a karaoke machine, and then she contrived to find Gregory a tuxedo with a white tie and tails. At the recital I attended, Mom bustled about, and in her finest clothes, both gourmet caterer and mistress of ceremonies, announcing each song and ensuring due praise and applause for Gregory. She included Annika in her remarks and asked her to sing as well, but it was Gregory's day, and he had fairly levitated with joy. "I feel famous!" he'd said. "She just brought me under her wing and cherished me," he would tell me later. "She made me feel like I was really important."

Now Mom starts a back and forth swaying with Annika and Lynne on one side and Aunt Jayne on the other. Annika gets up to get herself some water from the kitchen. "You have no idea how much I've learned from her," she says. "Most of all that you can always find the good in what happens." I get up for more *kuchen* myself. "She's so pretty," Silke says, nodding toward my mother, and I agree that she is. Today she is luminous. She is incandescent.

She is a tough old broad. She used to say that herself, when I was a kid, but back then I'd have told you surely my rough-and-ready commando father was the more obvious subject of a book. It took me a lot of learning to fully appreciate how fiercely brave—in the things that mattered, in the sense of feeling the fear and acting anyway—my mother really was. I don't remember my first meeting with my father, when I was nine. What I remember is how it affected my mother. I remember her sadness, and her anger. She wasn't able to listen as well as I would have liked, but she was willing and able to feel the big things.

After she read *Christopher*, and read it over the phone to my father's sisters Willa Kay and Diane, as well as Grandma Powell (who said, of her youngest son, "Well, that sonofabitch needs to see that"), she drove up Main Street straight to the Ace-Hi Bar, where most of Clark's recons were conceived. She found him at the bar, and began to read to him. Then she laid the Big Chief pages on the bar in front of him, and watched him turn to his appearance on the now-missing third page. The first sentences recounted how the boy's father came to meet him for the first time late one night, and how he promised to come again in a few days. Mom recalled the rest decades later, including the young author's shift from referring to himself as "Chris" to "the boy": *It was just like Christmas. But the boy waited all day. Thursday came and went. And it wasn't Christmas anymore. The boy went to bed and tears spilled on the pillow.* When Clark was finished reading, my mother took the papers from his hands and walked out.

I've never forgotten her description of how Clark left her at the Ranch: pregnant and far from home, his girlfriend waiting in his idling truck as he shook my mother "off his leg like a dog." Uncle Smokey went and talked to Clark, but soon he came back to my mother and said, "Sis, I wish there was more people in the world like you. You know I do. But he says he's not gonna marry you." In her despair she took a bottle of aspirin, which only made her sick.

She once told me that for years after our return to Rangley, she "felt too tongue-tied to say anything" around Clark. But at my college graduation, she walked up to him and said, "There were many times, Clark, when you broke your promises to Chris and we didn't have enough to eat, that I really hated you. But today I thank you for my son." I can still hear emotion, her conviction, as she repeated that to me.

"All's well that ends well," my father had mumbled, according to my mother. I can still hear her bemusement.

When shit got really scary, when it would have been easier to avoid, to drink, to resent others, to retreat from the heart's grave dangers, my mother always showed up. She knew her answer to the question we all have to answer: how shall we show up in the world, for ourselves and others, even and especially in the face of our fear and pain? That is the kind of warriorship, I realize, that always drew me in. "The essence of warriorship," the Tibetan teacher Chögyam Trungpa once wrote, "is refusing to give up on anyone or anything." Being a real warrior means opening up to the pain of others and of one's self.

The cancer took my mother's ovaries but it could not touch the mother in her. "Your mom is like a mother to me," Peggie had told me a few months earlier. "Even though she's not old enough to be." I was no longer surprised when a woman or girl told me something like that. But Julio? The day after my mother's death he wrote: *Amigo Cameron, I don't known to say…Inge was like a second mom to me.* And almost three years later he finished an email of updates on his travels with this: *Inge still in my heart, mainly when i walk, i remember her when she was calling Quasimodo to her rucksack … she was more than special to me …*

Here at my mother's party for her caregivers, Annika seems a bit lost, inside herself. As the musicians play "Somewhere Over the Rainbow", Mom fingers Annika's braided hair, rearranging the way the length of it lies. Annika watches Mom trace the German lyrics, in the songbook, with her finger. Later, she will say, of Mom, "She was the only one who just spent genuine one on one quality time with me. Just walking around town, but it was so nice. Her taking her time and having an interest in being with me." "Que Sera Sera" starts up, and Mom sings it with gusto, as I remember her doing when I was a boy. *Whatever will be, will be.* She grabs Lynne's hand and sways her arm back and forth. Lynne's other arm is around Gregory, who sways as well, smiling, at first.

Are Annika's eyes wet? Annika is facing away from Mom, brows knit, looking down and now and again at Gregory, whose features also reveal a struggle. Suddenly they are both crying. Mom sees them and wraps them in her arms, even as she bursts into tears herself. She holds them both like that for a long moment, and as they part she dabs at her eye and nose with a handkerchief and cries, with mock sternness, "*Stop* it! Both of you! *Stop* it! It's not my funeral! We're having a *pa*rty!"

Annika smiles through her tears.

Mom points toward me and the people behind me. "See what you started?" she says. "Everybody's bawling. Stop it!"

Christa's shoulder-length, raven-black hair has only a little grey in it. She's a portrait of dignity, and the picture of good etiquette, which is empathy in action. Now she is at once somber and quick to smile. Dark circles attend to her eyes' every glance. She and Fiona know this will be their last time with my mother. Only months after the death of her only surviving brother, Horst, she is watching the decline of her only sister. Once back in Germany, she'll return to the vigil for their cousin Renate, who will die before I try to call her again. My mother's visits to her family in Germany over the last dozen years had been punctuated by tears and misunderstanding. So had this visit. Mom said Christa and Fiona didn't spend enough time with her. They were always cleaning, cooking, organizing, shopping. They never just sat down and talked to her. Christa and Fiona objected to Mom's tone, with its way of demanding that things be different from what they were, and huddled defensively in the kitchen.

Now I watch Christa watching my mother, as both of them sing in German. Christa wipes her eyes and nose, out of Mom's sight. She is regaining control. Then she hears Mom's voice catch, and then Mom hears *Christa* and tears spring to Mom's eyes so that Christa turns and smacks Mom's side with her rolled-up sheet of lyrics, saying, as Oma had, "Na!", and Mom shakes her head, then smiles as I film them and cheer for their singing.

"A toast!" Mom cries. *"Ein Prosit. Tsiki Tsaki."*

My mother could seem self-absorbed, defensive, and prickly. But of course people aren't so simple: everyone she met also felt her friendliness and concern, her compassion and her willingness to give of herself on their behalf. Kindness really was her religion. One would need to turn to the kingdom of dogs to find a living creature as well-intentioned as my mother. Here is my mother's legacy, sitting all around her. "If you get nervous, just look at me. I'll help you," she is saying to Gregory, before conducting him through Beethoven's "Ode to Joy".

She launches into the next song, "Hänschen Klein", as she had on the Camino. She mimes the story, beginning with Little Hans' declaration that he's leaving home to get some peace. There's a modern version of the song where the mother protests so much that Hans never actually leaves, never becomes Big Hans. This is not the version my mother has committed to memory. In the original version, the mother lets Hans go in spite of her grief. Out into the world Hans goes, *mit Stock und Hut*, with stick and hat. When he returns seven years later, his sister and brother walk by him without recognition. Only his mother recognizes the Big Hans he has become, and Mom delivers the mother's recognition of her always-forgiven son with a triumphant flourish. "*Hans, mein Sohn! Grüß dich Gott, mein Sohn!*"

This is what love is, or rather, strives to be: ever-forgiving. Seventy times seven times we should forgive, and then more. Always, though it may be a thoroughly human struggle. Now we take off our shirts, hand them over, to the least among us. This is the mother, unique, for all we know, in all the universe. It was certainly mine. On Thanksgiving 2013, when both chemos had failed, under a year before Silke's party, Mom had sent me a card, letting me know how grateful she was for the many months I'd put my *life on hold* to help her through *this scary journey*. But she also wanted me to be free, if I wished it. *You can go now, son,* she wrote.

"No," I'd said aloud, to no one in particular, before closing the card. To love, very often, means to choose to limit our freedom.

At the end of "Hänschen Klein", after my mother has acknowledged the reactions of the people around her, she turns to me, toward the camera, and gives me a lasting look, her eyes shining. She knows she is near the end, and this is no everyday glance. She is looking at me, she is sending love to me in the future, every time I watch it.

In our albums there's a picture of my mother, about thirteen, riding a scooter in a polka-dotted dress and hand-me-down shoes. In this picture she's always looked to me a little like Anne Frank—her age, her face, her hair and the clothing of the time, the optimism of her smile, her boundless goodwill and humanity. One foot is on the scooter, the other straight behind her in an arabesque, like the dancers she admired. She's leaning forward, hands on the steering column, acting a bit, putting on a little show for her infant cousin, Brigitte. She is flying, just as she wanted some day to do as a foreign correspondent, and would do, as a stewardess and traveler. I think of that same German girl, rosy-cheeked, eyes shining and a bit overweight, turning around and around in the plaza of the cathedral of Santiago de Compostela, in Galician Spain, one late October day, and then I see her here, singing with all her heart on a Colorado afternoon, and my own heart is full.

Fin.

IF YOU LOVED
ORDINARY MAGIC,

Please help spread its message
of positivity and love.

As an independently published book, the success of
Ordinary Magic relies entirely on reader love—*your* love!

If you loved it (and even if you weren't so sure!),
please take just one minute to give it a review now,
wherever you shop for books online.

Long or short, favorable or critical, your review is the
best way to express your support—and to get the book
and its messages out into the world. Thank you!

STAY ATTUNED

Follow Cameron on Twitter: @cameroncpowell
Join the Conversation on Facebook: OrdinaryMagicBook

GET TO KNOW THE "CHARACTERS"!

Videos, pictures, and Cameron's newsletter: OrdinaryMagicBook.com

See the original video of Inge, singing incandescently at
her last party, and with the rest of the cast of characters
on the Camino de Santiago itself.

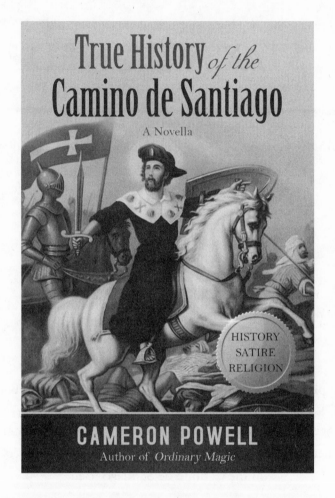

Read *True History of the Camino de Santiago*

Wherever fine ebooks are sold.

END NOTES

Page 1: *ditched the emperor of all maladies in a fiery lake of chemotherapy:* The phrase "emperor of all maladies" is most well-known from Dr. Siddhartha Mukherjee's singular achievement, *The Emperor of All Maladies: A Biography of Cancer.*

Page 6: *are all shared with other diseases:* Other symptoms of ovarian cancer include: persistent abdominal bloating, indigestion or nausea; changes in appetite, often a loss of appetite or feeling full sooner; feelings of pressure in the pelvis or lower back; needing to urinate more frequently; changes in bowel movements; increased abdominal girth; feeling tired or having low energy.

Page 6: *Crucially, this doctor also ordered the blood tests:* The standard of care for a patient reporting pressure on an ovary, in the U.S. at least, would have included an ultrasound scan.

Page 28: *Instead of chemo, she thought as she walked, I'm going to walk the Camino:* Please take note! My mother's decision to postpone a decision on chemotherapy was based on a number of factors that, quite frankly, are unlikely to apply to most patients with ovarian cancer. Among other reasons for her decision, her tumor's growth had been unusually slow and she was not symptomatic. And chemo had actually worked well for her before, which is not common with ovarian cancer.

Page 45: *Tomorrow we'll need to walk over 16 miles:* All distances are taken from the website at http://www.godesalco.com/plan/frances.

Page 95-96: *he had no doubt that the techniques he employed would be able to secure their convictions":* Murphy, Cullen, *God's Jury: The Inquisition and the Making of the Modern World* (Kindle Locations 359-361).

Page 111: *Carrie decides to take a picture of Mom and me walking side by side like this:* You can see the resulting image of the two of us on the book cover, with a teal ribbon added.

ACKNOWLEDGMENTS

In addition to thanking the people I've mentioned in the book, especially if you were nice to me, I'd like to thank all the readers who instilled in me a sense that this story might matter. There were many helpers in my Taj Mahal.

The original blog readers and friends who reached out with special encouragement: Andrew Arentowicz. Bruce Cady (d. 2017). Ahpaly Coradin. Tedd Determan. Jeanne De Sa. Andrew Dashiell. Laurence Egle. Rachel Mariner. Alejandro Pena Prieto (who made a long flight in the last week—*abrazos, amigo*). Marie Milnes-Vasquez. Willa Kay Powell. Jayne Kuck (nee Powell).

Many readers from around the world showed me their appreciation and hunger for this story, in comments and private messages: Fadya AlBakry, Paula Jane Amiss, Marion Anderson, Ute Anderson, Lisa Angst, Maria Arthur, Patty Arzuaga, Kerie Weiss Schwartz Berkowitz, Steffi Besser, Nikki Binns, Sonnen Blume, Gail Brannan, Carol Brannan, Uta Burke, Anika Brueckner, MarKay Carlson, Marina Chang, Bon Crawford, Diane Davis-Fox, Nancy Kalina Gómez Edelstein, Steffi Erbacher, Anne Fifield, Rebecca Freedman, Inge Jaeschke French, Shadlee Friesen, Jayme Gabossi, Antje Gebhardt, Renge Grace, Revi Renate Hammer, Karen Berish Heilner, Nancy Heitler-Kohl, Birgit Hoffschulz, Lori Alpino Holloway, Leslie Johnson, Harry Kassakhian, Charlie Kawasaki, Susanna Lisa, Laura Korman, Polly Kraetzer, Jody MacTavish, Eileen McCarren, Heather Maki, Jessica Martin, Krista Meier, Melissa Milburn, Garci Anne Moreno, Michelle Musselwhite, Stephanie Nobbs, Francesca Novak, Debi Pearson, Marie Perez, Regina Prentice, Kris Kelly Rivas, Elena Rodryguez Villar, Julie Roll, Denise Sanderson, Robin Sandell, Grace Santarelli, Pam Schunk (d. 2015), Katie Singer, Karen Sui, Waltraud Thompson, Karin Thrasher, Alison Tinsley,

Colleen Tomczak, Laura McGie White, Susan N Gerald Wilson, Joanna Maurer Winchester, the Teal Warriors Facebook Group, the German Girls Living in America Facebook Group, and others whose expressions of love and support I may have misplaced.

I want to thank the early manuscript readers who slogged through an unfinished product to give me feedback: editor Julia Scheeres and close reader Mary Dearborn; law school literati Christopher Ayres, Kate Nicholson, Lily Vakili, Adam Weiss, and Vikki Wulf; and Alessandra Cardarelli, Derria Banta, Joel Cantor, Laura Coffin, Meghan Conley, Ivona Datkova, Will Dove, April Glaser, Wendy LaTouche, Lisa Leslie, and Nancy McKibben.

People who helped shepherd the book toward publication include typists Lucija Williams (of Croatia and Wisconsin) and Oluseyi "Olu" Owoyeye (Nigeria); Naren Aryal, publisher, and Michelle Webber and Nina Spahn, project managers, at Mascot Books; cover designer Leslie K (Hungary).

In Boulder, I am indebted to The Little Yoga Studio, Bohemian Biergarten, Trader Joe's, and my caffeinated offices, Ozo and the Laughing Goat on Pearl, and the Sorority Starbucks on the Hill. In Telluride, I have to thank everyone who makes the most beautiful place in America also among the friendliest, and who helped me be more resilient during a challenging time.